CW01374028

THE SECRET AND SUBLIME

Other Works by the Same Author

The Wheel of Life
City of Lingering Splendour
People of the Sun
The Way of Power
The Book of Change (translated from the Chinese)
The Zen Doctrine of Huang Po (translated from the Chinese)
The Zen Teaching of Hui Hai (translated from the Chinese)

THE SECRET AND SUBLIME

Taoist Mysteries and Magic

by John Blofeld

London · George Allen & Unwin Ltd
Ruskin House   Museum Street

First published in 1973

This book is copyright under the Berne Convention. All rights are reserved. Apart from any fair dealing for the purpose of private study, research, criticism or review, as permitted under the Copyright Act, 1956, no part of this publication may be reproduced, stored in a retrieval system, or transmitted, in any form or by any means, electronic, electrical, chemical, mechanical, optical, photocopying, recording or otherwise, without the prior permission of the copyright owner. Enquiries should be addressed to the publishers.

© George Allen & Unwin Ltd 1973

ISBN 0 04 181019 8 Hardback
      0 04 181020 1 Paper

Printed in Great Britain
in 11 *point Baskerville*
by Clarke, Doble & Brendon Ltd
Plymouth.

To Mary Blackwell

Bibliographical Note and Acknowledgements

Works consulted include :

The Chinese text of the *Tao Tê Ching* and several English translations, of which I found Chen Lin and Yang Chia-Lo's *Truth and Nature* (Wan Kuo Shu Tien, Hong Kong) and D.C. Lau's *Lao Tzu, Tao Te Ching* (Penguin Classics) particularly helpful;

The Chinese text of *Chuang-tzû*, several Chinese commentaries and Burton Watson's excellent complete translation entitled *Chuang Tzu* (Columbia University Press);

Taoist Yoga (Rider) and *The Secrets of Chinese Meditation* (Rider) by Lu K'uan Yü (Charles Luk), both of which I found invaluable;

Creativity and Taoism by Chang Chung-yuen (Harper) which discourses charmingly on Taoist painting and art, as well as containing a chapter on the internal alchemy;

'Lu Hsi-hsing and his commentaries on the Ts'an T'ing Ch'i' by Liu Ts'un-yan (*Tsing Hua Journal of Chinese Studies*, August 1968); and *Sexual Life in Ancient China* by R. van Gulik (Brill, Leiden), both of which contain valuable material on dual cultivation (sexual) Yoga.

I am deeply grateful to Professor Burton Watson, Mr Lu K'uan Yü and their respective publishers for permitting me to quote from and summarize some of the material contained in *Chuang Tzu* and *Taoist Yoga*. Particulars of the use I made of it are to be found in the pertinent parts of this book.

Contents

Foreword		*page* 13
1	A Preview	19
2	Stumbling Upon Taoism: Some Taoist Recluses	34
3	Demons, Fox-Spirits and the Realm of Magic: Popular Taoism	58
4	Living in Harmony with Nature's Rhythms: Taoist Arts and Yogas	113
5	To Know and Not Be Knowing: Taoist Philosophy and Kindred Matters	152
6	The Nameless: Taoist Mysticism	181
7	Dragons to the West? Prospects	211

Foreword

Taoism, the progenitor of mystics, philosophers, yogins, magicians and, incidentally, the world's first hippies, was a mystical religion, a philosophy and a way of life that persisted for well over two thousand years and had roots going back four or five thousand, but recent events in its homeland seem to have inflicted a mortal wound, if not killed it outright. True, there are some Taoist monasteries functioning in Taiwan and Hong Kong and some partially Taoistic temples and cults among overseas Chinese communities in south-east Asia, but one does not know whether any monasteries have survived as genuine inheritors of the Taoist tradition as opposed to commercial enterprises or holiday resorts lightly disguised. Their number, too, is insignificant by the standards that prevailed right up to 1949, the beginning of the communist régime.

Saddened by the demise of an ancient system at once so colourful and benign, I offer this book as in some sort a memorial to its departed splendours. This is a time when the increasing open-mindedness of Western people, especially the younger generation, is leading to more sympathetic study of Eastern traditions, to greater humility in the approach made to them, and to new readiness to recognize excellence where excellence exists in unfamiliar forms. Therefore this book is written with love—love for my Taoist friends of yore and love for those readers who feel drawn to them even if they cannot help smiling at some of their beliefs.

The great Taoist classic, the *Tao Tê Ching*, opens with the pronouncement: 'The Way (Tao) that can be expressed in words is not the Eternal Way; a name that can be uttered is not the Eternal's name.' Ha! From such an opening it at once appears that Taoism was concerned with the mystery of the Ultimate. Indeed it was, though with many, many other things besides. Those famous words point directly to the nameless truth which is the high goal of all mystics, be they dapper professors with pearl tie-pins or bearded hippies without shirts. I do not say that Taoism offered the swiftest or surest route to mystical experience, but it was a way with an immense appeal for certain kinds of people. If curious rock-formations remind you of strange animals in the throes of creation; if the blossom of crab-apple or winter-plum bears a message that goes beyond mere prettiness; if water

FOREWORD

tumbling into a mountain pool fills you with inexplicable rapture; if walking in the rain makes you long to dance and sing; if a vista of rocks, pine trees and purple hills seems to hint at what the poet Li T'ai-po calls 'another universe, a realm of Immortals' –, then you have the makings of a Taoist – one who, living in accord with nature's rhythms, may be drawn at last to seek union with the Sublime Tao (known to other mystics as the Godhead, *Sunyata* or Nirvana).

It goes without saying that not every recluse dressed in antique Chinese robes, wearing a top-knot secured by a jade peg and living in a hermitage or monastery, consciously entertained that supremely exalted aim. Truly dedicated sages, accomplished yogins, simple-minded dabblers in real or imagined marvels (and even charlatans, perhaps) were sometimes to be found within the same community. Taoists, being tolerant kindly men, were not likely to drive anyone from the monastery gates for lack of spiritual qualifications or even to punish a colleague for misbehaviour, the use of punishment being one of the characteristics of conventional society they most deplored. Visitors, too, were always welcome. Each community had its guest-rooms; no charge was made for bed, food and wine, it being assumed that a guest would freely offer what he could afford. Someone so unappreciative of warm and generous hospitality as to leave no offering at all would still be seen on his way with smiles and bows as though it did not really matter if the recluses were left with nothing to live on but air and dew, for they were a courteous people with modest expectations to whom hardship came easily.

As to Taoism's being the progenitor of the first hippies, close on fifteen hundred years ago there flourished some widespread Taoistically-minded communities known as the Light Conversationalists. Their prescription for discovering whether life had meaning, and if so what, was to live in frugal but happy accord with nature's rhythms, which generally involved fleeing from places where man-made laws imposed artificial limitations on people's spontaneity. They rather hoped to discover true understanding of life's meaning by seeking it in the stillness of their own undisturbed minds; meanwhile, just in case life might offer nothing meaningful to understand, they enlivened their days with wildly unconventional behaviour and by conversing at a deliberately fantastic level for the fun of it; yet, though the Confucian establishment mocked them, they were entirely serious in their underlying aim and in their opposition to every sort of threat, coercion, punishment or violence. They were free souls born to smile contentedly at each fresh recognition of their kinship with nature. Needless to say, the Confucian rulers were appalled by the spread of these groups and made sure they did not flourish long; even so, the whole Chinese people were until recently influenced to some extent by somewhat similar Taoistic and therefore unconventional ideas, which have much in common with those of the younger generation in the West today. Rigid Confucian-style conformity, which has found its apotheosis in Maoism, was paralleled in traditional Chinese society by a refreshing streak of nonconformity and freedom, even eccentricity, of behaviour.

Now for a word about myself and my approach to this book. During the seventeen years I spent in China, my frequent wanderings took me across its mighty rivers – once in midwinter I slithered across the Yellow River on my feet – and deep into those mountains which were especially sacred to its venerable religions. Though primarily interested in Buddhism, I did not fail to visit as many Taoist hermitages and to cultivate the friendship of as many different kinds of Taoists as possible. The experiences that befell me, coupled with some reading of Taoist works in Chinese and/or in English renderings, have provided the substance of this book. As I have said, my fear that Taoism may be on the point of vanishing from the earth has persuaded me to regard as something of a sacred duty the task of recording my memories of it as a living force remarkable for the variety and interest of its manifestations. If (as is all too probable) my record contains serious errors and omissions, or if in striving to entertain the reader I have dwelt at too great length on some weird but relatively unimportant aspects, I beg forgiveness of my Taoist teachers and of Taoism's guardian deities.

What I have written is partly intended for those now travelling the world as I used to travel through China, possessing very little money or luggage, but managing to come close to the local people. Living was fortunately cheap in those days, my monthly expenses being around five pounds (then $20 US) when on the move and much less when I settled for a while in some hermitage or monastery. My mode of travelling was to walk, ride on muleback, take passage in small river-craft or country buses, put up at cheap

FOREWORD

inns (one-and-threepence or $.25 US a night) and eat in the simplest cook-shops. I mention this because I like to believe that, for as long as the world contains wanderers and wonderers who are frugal in their habits, lovers of people in their endless variety, sincere in their pursuit of truth and able to laugh at themselves, the spirit of Taoism will live on.

Regarding my manner of presenting the materials thus gathered, I hope it will be clear that this book is not fiction masquerading as fact, but fact here and there very thinly disguised by fiction. As to the need for such a disguise, by pretending that stories heard and experiences encountered in many widely-scattered places related to just a few people or hermitages, I have sought to spare the reader many needless digressions such as accounts of journeys and of intervening activities unrelated to Taoism. For much the same reason I have put the teachings gathered from many hermits into the mouths of just a few, who should be regarded as composite characters. Naturally, after the passage of so many years – nearly all the events recorded took place in the nineteen-thirties – I have had to reconstruct most of the conversations and some of the background details and even to invent appropriate names for hermitages and recluses whose real names escape my memory. However, even the smallest details of conversation, personalities, events and backgrounds possess at least poetic truth in that I have fabricated nothing that is not strictly in line with what I saw with my own eyes and heard with my own ears while in a Taoist milieu.

Only in dealing with the more advanced yogas and with the higher flights of Taoist mysticism and philosophy, or else with purely historical matters, have I supplemented my memories of actual events and conversations with knowledge culled from written sources. My purpose in sometimes weaving matters heard and matters read into the form of reported speech has not been to deceive the reader but to make the presentation more vivid and especially to re-create the very atmosphere in which I myself first encountered the higher teachings.

My English renderings from the *Tao Tê Ching* are my own, but of course I am deeply indebted to the previous translators for their suggested interpretations of the more obscure phrases. For the *Book of Chuang-tzû*, I have in most cases stuck rather closely to Burton Watson's translation, finding it as faithful to the original

FOREWORD

as one could hope for and almost as racy in style, although perhaps inclined to reject the mystical and yogic implications of those passages which are also open to alternative constructions. Most ancient Chinese works contain phrases or even whole passages at whose meaning the translator is sometimes compelled to guess; Professor Watson's renderings of such debatable passages strike me as being highly plausible and they are based on a much higher level of classical Chinese scholarship than my own. As to Taoist manuals on yoga, I have not even attempted to render passages into English; whole paragraphs may be variously read as pertaining to government, military affairs, alchemy, non-sexual or sexual yoga – sometimes because the author wished to hide the true meaning from non-initiates liable to abuse the yoga, but often because he held the Taoistic belief that, since the same principles or cycles of movement govern all conceivable activities, what applies to one activity applies to every other. To supplement my yogic knowledge, I have had to rely, therefore, on the interpretations provided by experts, particularly, Lu K'uan Yü (Charles Luk).

In poking a little fun at scholars, an amusement in which many a Taoist has indulged over the last two thousand years or so, my shuttlecocks have been aimed only at those un-Taoistically-minded writers who insist that every aspect of Taoism other than its philosophy is a perversion of the teachings of the sages. How the sages themselves would have laughed at such discrimination! To draw hard and fast lines separating the myriad embodiments of the Tao is the very negation of Taoist principle. Purely for the reader's convenience, I have written separate chapters on Taoist magic, yoga, philosophy and mysticism; but I beg him not to take these distinctions as ultimately valid. Almost all the Taoists I encountered were 'magicians', yogins, philosophers and mystics all in one, but with differences of emphasis. I never came across one who disbelieved in the existence of gods and spirits, though quite a few attached little importance to such beings, holding (with Buddhists) that an individual's ultimate development depends upon himself. Gods and demons, if left well alone, are less likely to complicate the issue by kindly meddling in the one case or malevolent muddling in the other.

What practised meditator has ever been so entirely free from the attentions of demons as not to believe in them? Giving some

FOREWORD

of them Greek names such as Neurosis or Psychosis does not alter the fact of their existence. These denizens of the dark unconscious are never far away; efforts to placate them can rebound; like blackmailers, they are insatiable, for which reason some Taoists were inclined to agree with the Confucians that, in the matter of supernatural beings, it is best to be respectful when an encounter is unavoidable and otherwise to keep one's distance. Maintaining this attitude has, I think, served me in good stead. Western writers fond of probing too deeply into the affairs of Chinese or Tibetan demons have been known to meet disastrous ends.

JOHN BLOFELD
The Garden of Immortals
1972

Chapter 1

A Preview

What is Taoism or what was it? How may it be defined? Perhaps there is not and never has been anyone able to define it with authority. To certain Chinese scholars, Taoism meant the philosophy contained in a couple of volumes, almost two-and-a-half thousand years old, bequeathed to posterity by the sages Lao-tzû and Chuang-tzû, together with some surviving fragments of the teachings of Yang Chu and a handful of fellow philosophers who also flourished well before the Christian Era. To most ordinary Chinese people, Taoism meant teachings covering a great range of occult practices alleged to have originated with no less a person than the Yellow Emperor (third millennium B.C.) and the three immortal ladies who advised him in skills both mystical and erotic. To yogins steeped in the arts of rejuvenation, prolonging life and achieving one of several kinds of immortality, it meant both of these, together with the teachings of Lieh-tzû, Ko Hung, Kuo P'o, Wei Po-yang and other sages and masters of the secret (internal) alchemy who appeared in successive dynasties. To mystics seeking union with the Sublime Tao, it meant the esoteric aspect of the teachings of both the philosophical and yogic treatises, assuming that the distinction sometimes made between them is valid. To the bulk of Taoists it meant all these things together. I accept the view of this last group and have endeavoured to do justice to all aspects of the heterogeneous yet elusive body of learning and practice called Taoism. 'Oh!' exclaim the scholars, 'you are surely not going to profane the name of Taoist by giving us a lot of fanciful talk about gods and demons?' That, dear scholars, depends upon your point of view. First, if you arraign that approach as unscholarly, permit me to recall that the *Tao Tê Ching*, a classic which enjoys your high esteem, contains the words: 'Get rid of the wise, discard the learned and the people

19

THE SECRET AND SUBLIME

will benefit a hundredfold!' Second, one should bear in mind that Mr Lu K'uan Yü, a modern interpreter of Taoism whose wisdom and erudition are well known, prefaces his work *Taoist Yoga* with a dedication to his 'godfather, the Deity Pe Ti, ruler of the Northern Heaven', from which it follows that even scholarly men may believe in gods (and demons).

However, out of deference to the learned, I shall give Lao-tzû and Chuang-tzû first place in this preview, all the more willingly as I admire them immensely and must confess to having little reliable information about the Yellow Emperor and his three immortal ladies, who preceded all other known Taoist sages by a couple of thousand years; for, having flourished four-and-a-half millennia before we were born, they belong to what is generally described as the legendary period of Chinese history, concerning which facts are sparse.

The philosopher Lao-tzû (the Aged Master) was, according to the historian Ssû-ma Ch'ien, born in Hu county in the State of Ch'u in the sixth century B.C. Surnamed Li and given the name Êrh, he was also known as Li Tan. Popularly credited with looking old at birth 'as a consequence of having stayed some seventy years in his mother's womb', he subsequently became a historian and was put in charge of the archives of the State of Ch'u. There, hearing of his immense learning, Confucius paid him a visit and requested instruction in the ancient rites, only to receive a telling rebuff. Lao-tzû explained to that highly decorous but rather pompous sage that the rites were merely words left by people whose bones had turned to dust; it would be best for Confucius to rid himself of his 'arrogance, lustfulness, ingratiating manners and excessive ambition'. According to one tradition, Confucius, far from waxing indignant, spoke of Lao-tzû in the highest terms, likening him to a dragon ascending to heaven on wind and clouds. Unfortunately this high opinion was not shared by the princes whom Lao-tzû served. To quote his own words: 'Few understand me. Those who calumniate me are honoured. Therefore must the sage disguise himself in coarse garments, hiding in his breast the jade of wisdom.' Seeing the sad decline into which the State of Ch'u was falling, he mounted an ox and departed westwards through a pass, whose keeper begged him to record his wisdom before leaving the world behind, whereupon he dashed off the two volumes of the *Tao Tê Ching* (amounting in all to only five thousand characters) and left for an unknown destination. Nevertheless, it is variously recorded that Lao-tzû lived to a hundred and sixty or over two hundred years of age.

Some scholars, including Dr D. C. Lau, to whose rendering of the historian Ssû-ma Ch'ien's account of Lao-tzû I owe many of the foregoing details, express serious doubts as to whether that sage existed; others aver that, if he lived at all, it was probably several centuries later than the period ascribed to him by tradition; they are inclined to suppose that the *Tao Tê Ching* was the product of some other sage, or a compilation of the aphorisms of several sages. Yet other scholars, including Lin Yutang and Lu K'uan Yü, suggest that the Lao-tzû legend accords more or less closely with the facts. Who am I to make a judgement? It is enough for me that people *believe* that Lao-tzû was a senior contemporary of Confucius and the sole author of the *Tao Tê Ching*. What difference could it make to Taoist believers or to us if one or both of those traditional suppositions proved wrong? If it could be proved that Jesus was not a historical figure, would that alter the tremendous impact made on history and on people's hearts by words firmly believed to be those of Jesus? Furthermore, in the case of the ancient Taoist sages, the evidence adduced to prove that they did or did not exist, that they did or did not write the works ascribed to them, is so slender that the best of scholars is reduced to making intelligent guesses. One thing is sure – a person or a concept labelled Lao-tzû made a very deep and beneficial impression on the evolution of the Chinese people. As ancient traditions are often found to contain more truth than the iconoclastic works of scholars ill-supplied with factual materials, I prefer to suppose that Lao-tzû existed in the sixth century B.C. and wrote the classic known variously as the *Lao-tzû* or the *Tao Tê Ching*, thus aligning myself with the vast majority of Taoist believers.

The second sage allowed by some scholars to have been one of the 'founding fathers of Taoism' was Yang Chu (fourth century B.C.?) whose thoughts survive only in the works of others. Accused of beast-like anarchy by the Confucian scholar Mencius, he seems to have offended that worthy man by his doctrine of *wei-wo* (literally 'for myself'), but Taoists find no fault with his mystical doctrine of individualism based on effortless accord with nature. Yang Chu, from what little we know of him, was opposed to busybody-like interference with the affairs and thoughts of others, and regarded an official career under prevailing conditions as both useless to the community and dangerous to oneself; so it is recorded of him that he would not have accepted the Empire even at the price of one hair! The true mystic, though full of compassionate concern for the welfare of all beings, cannot help being immediately preoccupied with his own progress, since liberating the mind from the delusions conjured by the senses is something neither god nor man can do on his behalf; self-cultivation is needed before one can benefit the world, and self-realization must come before one can claim to know or teach truth.

The third in point of time, but second in the hierarchy of Taoist philosophers, was Chuang Chou or Chuang-tzû (born in Honan in the fourth century B.C?) whom, though very few details of his life are known, even the scholars credit with being the author of some parts of the book which bears his name, no doubt regarding the possibility of his having written all of it as a theory altogether too naïve to merit serious attention. But, again, does it matter? What matters exceedingly is that the book attributed to Chuang-tzû exists and is replete with insight, wisdom and humour that have benignly influenced generation upon generation of human beings.

The fourth reputed 'founder', Lieh-tzû, though a book said to belong to the Han period (second century B.C. to second century A.D.) bears his name, is not generally allowed to have existed at all. Thus he seems to have outdone those Taoist adepts who vanished into thin air, by never having emerged in the first place! In any case, the book of Lieh-tzû contains a chapter on Yang Chu and this constitutes one of the rare sources of information on that sage, whose alleged egoism consisted of determination to follow his own reasoning and impulses – a doctrine that could be dangerous, but surely not in the case of one whose joy it was to live close to nature and to be inspired by its harmonies and rhythms?

As to the word 'Tao' itself, it is a term of great antiquity long used by different philosophers in as many senses as the word 'God' is employed by different schools of religion. Literally meaning 'way' or 'path', it was later used by the Confucians to mean the divinely ordained path of rectitude; by the Buddhists as an equivalent of *Fa* (Dharma, Doctrine of the Buddha); and by the

Taoists to mean a combination of the undifferentiated unity from which the universe evolved; the supreme creative and sustaining power which nourishes the myriad creatures; the way in which nature operates; and the course which men should follow in order to rise above worldly life and achieve harmony with the Ultimate. It is what Christian mystics call the Godhead and what Buddhist sages mean by *Sunyata*, that mysterious void in which all things have their being.[1] Of this Way, the *Tao Tê Ching* has much to say, as for example: 'The Way that can be expressed in words (literally the *Tao* that can be *Tao*-ed) is not the Eternal Way ...' 'There is something evolved from chaos, antecedent to heaven and earth, silent and vast, spontaneous and immutable, omnipresent and eternal, which can be regarded as the Mother of Heaven and Earth ...' 'The Way gave birth to one, the one to two, the two to three, the three to all the myriad objects which, carrying the *yin* (negative female principle) and embracing the *yang* (positive male principle) owe their harmony to the blending of these two ...' '(Mere) mouthing about the Way makes it seem insipid, tasteless; (for it is so subtle that) the eye cannot behold it; hark and you will not hear it; yet its functions are inexhaustible ...' 'Its summit does not dazzle, its base is not obscure. Intangible (in a manner) not to be described, it leads back to the state of void. Thus one speaks of a shape that is no shape, of an image that has no form; one speaks of what is indistinct, shadowy. Stand before it, you will not see its head; follow it, you will not see its tail. By holding fast to this primordial Way, the present can be governed. Awareness of the primal origin is called (bearing) the imprint of the Way.'

To understand why the work attributed to Lao-tzû bears the title *Tao Tê Ching*, it is necessary to have some knowledge of the term *Tê*, power. (*Ching* simply means 'classic' and can be discarded if we choose to use some such English title as *The Way and Its Power*.) In fact, *Tê* does not mean exactly power, but rather virtue – to Confucians, virtue in the moral sense; to Taoists, in the biblical sense of the virtue that went out of Jesus when the woman touched his robe. To Taoists, *Tê* also connotes the nature of an entity, that which empowers it and makes it what it is. In other words, it is the Tao as embodied in each separate

[1] In early Chinese translations, St John's Gospel begins: 'In the beginning was the Tao.'

creation. Christian mystics may see an analogy between the Tao and God, the *Tê* and the Holy Spirit or the Christ Within, though of course there is no vestige of anthropomorphism in either of the Taoist terms. Mahayana Buddhists may perhaps equate *Tê* with the Buddha-root enshrined in the heart of each sentient being.

Another peculiarly Taoist term that needs clarifying is *wu-wei* (non-action). This does not mean quite what it says, but rather not going beyond spontaneous action that accords with needs as they arise; not indulging in artfully calculated action and not acting with the intention of exceeding the very minimum required for effective results. Thus, profit-motivated action is totally excluded. *Wu-wei* is based on the mystical concept that, if we keep still and listen to the inner promptings of the spirit, we shall act spontaneously, correctly, efficaciously, yet hardly giving the matter a thought, just as branches naturally bend towards the sun or as kittens make an untaught response to scratching noises.

Most Taoists in my day subscribed to what was called the Yellow Emperor's School, yet revered Lao-tzû and Chuang-tzû profoundly and did not think to cast doubts upon either their existence or the authorship of the works attributed to them, thus displaying a contentment with things as they are (or had become). Their disinclination for learning unproductive of peace of mind was more closely consonant with the spirit of those works than the sometimes destructive researches of scholars dedicated to the search for 'pure Taoism'. Of poor Lieh-tzû, who is declared not to have existed, it may be that, like both my great-great-great-great-grandfathers (who most certainly did exist), he chanced not to have his biographical details recorded by a sufficiently reliable source. Concerning the later masters of the Yellow Emperor's School, we have enough details to fill a large volume, but it is difficult to distinguish between fact and legend. The following account of Ko Hung is fairly typical and the very important Heavenly Teacher Chang is dealt with at some length in another chapter.

The Master Ko Hung, who lived around the beginning of the fourth century A.D., was a scientist of considerable renown. It is to some of his disciples that we owe the work called by the Master's nickname, Pao-p'u-tzû (the Master Who Embraces

Things in the Rough). From it we learn that he found the society of his day too frivolous and his fellow Taoists somewhat overcredulous; for example, he pointed out that, while the sexual form of yogic alchemy on which some of them based hopes of being able to transmogrify their flesh into a virtually immortal adamantine substance was all very well as a means of prolonging life and guarding one's health, it was no way to set about attaining immortality, nor yet, as was popularly supposed, a means of securing good fortune in the form of wealth and rank. However, he came to place great stress on the internal (or *kundalini* type of) yogic alchemy. Certain of his followers have interpreted his teachings on that subject as referring obliquely to the sexual variant – a natural error, if indeed it be an error, in that his yogic manuals were written in a sort of code language that could be interpreted at several levels. So convinced did he become of the importance of yogic alchemy and so high were the hopes he ultimately reposed in it, that he came to believe in transmogrification of man's fleshly body as a sure way of achieving immortality, if only one could discover the right formula. Towards the end of his life, he settled upon Mount Lo-fu and devoted himself to searching for the precious formula. It is written that, in his eighty-first year, he vanished from human ken, leaving his clothes behind him, this being the usual manner of hinting at a sage's transmogrification. His personal life must have pleased even his non-Taoist contemporaries, as he combined his devotion to 'alchemy' with ethical views derived from the Confucians. Incidentally, modern scientists interested in the development preceding the point at which alchemy gave place to chemistry esteem Master Ko Hung as a fellow-scientist remarkably knowledgeable by the standards of his day.

We may now assemble a few of the principal sages and others to whose efforts the development of Taoism was due (see overleaf).

It will be noticed that mysticism and philosophy permeate all branches; in fact, any threefold division is arbitrary; certainly a great many Taoists would have roared with laughter at my presumption in making it. From the five-thousand-word *Tao Tê Ching* alone, it is possible to derive mystical, cosmological, religious, philosophical, ethical, yogic, naturalistic, political, educational and even military lessons, as well as hints of magical practice and at least one piece of information of importance to

THE SECRET AND SUBLIME

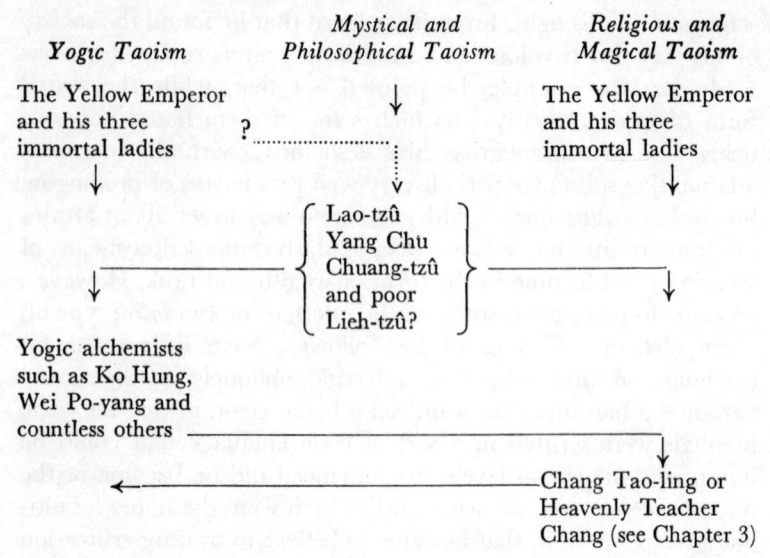

Yogic Taoism	Mystical and Philosophical Taoism	Religious and Magical Taoism
The Yellow Emperor and his three immortal ladies ↓	↓ ? ⋯⋯⋯ ↓ Lao-tzû Yang Chu Chuang-tzû and poor Lieh-tzû?	The Yellow Emperor and his three immortal ladies ↓
↓ Yogic alchemists such as Ko Hung, Wei Po-yang and countless others		↓

←——————————————————Chang Tao-ling or
Heavenly Teacher
Chang (see Chapter 3)

adepts in the white-tiger/green-dragon (sexual) yoga. In the book of Chuang-tzû, too, most of these elements are present, but mystical or quietist philosophy plays a larger and more emphatic part. That the notion of a plurality of gods is not an extraneous addition to the teaching of Lao-Chuang can be judged from several references in the *Tao Tê Ching*, such as: 'The gods derive their powers from the One.' I have never understood why so many Westerners think it more reasonable to believe in one god than in many. The Taoist (and also the Buddhist) view is quite to the contrary—namely that the Supreme Being is not a being but a Non-Being which cannot possibly be concerned with whether Mr Wu has a fine day for his wedding or little Wang passes his primary-school examination; but that there are indeed a goodly number of divinities, from the high gods, who, though not truly immortal, endure for aeons, to nature-spirits whose paltry life-spans can be numbered in centuries, to say nothing of the many categories of demon. Western man has forgotten those hierarchies of beings variously known as gods or angels, demons or goblins, once manifest to the entire human race under various names and guises, as evidenced by the scriptures of every world-religion; but this does not mean that those beings have forgotten Western man, at whose expense they continue to amuse themselves, assisting or plaguing him according to their whim, bestowing what he takes for a run of good or bad luck, or sending him off gibbering in headlong retreat to the magical protection promised by the psychiatrist's den. Not that those Taoists whose main interest was in mysticism or yoga were greatly concerned with the spectacular array of divinities, fiends, nature-spirits; majestic beasts such as dragons, lion-tailed *ch'i-lin* (Chinese unicorns) and multi-hued phœnixes; or foxes able to assume the form of lovely maidens to the great confusion of lascivious young men. If they offered them incense, flowers and tea or (in the case of demons and fox-spirits) a little wine and flesh, that was no more than prudence, since they lived in communities where some of their rasher colleagues actually invited commerce with those exotic beings. Certainly it was not supposed that divine or demonic intervention was a means of promoting success in yoga or of hastening one's progress towards mystical union with the Ultimate. Of gods the best that could be expected was a little intermittent and uncertain help in gaining wealth or fame, which thoughtful Taoists regarded as being in any case not boons but sources of perpetual disturbance. On the other hand, the existence of such beings was never doubted, nor is it likely to be disputed by anyone who has entered the magic portals of the Taoist world. All that remains in doubt is whether those beings really inhabit mysterious hidden realms and mountains, caves, pools and groves independently of the beholder; whether they dwell wholly in our minds; or whether they are at once to some extent objective entities and yet in some sense the product of our own subconscious, as Jung would have it. Who can say? If this is a riddle, one has only to pass through the mysterious portals to discover why such beings cannot be laughed out of existence, why accepting them without seeing them and seeing them without accepting them both make good sense. If this book allots disproportionate space to them, that results not only from a desire to entertain, for I recognize that serious readers interested in following the path to the contemplative's ardently longed-for goal may be impatient of my detailed descriptions of what could be called mere wayside scenery; the problem is that I have less to say about the core of the sacred teachings, as there are many matters in which I received no advanced instruction and others in which such instruction was, for certain good reasons, imparted under the seal of silence.

With the approach of the year 2000, in almost every corner

of the globe, the contemporary values of the modern Western world are growing predominant. Unless one goes to the Himalayas, where the Tibetans in particular still preserve something of their ancient wisdom, it is now scarcely possible to enter that eerie world peopled by gods and demons who are none the less powerful for perhaps not quite existing in a fully objective sense. The disappearance of that world is a pity. Just a few decades ago, by visiting many uncommercialized parts of Asia, one could travel backwards in time, which was to my mind far more attractive and certainly more profitable than journeying in space to a lifeless orb. Also, the secret gateway rose unobtrusively amidst poetically beautiful surroundings that were in themselves a joy. The founders of Taoist hermitages, for example, had a genius for choosing spots abounding in mountain torrents, limpid pools well suited to be the haunt of dragons, ancient pines and cedars, and curious folds of rock concealing mysterious grottos. Their dramatic loveliness was there for all to see. Not so the magic portals; for they, being conjured from the mist, displayed their rainbow colours only to those with eyes to see and, even then, not often; one might spend months or years in their vicinity and discover nothing more astonishing than the sweetness of the smiling hermits who guarded their secrets. Visitors, unless they cultivated appropriate attitudes, such as humility and a sense of wonder, might search for them in vain and come away echoing the English colonel who, after visiting Mount Lo-fu, exclaimed petulantly: 'The whole bag of spookish tricks and yogic mysteries is unmitigated moonshine!'

If wisdom were the traveller's goal, the rest of his lifetime might barely be sufficient for his quest, though he might sometimes stumble quickly upon clues to it, thanks to having discovered the right teacher and companions. First, affinities had to be established, all the more so as visitors from the West had acquired a sad reputation for arrogance and mockery. A newcomer had to show himself worthy of the privilege of being guided through the dim portals; until then, he was likely to remain unaware of strange occurrences happening under his very nose.

Even those Westerners who approach Eastern traditions with a courteous humility and a sincere desire to learn are at a disadvantage; our education and upbringing have disposed us to exclaim: 'I dig that stuff about yoga and meditation; but, hell, don't try to put it over that the air is thick with gods and goblins!' Personally, I found it better to be overcredulous rather than frankly disbelieving. Disbelief can so easily lead to both arrogance and ignorance; besides, the Taoists (like the Tibetan Buddhists of today) had inherited traditions so antique that their origin was lost in mist; it was bewildering to discover that the precious means to Liberation or union with the Ultimate, such as meditation and high yoga, were intertwined with other mysteries, fascinating in their way no doubt, but surely of trivial consequence. I remember trying to separate them, thinking 'I'll go for this, but not for that.' There seemed no harm in attempting to evaluate different kinds of experience, so long as I refrained from criticism and mockery; but, as often as I dismissed allegedly supernatural occurrences as spurious, something would happen to make me wonder, especially when I had dealings with oracles. The Lama Govinda, in writing of Tibetan spirit-possessed oracles, who function in much the same way as their Taoist counterparts, adduces the testimony of a European savant new to such manifestations and by no means predisposed to believe uncritically. To requote the passage in part, Amaury de Riencourt writes in his *Lost World*: 'I was stunned, stupefied . . . by some indefinable conviction that I had seen an occult performance . . . The performances of the oracles had opened to me the gates of a new and entrancing world . . . the mysterious world of magic and psychic forces, the universe of yoga and of what lies beyond.'

Some demonstrations of spirit-possession or psychic powers move a curtain from beyond which strange 'energies' impinge upon one's consciousness too forcefully to admit of outright disbelief. In any case it is best, I am sure, to suspend judgement and abandon preconceived notions, for a mental reservation to the effect that half of what one sees and hears is nonsense is easily intuited by people much given to contemplative exercises; and so condescending an attitude is not endearing to those who might otherwise teach us something of great value. The appearance, manner and speech of some of the Chinese and Tibetan sages I met so convinced me of their high wisdom and integrity that I felt bound to respect the totality of their beliefs and practices, including those which, judged superficially, seemed to me of doubtful value. Only by immersing oneself in the ideas and practices they taught could one become qualified to make the distinctions implied by acceptance or rejection.

There is also the matter of environment or mood. When walking down London's Bond Street or sitting at my office desk in the heart of Bangkok's concrete wilderness, I am inclined to relegate gods and demons to the realm of dreams and imagination. Were my secretary to become possessed by a malevolent demon or to rise in the air with mysterious rays emanating from her body, I should be absolutely astounded; the familiar click of her typewriter and hum of the air-conditioner prohibit such expectations. On the other hand, when seated late at night in my Buddha-room, when wandering on some mountainside gazing down upon a fantastic medley of temple-roofs or exploring a sacred grotto in which the effigies of mysterious beings glimmer faintly in the light of votive candles; when listening to the high sweet tinkle of Tibetan *dorje-bells* and spirited rattle of prayer-drums, or the thunderous roar of *radongs* and the ear-splitting clash of giant cymbals, or the thin, eerie melody of a Taoist flute—when my senses are flooded by unearthly sights and sounds, I remember secrets known in childhood or perhaps in former lives, precious secrets tragically forgotten. At such moments, the store of knowledge so painfully gathered at school and university strikes me as a largely worthless clutter of facts and shallow views that lead to the frittering away of one's life on vain pursuits. Preconceptions, scepticism and prejudice fall away like a shower of withered bamboo-fronds in a gust of wind; fallible logic gives way to wordless intuition. An inner stillness supervenes; everything within my purview, down to the smallest blade of grass or insect, takes on a freshness and a beauty hitherto unperceived. At times like these, shining gods, grimacing demons, sinuous dragons and those strange monsters which lurk beyond the threshold of limited consciousness are apt to manifest themselves. Nor are they frightening. Let a demon gobble and gibber however menacingly, one recognizes him as a long-time companion—even as a potential ally—and says with a smile: 'So *there* you are! I had almost forgotten you, friend!'

If for the sake of convenience we speak of Taoism as having had three distinct levels, then the middle one may be called yogic Taoism. The purpose of the yogins was to achieve health, rejuvenation, a vigorous old age, long life and even physical immortality by a combination of meditation and yogic exercises based on the so-called internal alchemy. Visualization, breathing and other physical exercises were involved; but, as with the yogas of other religions, the methods were kept secret, being transmitted partly by oral instruction and partly by manuals couched in alchemical terms. Taking the manuals at their face-value, some Taoists did in fact seek formulas for transmuting base metals and for compounding an elixir that would confer radiant health and immortality. Certain of their colleagues probably smiled into their sleeves at such simple-mindedness, but who knows how many of the professed alchemists were not just pretending, for the benefit of outsiders, to be engaged in an external search for the exotic formulas popularly associated with longevity? In any case, as Professor Needham has pointed out, their alchemic experiments were to prove of considerable scientific value. As to the yogas based on 'internal alchemy', which required the co-mingling of generative force (*ching*) and spirit (*shên*) by means of cosmic breath-vitality (*ch'i*), they included sexual yogas of Tantric type that were frowned upon by not a few Taoist adepts and were positive anathema to the government authorities.

Taoist philosophers (as opposed to yogic adepts) are credited by some scholars with having sought no higher goal than a pleasant life secured by withdrawing from the world to avoid the dangers inherent in the political life of the Empire and by cultivating their inborn affinity with nature. Be this as it may, a good many of those philosophers seem to have been mystics of the highest order who had set their minds on that high goal which has shone like the Holy Grail before the eyes of contemplatives everywhere. Initiates of the ancient mystery cults, Egyptian, Mithraic and Eleusinian, perceived it, as did the sage Plotinus and, in later centuries, Master Ekhart, St John of the Cross in Europe, and the Sufi mystics of Persia and Morocco. As for eastern Asia, among Hindus and Buddhists, as well as Taoists, the strand of mysticism has always been strong. Men who have raised their eyes so high transcend tradition, reaching out to what has been called the Truth beyond religions, which is precisely what was often meant by the term Tao. Whether union with the Ultimate is regarded as an *attainment* or as a *realization* of a union never interrupted from the first (this latter being the view of most schools of Mayahana Buddhism, including Zen and Vajrayana), the character of the mystical experience is, of course, one and the same. The Taoists, rightly conceiving that, since names are by their nature limiting, the Illimitable must be nameless, chose the provisional name Tao which, since its primary meaning is Way, carries with it the subtle implication, so familiar to Mayahana Buddhists, that the goal and the path to it are in essence one. Moreover, all mystics are agreed that whatever name they use for the Ultimate – Tao, Godhead, *Sunyata*, etc. – can at best be a makeshift, since nothing can be predicted of a state beyond time and space that transcends all dualities. Even to say that It exists or does not exist is to belittle It, since each of those terms excludes its opposite and is therefore finite. The nature of the goal can be known only to those exalted beings who have realized it for themselves.

If one can accept the identification of the source and being of all with mind, in which supposition some physicists now support the mystics, then ten thousand obstacles to understanding vanish and everything falls into place. Even miracles are explained – by mind, disease is cured; breath, blood and semen are marvellously controlled; flesh is made impervious to fire; objects are caused to appear and vanish; barriers of space and time are conquered in a flash. Conversely, if this perception is rejected, then mystics and their admirers (including the present writer) may appear as charlatans or fools! Acceptance requires that we regard this universe not as illusory in the sense of not existing, but as a reality which, filtered through our faulty senses, is apprehended as other than it is, with the result that we falsely assume each entity to have its own being, instead of recognizing all of them as interdependent, transitory semblances with no true being outside the Tao. When Dr Johnson kicked a table to demonstrate his conviction that it was as solid as it seemed, he left out of account that such a kick might be delivered in a dream with apparently similar results and yet prove nothing of the sort.

That successful yogins, Taoist or otherwise, develop what are sometimes called supernormal or even magic powers is an undoubted fact; but what is or is not magic depends, of course, on one's point of view. For example, as one enters the little wooden cottage where I live, the eye is caught by a magnificent Mongolian painting of Amitayus Buddha hanging above a magic box in which, for my eleven-year-old daughter's pleasure, I cause to be conjured up mysterious glimpses of events taking place far away; the sight of them would have made my grandfather break out in a sweat of fear, whereas my daughter can scarcely imagine a television-free world.

Those who do not understand the powers developed by yoga suspect conjuring or fraud; yet most people who are prepared to undergo the severe rigours of yogic training – often including from three to seven years spent in solitary confinement – can certainly acquire them. Not that such powers are important; rather they are hindrances to progress, since they distract the mind from its true goal and draw unwelcome attention. This is the reason why spectacular miracles are seldom seen; those able to perform them guard their powers from the eyes of the profane, whereas those eager to display them are generally too shallow-minded to attain them. Hence travellers merely hoping for demonstrations of supernormal arts are doomed to disappointment or to becoming the prey of charlatans; whereas those who thirst for true wisdom and therefore set little store by marvels are likely to behold sights which to those others remain quite maddeningly elusive.

Away now with abstract discussion; let people and events speak for themselves!

Chapter 2

Stumbling Upon Taoism: Some Taoist Recluses

In my early twenties, I was fortunate enough to spend some years in Peking. In those days, arriving there from the West was like travelling back to another century. *Everything* was different – streets, houses, gardens, people, costumes and household objects, as well as language, food and manners. Within the battlemented walls of that ancient city a large measure of China's traditional culture still survived; the old ways had not yet been shattered by modern innovations; the devastating Japanese occupation was still to come; as for communists, they scarcely, if ever, entered people's thoughts. Innumerable rays of the past splendours of the imperial capital continued to shed their light.

With so much beauty lying about me, I was seldom tempted to venture beyond Peking's outer gateways, but now and then I would visit a lovely range of hills rising to the north-west of the city; and once I happened to pass a night there in a small Taoist temple that lay securely in a sheltered fold. It was autumn. The trees cascading down the hillsides presented a gorgeous display of scarlet, crimson, copper, bronze and gold, interspersed with the dark-green foliage of ancient cedars noted for their silvery-white bark. The aged temple showed signs of neglect, but its mossy tiles and weathered grey-brick walls still resisted inclement weather after five whole centuries of existence. It was inhabited by a solitary recluse, a dignified figure clad in Taoist garb who looked about eighty. His face was a network of wrinkles, his grey beard was flecked with white, but his movements had the grace and alertness one comes to expect of elderly Taoists, whose extraordinary exercises preserve health and youthful vigour for many decades. I admired his antique clothes – a long robe of bronze-coloured cloth with enormous flapping sleeves resembling the wings of butterflies, and a curious stiff hat from the centre of which protruded a topknot of grey hair secured by an elaborately carved peg. A pretty ten-year-old child, long-haired and wearing a sky-blue robe, appeared; it was impossible to determine whether it was a boy or a girl. This child served us with pale-green tea in thick earthenware bowls, and some saucers of pine kernels, melon seeds, and sweetmeats made of rice flour. My host, whose name was Ch'ing-t'an Hsiên-jên, (the Immortal of the Limpid Pool) soon called for heated wine, which the child brought in a narrow porcelain jar placed in a bowl of warm water to maintain its temperature at a higher level than is common for Western-style wines. Yellowish-green in colour, the mild wine tasted delicately of herbs. At first our conversation followed the usual stilted lines, host and guest courteously requesting details about each other; but when he perceived I was eager to learn something of Taoism, the recluse became less formal. Between the first and second jars, he persuaded me to don a padded Taoist gown as a protection against the evening chill, and led me into the main courtyard where he showed me several curious objects, including a rockery composed of fantastically shaped stones brought by some long-departed emperor from close to the frontier of Burma. This cunningly fashioned landscape, complete with mountains, grottoes, pools and winding river, produced the illusion of a distant scene. Half-closing my eyes, I could imagine a great range of mountains with contours pleasingly grotesque.

'And this!' he said, pointing to a plinth on which stood an oblong basin of dull-coloured earthenware containing a landscape created on a truly minute scale; clearly the work of a gifted artist, it was perfect in every detail. Idly I asked why the plinth was so tall and his answer plunged me into a world of fantasy.

'You see, it is not just an ornament, but the present dwelling of the Great Master Po Yün who was abbot here three hundred years ago. It would be disrespectful to place it closer to the ground.'

'You mean his spirit lives here?'

'Certainly. His body, too. It is his whim to be tiny and he is generally invisible; but, as you see, the Immortal eats and drinks like humans, though very little and not often. He chose to assume the stature of a very small dragon-fly, so they say.'

I gazed at some of the tiny dishes and at three empty goblets no bigger than daisies, noting that one of the dishes contained finely chopped minced vegetables and mushrooms. Naturally I could not make myself believe in the existence of that minute, invisible being; but out of courtesy, bowed low before his 'dwelling', thus winning from my host an approving smile. This fantasy was the one irrational feature of his otherwise admirably sane and lucid conversation. With Taoists one had rather to expect such anomalies – a sure taste for beauty and a capacity for profound mystical or philosophical thought mingled with the most puzzling ingredients. I was sure that the old gentleman was not joking but I have never known what he really meant. Shyness prevented me from pursuing the matter further. Leading me back indoors, he broached a second little jar of heated wine; its contents gave me the courage to ask him why he, too, bore the title 'Immortal'.

'My disciples are foolish,' he smiled. 'They choose to think I shall live forever in this body. Such simple-minded people! When the ancients spoke of the possible transmogrification of the human body, they were hinting in guarded terms at a much more subtle reality.'

'And yet, Your Immortality, I have heard that certain learned Taoists do believe they can transmogrify their mortal flesh into spirit able to fly through the air and endure for aeons.'

'No doubt, no doubt!' he answered, by no means disconcerted. 'It would not do to contradict them. I spoke thoughtlessly.'

He fell silent and presently we turned to other matters.

'Tell me,' I said, when for the tenth or eleventh time we had completed the antique ceremony of rising from our seats, carrying the tiny wine-cups to our lips with the fingertips of both hands, quaffing them solemnly, bowing low to each other and resuming our seats, 'what exactly do Taoist recluses do?'

'Such a question!' he roared in mock indignation. 'Be very sure we do not.'

'Do not what?' For a moment I thought my understanding of his Chinese was at fault, but suddenly he laughed and said :

'*Wu-wei* (non-action) is our cardinal principle. You must know that asking a Taoist what he does is like asking a Confucian how he sins!'

'I beg Your Immortality's pardon,' I replied, joining in his laughter. 'Perhaps I should have asked what exactly it is that you do not?'

'Much better, my young friend. I like you. Chinese youths these days mostly treat us as if we were innkeepers with nothing better to occupy us than looking after travellers. I shall tell you a secret. We *do* as well as *don't*, but then, you see, it is a special Taoist kind of doing. Not to do at all would make a recluse as useless as a dead pine-tree. Do you know the meaning of the Sublime Tao?'

I nodded. 'The Sublime Tao is what we Westerners call Ultimate Reality. At least I think so. Is it not the totality of being, the beginning and end of all existence? From the Tao we come; to the Tao we go – something like that?'

'Something like that,' he repeated. 'You may be – forgive me – a barbarian, but you do apprehend a fragment of the meaning, which is more than can be said for those noisy undergraduates from Tsinghua who visit these hills at weekends. Permit me to expound *wu-wei*. It only appears to mean "action rooted in not-ness". What it really means is "action rooted in non-being". And what is non-being? It is the Great Non-Being, a name for the Sublime Tao which is the formless matrix of a myriad forms. As I interpret it, *wu-wei* simply means "action rooted in the Tao". What we shun is calculated activity, which can never be spontaneous, harmonious, free!'

His voice had taken on a liturgical solemnity and this lapse into a priestly rôle seemed to amuse him, for he smiled deprecatingly and went on more softly:

'Activity in itself is not harmful, but it must be just an instinctive response to immediate needs. Calculation or self-interested forethought leads to demon-action. Only activity proceeding from a mind that resembles a calm, deep pool of stillness can be free from undesirable results. Therefore I rise two hours before dawn and sit in meditation until noon, cultivating perfect inner stillness. When no thought moves, I feel the pulsing of the Tao. Then I am one with the plants whose sap pulses through their leaves, one with the stars pulsing with the glowing energy of fire. Because my thoughts are stilled, the Tao flows through me, its movement unimpeded. My words and actions are a natural, uncalculated response to present circumstances. A tree growing in the shadow of a wall does not think "in order to live, I must bend my leaves towards the sunshine and drink the water with my roots". It does those things spontaneously. Its spontaneous activity proceeding from stillness fulfils its needs.'

'Does the Tao resemble Shang-Ti, the Supreme God of the Christians?'

'Certainly not. The Tao does not declare: "Let this or that be so" or "I shall do thus and thus". Nor is it separate from spirits, people, animals, rocks or plants. It is not just the source of being, but the being of all beings, the fullness and the nothingness of all things. Acting spontaneously, exerting no will, it acts gloriously. By according with its action, I, who am eighty-three years old, may hope to live perhaps for another thirty years — another fifty even; but not many people attain that great age in their fleshly bodies. Flesh must die, for the Tao, though changeless, is ever changing and none of its myriad creations endures long.'

'Why then do Taoists think so much in terms of immortality?'

'By personal immortality is sometimes meant relative immortality, the ability to endure a few aeons in some bodily or spiritual form. What are aeons in comparison with the everlasting Tao? Only the Tao as Being-Non-Being is truly immortal; the entities it forms never cease to change. Their constituents must ultimately dissolve.'

'Could a Taoist achieve even relative immortality if he were living in Peking or some other great city?'

'It would be more difficult. What is needed to prolong life even by a few decades is perfect serenity, the result of freedom from restriction. How is that possible in a city where man-made laws and man-made custom compel us to behave like demons?'

It had grown late. Before leading me to my bedroom, he offered to give me some yogic teaching in the morning, breaking his meditation to explain its principles. Such an opportunity was too rare to be missed, even though it entailed rising hours before dawn and though autumn nights in those hills were, by my standards, bitterly cold.

When he came to call me, I was asleep on the hard wooden bed, wrapped in a cocoon of wadded quilts. Teeth chattering, I donned the robe he had lent me, throwing a quilt over it like a cloak. As for the Immortal, he seemed scarcely to notice the cold. Wearing nothing over his robe, which was but lightly padded, he led me to his own room, where the image of a youthful deity enthroned behind a simple altar gazed down on us. The painted eyes seemed fixed on mine with a disconcerting expression of faint surprise. Lighting incense and candles, my host signalled to me to join him in making three full prostrations. Then he stood chanting melodiously the words of a sacred text lying open on the altar. To mark the rhythm he tapped a mallet against a hollow block of wood identical with the wooden-fish drums used in Buddhist temples. When this short rite was finished, he ordered me to sit on his bed with a second quilt about my shoulders and made sure that I was comfortable. Taking up a position cross-legged on a cushion placed on the ground, he embarked on some curious breathing-exercises so that the *ch'i* (universal psychic vitality) would circulate freely through his body. At the beginning he made violent motions of the arms, his sleeves flapping like wings. The next stage consisted of a rotating movement made by the muscles of his abdomen; despite the cold, he lifted up his robe to reveal his stomach, which looked as if it might contain a writhing python. Presently he grew still and his breathing subsided until no sound was audible. Simultaneously all movements of his body ceased. To all appearances, I was alone with a corpse sitting upright on the floor. How long this endured, I do not know. Barely able to keep awake, I saw the room grow light, and presently noticed that his eyes, long shut, were open and fixed on me.

'So you see, my young friend, how it is done. The preliminary exercises were designed to induce circulation of the *ch'i*. Later, I grew calm and my breathing became imperceptible even to myself. Meanwhile, my consciousness was directed to my nostrils, to promote awareness of the rhythm of my breathing. Next I concentrated on the Mysterious Gate of the Square Inch, which lies midway between the eyes; there it normally stays unwaveringly until noon.'

'What do you feel at such times?'

'*I* have no feeling. Though bliss arises, it is not *my* bliss, but an attribute of the Tao shining through that ghost, my body.'

'And then?'

'What else? Go now to have your breakfast. I shall re-enter absorption in the Tao and so remain until midday. If you are obliged to leave earlier, pray excuse my not seeing you off, for, when you come to think of it, *I* shall not be here.'

Dismissing me with a wave, he resumed his meditation. When

the child came in to serve my breakfast of millet-porridge and pickled bean-curd, I was still doubtful whether it was a boy or a girl. In answer to my question, came a high-pitched giggle.

'A boy, of course. Can't you see? Grandfather will laugh when I tell him.'

'So you are grandson to the Immortal of the Limpid Pool! You must be proud.'

'Yes, yes. I'm the lucky one of the family. All my brothers and sisters go to school to learn nonsense, but Grandfather keeps me beside him to learn *real* things. I'm going to be an Immortal with a body of pure white weightless jade. I shall be able to fly like a bird – no, an airplane, all over the world.'

'Did your grandfather tell you that?'

'Oh, no. Everyone says so, though. Grandfather just smiles when I ask him. He knows it's true, but he's afraid of my being proud, you know. Still, I'm a Taoist, so I'll never be proud. Pride's just silly. I shall love being able to fly, but then anyone could do the same if he had Grandfather to teach him – even a girl, I should think.'

'What do you know about the Tao?' I asked with deep interest.

'The Tao? Oh, the Tao is big, big, big.' He spread out his arms to show me. 'Everything you see or hear or touch has the Tao. It's everywhere – in me, in you. No, that's wrong. Grandfather says it *is* me and you. I can fly from here to the Dipper Star, but not get away from the Tao. Do you know what Grandfather said yesterday?'

'What was that?'

'Someone rode up here, you see, and his horse left its yellow droppings outside our gate. Grandfather was pleased when I asked if those droppings were the Tao. He called them beautiful. I said, "Grandfather, they stink," and he said, "Yes, Little Five, they stink of Tao." I was shocked, you know, but Grandfather says if I keep my nose clean, everything will smell as sweetly as flowers.'

I grinned. 'Why do you laugh at me?' he asked indignantly. 'If Grandfather says so, it must be true. Perhaps your nose needs cleaning, too.'

'I'm sure it does, Little Five. If your grandfather became my teacher, I'd learn how to make it clean once and for all.'

I left soon after breakfast, climbing further into the hills so as to reach a large Buddhist temple which was the real object of

SOME TAOIST RECLUSES

my journey. The sun-dappled ground was carpeted with leaves and the birds were chorusing Taoistic approval. Following the narrow pathway, I reflected on what I had learnt, already wondering whether certain aspects of Taoism could be woven into a non-Taoist's way of living, and very curious about the whole subject.

Visits to other Taoists followed; the more I came into contact with Taoist recluses, the more I found their beliefs to be an extraordinary mixture of lofty wisdom and what struck me then as laughable or even puerile fantasies. This is well illustrated by my meeting on Mount Nan Yeo with a certain Pien Tao-shih, and so I shall relate the story in some detail. Nan Yeo, most southerly of Taoism's Five Sacred Peaks, is in Hunan province. Monasteries and the cells of anchorites cling to its precipitous slopes in profusion; buildings on the upper slopes are, as often as not, veiled by mist and clouds or, as some would say, by the breath of dragons. While making for a celebrated temple about halfway to the summit, I lost my way; a thick white mist descended, causing me to take a wrong turn and follow an undulating path curving round to the cold north face of the mountain where habitations were sparse. Unlike the route I had diverged from, it led past no shrines or buildings, but was solitary and wild. Presently the mist deepened and I wondered uneasily whether I should find shelter for the night. Stories of bandits, wild beasts and demons came flooding into my mind, so that I was overjoyed to find that the path stopped short before a low grey wall. There was a moon-gate with panels of faded scarlet lacquer beneath an oblong board bearing in gold calligraphy the legend: 'Yün Hai Tung (Grotto of the Sea of Clouds)'. I was just in time. One of the gate's two leaves stood slightly ajar, but already a Taoist greybeard was preparing to bolt it for the night.

'Ho there, Distinguished Immortal,' I panted. 'I was hoping to find shelter.'

He pushed open the gate, and, peering at me curiously through the wisps of cloud, hurried forward to make me welcome with elaborate courtesy. Raising and lowering his clasped hands effusively, he addressed me in archaic manner.

'Welcome, sir. Welcome to such poor comforts as our humble dwelling can offer. Night is upon us. If you will deign to accept frugal meals of coarse vegetables and cold spring water, we shall endeavour to make your visit bearable for as long as you care to honour us with your illustrious company.'

'No, no, this humble person dare not put you to such trouble,' I answered politely, but a chilly rain was falling and I hurried towards the ancient wooden gates. Stepping over a high sill, I entered a courtyard with rows of one-storey dwellings to left and right and a medium-sized shrine-hall opposite the gate. The greybeard shouted to make my presence known and an elderly man hurried out of a doorway to receive me. Dressed in a simple robe of blue cloth, he wore a most peculiar hat, tall and rectangular, which hid his topknot completely. Despite his years, he possessed a certain youthful grace of movement and eyes of extraordinary brilliance. To my relief, he did not keep me standing in the icy rain exchanging compliments, but seized my hand and pulled me under the broad eaves, calling for someone to attend to the 'distinguished guest'. Later I discovered he was the Abbot. Meanwhile a couple of young boys, also in Taoist garb, came running out to lead me to a guest room.

The hospitality of that hermitage, though less than luxurious, was heart-warming. My room, which adjoined the shrine-hall, was small, but it was furnished with heavy old wooden pieces, including a great bed boxed in on three sides and curtained on the fourth. I noticed a couple of wall-scrolls, one displaying fine calligraphy in the ancient seal-style, the other depicting an elderly sage apparently feeling quite at home, though seated on a cloud-girt rock. On the table near my bed stood a porcelain vase containing a few branches of some sort of fruit-blossom. One of the boys brought me a copper hand-basin of pleasantly hot water. Bowing low, he urged me to wash quickly, hinting that delay would mean keeping everybody trom their dinner.

As soon as I entered the refectory, eight or nine recluses converged upon the round table, insisting that I take the seat of honour facing the doorway; however, in view of my youth, etiquette required that I accept it only after making a great fuss, and so at last the Abbot seized my arm and literally forced me to sit where bidden. The food consisted of some five or six dishes; as they had certainly had no time to prepare anything special for an unexpected guest, it was clear that these recluses did themselves fairly well. Rice was not brought in until the close of the meal, as the serving-lads kept refilling our wine cups from heated pewter containers, and it was a rule not to serve rice until all had finished drinking.

From what I remember, there was little difference in the appearance of my hosts, except as regards age. All wore the traditional Taoist habit, but there was a pleasing variety of colour, and the Abbot, who had changed his strange hat for another with a hole at the crown, now displayed a hair-peg of heavy white jade. We drank a fair amount of the darkly yellow wine, but it was so mild that I felt no effect beyond a comforting mellowness. The food consisted largely of vegetables, but there were slivers of meat which could not have been the case in a Buddhist monastery, and the pumpkin soup, served in the vegetable's thick green rind, contained the flesh and bones of a whole chicken. Following the usual custom, my hosts kept apologizing for what they described as the execrable food and each time it was up to me to find new ways of declaring that it was a veritable banquet.

It would have been bad manners to ask erudite questions at table; even so, the level of conversation revealed that these were not innkeeper-type recluses of a kind sometimes found in more accessible monasteries, but men well-versed in Taoist literary works. Indeed, my coming upon that little hermitage proved a great piece of luck. By the end of the meal I had decided to stay on for several days so as to learn more about the Tao – the Mysterious Womb of the Myriad Objects.

It turned out that the Abbot was a serene but rather taciturn man; however, when I sought him out the following morning, he kindly sent for a relatively young colleague called Pien Tao-shih, whom he ordered to remain entirely at my disposal for the duration of my stay. My new mentor's cell was furnished with little more than the barest necessities, but I shall never forget it. To relieve the room's austerity, he had laid out a few treasures on the top of the bookcase, including a piece of stone shaped like one of those fantastic mountains in Chinese landscape paintings; this rested on a finely carved blackwood stand. There was also a small bronze ox fashioned of creamy jade, but what held my eye was the strangest kind of picture I had ever seen. Mounted elaborately on a strip of fine grey silk and brocaded rollers, it consisted of a vertical panel of off-white paper, completely blank. Watching my expression, Pien Tao-shih said smiling:

'No, it is complete. The best of paintings hanging from one's wall becomes so familiar that one doesn't notice it for days on end and its beauty seems to wane. On this picture, I imagine whatever scene I choose. Today it happens to be a pine-shrouded waterfall; tomorrow I think I shall decide on a tortoise or a crane. On your last day here, there will be a portrait of you riding away on – what is it to be, a horse or a camel?'

'An elephant!' I cried.

'Magnificent! A snow-white elephant with pink eyes and a pale-grey tail. You will be wearing a purple robe with an exceedingly wide black hat and carrying a paper parasol.'

'Thank you. I am eager to receive some teaching about the Tao. Before we get down to it, I wonder if you would care to show me the sights of your distinguished hermitage?'

He led me through the shrine-hall, an oblong building running the whole width of the courtyard. Grasses were sprouting from cracks between the green tiles on its heavy upward-curving roof, which was supported on faded red pillars of wood. Three of the walls were of dark-grey brick: the fourth, which faced the courtyard, was composed of a long row of wooden doors, their upper halves latticed with translucent rice-paper. As only one of the doors stood open, the interior was gloomy. The three statues and their altars had a shabby look. In the centre was an effigy of Hsi Wang Mu (Royal Mother Residing in the Western Heaven), her gilded flesh shrouded in robes bedecked with seed-pearls. To her right was an effigy of Lü Tung-pin, a Taoist Immortal regarded as the hermitage's patron deity. His painted face, lightly bearded, looked calm and benign, unlike the fierce red face of Kwan-Ti, the deified warrior, enthroned on the left. Pien Tao-shih bowed perfunctorily to the effigy of Lü Tung-pin and we walked through a small back-door that led straight into the grotto.

Here, too, it was gloomy. The water in a pool at our feet looked almost black. On the farther side were some rock-formations with niches containing demonic figures of mud-filled plaster in various stages of decay. Altogether the effect was dreary; yet, for a reason that escaped me, the grotto's atmosphere inspired a notable feeling of serenity.

'Is that surprising?' inquired Pien Tao-shih. 'This is our meditation cave and has been so for centuries. Who knows how many gifted sages – Immortals even – have given it something of their peace?'

Feeling chilly, we soon returned to his cell and one of the boys brought in a brazier of glowing charcoal complete with tripod and kettle. Pien served tea from a very plain but quite attractive old teapot which was never washed, so that its porous interior, encrusted with the deposits of many thousand brewings, gave even quite ordinary tea-leaves an exquisite flavour. When we were settled comfortably with our tea-cups, he talked and talked with a kind of gentle enthusiasm. Of the many things we discussed on that occasion and during the rest of my stay, I particularly remember the story of his life, which had already embraced many aspects of Taoism.

His father, though deeply immersed in Taoist learning, had been strictly a *Tao-chia*, an upholder of Lao-tzû's philosophy, who avoided all commerce with invisible beings, since to approach gods would be presumptuous and to approach demons, dangerous. Young Pien, however, had become intoxicated by the contents of the library in his ancestral home, which contained hundreds of treatises on magic, alchemy, exorcism and similar pursuits. At the age of fourteen, he had run away from home and implored the first man he met wearing Taoist robes to accept him as a pupil-servant. Unfortunately his new master had turned out to be a married man living at home with two wives and a brood of children, whom he supported in luxury by operating a shrine dedicated to an Ever-Rewarding Sky Dragon situated in the heart of the city. There he practised magic, divination and the concoction of medicinal potions for his clientele.

'The man was a charlatan?'

Pien Tao-shih reflected. 'That could be so. In some ways undoubtedly, yet not altogether. He had made himself truly invulnerable to steel and poison. A charlatan could not do that. Also his charms and predictions worked when he really took pains with them for his wealthier clients. I disliked him only because he was unprincipled in perverting sacred knowledge for commercial gain.'

Saving up his wages, young Pien had one day slipped away and travelled up the Yangtze River to one of the great temples built close to its banks. For a while he had been content there, living in a community of over a hundred recluses, some of whom were monks whereas others were married and went home to their families for a few months each year. The monastery had departments where esoteric studies were conducted – a system of medicine combining herbal remedies with magic charms, alchemy, the evocation and casting out of demons; various kinds of divination including the use of spirit-possessed human oracles; and a very small department of chess where a game with three hundred and sixty pieces was taught. Some of his colleagues specialized in attaining psychic powers, but Pien was not very informative about this.

'It sounds a wonderful place,' I remarked. 'What persuaded you to leave it?'

He looked surprised. 'You can see such things in most big monasteries, I suppose; though, for an outsider, it might be different. Sincere followers of the Way are not fond of display and false ones soon cease to be impressive. I left because none of those things is important. Most of my colleagues were frittering away their time on the pursuit of trifles, don't you think?'

One day luck had come his way. A visiting recluse from his present hermitage had described his community as a congenial little band dedicated to the uninterrupted practice of Taoist yoga and meditation aimed at achieving healthy and serene longevity that would culminate in nothing less than immortality. Living on an unfrequented part of the mountain, they were visited by enough travellers and pilgrims to contribute to their support without constituting a continual distraction.

'And so I followed him here,' Pien concluded. 'It is a perfect life, you see. Living without women is difficult at my age; living with them is even worse. So some of us have reached a compromise, going off to Hêngyang city for two or three months a year, but otherwise living as recluses and pursuing worth-while goals.'

'Isn't it expensive? You say you don't have many visitors.'

'Oh, you are wrong. On the Festival of Hsi Wang Mu, pilgrims come in their hundreds. It is true their donations are small, but then most of us have private incomes. At first I did some clerical work for the Abbot in return for my board and lodging, but presently my father died and I inherited a portion of his property with which I bought a permanent place in the community that leaves me free of such duties.'

'Can you summarize the beliefs, the philosophy of this community? I mean, what is the theoretical basis of your yogic practice?'

'Naturally we revere the teachings of Lao-tzû and Chuang-tzû, ordering our lives accordingly. As you know, Lao-tzû's *Tao Tê Ching* is the foundation of all. It teaches us to submit ourselves to nature's promptings, once we have learnt to distinguish them instinctively from self-will. And from Chuang-tzû I have learnt how to deal with needs as they arise and leave all else alone, quietly according with the Tao, whose spotless, undifferentiated unity suffuses all. The key to inner serenity lies in three words: "Make no distinctions." '

Pien Tao-shih tried his best to instruct me in the essentials of the higher Taoist philosophy, hoping to make it clear that the Tao, besides being the matrix, the plenum of the myriad phenomena, is also the Way in the sense of a path. Whether because my knowledge of Chinese was inadequate or my powers of perception too poor, I could scarcely follow him. While dealing with such subjects, he struck me as an unusually erudite scholar; yet when the conversation turned to his conception of immortality he seemed to descend to an altogether different plane. There were moments when I could barely hold back from affronting him with laughter!

'Immortality', he announced forthrightly, 'has nothing in common with Buddhist notions of reincarnation, although many Taoists do confuse them. It means exactly what it says—no death, at least not for many aeons. I myself fully intend to transmogrify my flesh into a shining adamantine substance, weightless yet hard as jade. That is the only sure way; for, suppose we were – like so many recluses – to aim at creating a spirit-body to inhabit after death, imagine the frantic scurryings of the ghosts of those who died in the mistaken belief of having completed that difficult task in time! How they would rush about, seeking in vain some vehicle to save their *hun* and *p'o* (higher and lower souls) from gradual dissolution into nothingness! How pitiful! Whereas, by transmogrifying my present body, I shall leave no room for error.'

Literal belief in transmogrification? In the twentieth century? I could scarcely credit my ears. To doubt the loftiness of Pien Tao-shih's intelligence was no more possible than to impugn his sincerity and dedication; but surely a ten-year-old school-boy would have sense enough to ridicule the notion of transmuting flesh and blood into a physical substance able to exist for aeons! Was it possible that poor Pien had such unswerving faith in some tattered old books and deluded teachers as to accept at its face-value this incredible interpretation of whatever the sages had really meant by immortality? At any rate he continued:

'Our Abbot, the Immortal of the Onyx Cleft, and most of the recluses here seek spiritual immortality. They practise the inner alchemy in order to fashion spirit-bodies that will be perfected before they die; whereas my own dear teacher, the Dawn Cloud Immortal, is instructing two or three of us in the secret of secrets.' Eyes shining, voice betraying reverential awe, he bent forward and whispered: 'Within another three years or so, the transmutation of our flesh will be complete!'

Hastily I dropped my eyes; yet, though sensing my scorn, he met it not with anger but with pity.

'Oh, *why* can you not believe, you and the rest of them? Why, why? On what grounds? We have sacred texts that set forth clearly the alchemy of fleshly transmutation, and everyone knows that Lü Tung-pin, the patron of this hermitage, achieved it. Then why not me – or you?'

Fortunately Pien, like all true Taoists, was incapable of being disgruntled. Gazing at me fondly, he hurried on: 'Dear friend, stay longer on this mountain and free yourself from those worldly obscurations that have, if I may say so, dulled your mind. Mount Nan Yeo is a strange and holy place. The air is impregnated with the effulgence of legions of accomplished sages who have lived among its peaks and grottoes since time began. There are times when you can sense a palpable effulgence emanating from them. By rare good fortune, you may even meet one, for they occasionally appear to travellers in the guise of mortals. Surely you have noticed *something* of the mountain's atmosphere? No streams in the world are so limpid as ours, no rocks so evocative of mystery. Standing alone of an evening on these sacred pathways, you can *feel* the pulsing of the Tao. From our teacher, we learn secrets once known to every living being, until man by his rude busying and bustling disturbed the natural harmony. Stay here and clear your perceptions of the ugly nonsense taught in schools and cities! Learn to see things in perspective. You will admit that a tiny seed you can barely see when held in the palm of your hand has the potentiality of becoming a great tree; is transmutation of the flesh a greater marvel? Free your mind of useless calculated thought and I shall petition our patron, the Immortal Lü Tung-pin, to instruct you in a dream.'

'Pien Tao-shih,' I answered gravely, 'I doubt if the Immortal will bother with a barbarian from the West, but if he does deign to visit me in a dream I shall of course be highly honoured.'

At this point, a serving-boy came in to call us to the midday meal. Afterwards, as we were strolling across the courtyard, I remarked: 'This morning, while speaking of many things, you mentioned alchemy. Do Taoist sages really practise the transmutation of base metal into gold? Some say the true alchemy is something more subtle.'

His smile broadened. 'So even you strangers from the West know the gold-cinnabar pill is not a drug. Wonderful!'

Full of enthusiasm, he hurried me back to his cell, where he produced from among some piles of books kept in ivory-hasped boxes a ragged volume finely printed an flimsy paper. It bore the title *Ts'an T'ung Ch'i*, which I took to mean something like *The Ts'an Agreement* or perhaps *The Agreement of Three*.[1] Below it, was printed the subscription *True Original Text of the Taoist Immortal Wei Po-yang of the Han Dynasty*, from which I calculated that the text had been in existence for close on two thousand years. Leafing through its pages, I found I could not make head or tail of its contents.

'What is it?' I asked.

'It is written in a cryptic language. Call it a book of philosophy or of ideal polity and you will not be wrong. Call it a detailed manual of alchemy and you will not be wrong; everything is there for the mixing of the elements that produce the gold and cinnabar pill. But look at it another way and you will see that it is a case of White Tiger and Green Dragon.'

My blank look seemed to disappoint him, for he said: 'Perhaps I should not tell you. After all, you know less than I thought.'

Falling silent for a while, he presently announced repentantly: 'White Tiger is lead, but also semen. Green Dragon is cinnabar, but also the woman's sexual fluid.'

My comical astonishment restored his good humour. Metaphorically my hair was standing on end. Nothing I had read or heard so far had prepared me for such a disclosure. In Buddhist

[1] It really means *Three Correspondences in Union*.

monasteries, though none of the monks would be likely to share the attitude of those Christian clergy who see sexual joy as positively sinful and allow it only grudgingly, even to married couples, it was always taken for granted that chastity is essential for those dedicated to rapid spiritual progress.

'The lead and the cinnabar', Pien continued, 'must be properly blended. Their product is not literally a pill, as you seem to know, but a kind of tiny foetus that grows within the male (or female) recluse's body. Rightly compounded, it has miraculous properties. How old would you say I am?'

'Rising thirty?'

'I am forty-five, and no one knows the age of my teacher whom you have seen and probably took for a man still in his early sixties.'

Pien Tao-shih did not seem capable of lying; so I was impressed.

'You see? I have been on the Way a mere twenty years, and already – ! The gold-cinnabar pill is the great preserver and rejuvenator of youth. Doubling man's life-span is the least of its properties. One who can find devout ladies to help him, especially if he embarks upon the task while young, can quite easily achieve transmogrification. You must know the old legend of the Royal Western Mother, how she attained the stature of a goddess at the cost of a thousand young men's lives? Unwittingly she deprived them of their entire stock of vital energy. That, if true, was monstrous. But male recluses need not be deterred by compassion for their female partners, since a woman's supply of vital essence is inexhaustible.'

All I could gather from Pien's explanation was that the sexual yoga involved conducting sexual intercourse as often as possible within the limits of special times and seasons of the year, using a technique based on carefully numbered thrusting movements and rigid abstinence from orgasms. Without permitting his own *yang*-fluid to leave his body, the adept must cause orgasm after orgasm in his partner, so as to absorb her *yin*-fluid and, by uniting the *yin* and *yang*, create a sort of cell or embryo within himself; and there was something which had to be drawn up to the top of the head.

It would have been wrong to think of Pien Tao-shih as a laughable character. He had mistaken the nature of the final goal, confusing mystical union or spiritual immortality with literal transmogrification; but I did not suppose his devout practice would necessarily prove fruitless. Of those Taoist recluses who, at a very advanced age, possessed extraordinary strength and vigour, there was no means of knowing what proportion of them, if any, had achieved this result by sexual alchemy rather than by other means.

Nor can Pien Tao-shih be reasonably accused of licentiousness. Nothing, I am certain, could have been further from his mind than mere physical satisfaction. He was joyful because he believed he had found a yoga that would surely lead to the transmogrification for which he longed.

Before leaving the hermitage, I plucked up courage to ask on which part of the mountain the recluses housed their female partners. Pien's eyes shone with laughter.

'No, no, there's nothing like that. The local peasants would think us devils and have the authorities imprison us all, don't you think? I am married, you see. The Abbot sends me back into the world during certain months every year to enable me to practise night and day. My wife co-operates to the best of her ability, realizing that pious girls, happy to devote their lives to donating energy to recluses, are rare these days.

I did not really understand much of this, nor did I pursue the matter until some years later. Towards the end of my visit, there occurred what seemed to me a mildly extraordinary incident. The Immortal Lü Tung-pin appeared to me in a dream as Pien Tao-shih had promised. Unfortunately, though the dream was both vivid and long, by the time I saw Pien, I could recall no more than one brief fragment. This was of a handsome lightly bearded youth, easily recognizable from the statue in the shrine-hall, greeting me with a burst of laughter. His gaiety had proved infectious. I, too, had burst out laughing. Though unable to recall what language we conversed in, I was left with a clear recollection of a few seemingly inconsequential words.

'You have come,' he said.

'Yes, yes, but how did I get here?'

'It doesn't matter, does it? Especially as you ought not to be here at all.'

Again our laughter exploded and then he added: 'It's simple, isn't it? Everything seen from here is simple! My advice is to take the longer route.'

Before breakfast I ran to Pien Tao-shih in great excitement and asked for his interpretation, only to discover how little I remembered of the dream. Reproachfully, he strove to think out what the Immortal's advice had referred to, but in vain.

The most sensational moments of my visit resulted directly from that dream. Early in the morning on the day before I left, Pien, looking at once secretive and gay, suggested a walk. The rain and mist of the last few days had cleared and a watery sunshine pierced the white clouds shrouding the peak; but his choice of route quickly dispelled any lingering supposition that the weather had anything to do with our expedition. Instead of making for one of the interesting hermitages, shrines and temples on the other faces of the mountain, he kept to a steep path overgrown by weeds and nettles, that led straight upwards. Presently we emerged on a broad ledge sheltered by rocks which really did resemble what he described as living beings emerging from the uncreate, though personally I should have called those beings monsters. With some imagination, one could see the rocks slowly writhing in strange contortions from which the heads and limbs of these monsters were imperceptibly emerging. Turning a corner, we came upon a small hollow where stood a solitary pavilion, dilapidated yet seemingly inhabited, for smoke swirled from a lean-to adjoining the main structure.

'Dear friend,' announced Pien portentously, 'you are about to behold a youth already regarded as an Immortal – Hsüan-mên Hsien-jên (Fairy of the Mysterious Portal).'

Among Taoists, the title rendered Fairy or Immortal may generally be taken to imply a degree of wishful thinking, and so I was quite unprepared to meet a truly extraordinary being. An elderly servant, running from the lean-to kitchen, ushered us into the pavilion which, though it comprised but one room, surprisingly contained no bed – just a heavy square table, a few chairs and many shelves of books. Facing the door was a shrine enthroning a benign deity whom I could not identify. As we entered, a youth rose gracefully from a meditation cushion before the shrine to bid us welcome with the antique courtesy to which I was growing accustomed. By the time I had finished returning his elaborate bows, half-ashamed of my untutored awkwardness, I was, as it were, caught up in a dream. The youth, whom I judged to be about eighteen, was perhaps the most beautiful human being I had ever encountered. To see him was to love him. I doubt if there was anything sensual in this strange attraction; I had no inclination to touch or embrace him, just a tangible joy in his presence and a longing to win his approbation. It was a feeling not far removed from worship. Smiling charmingly, he waved to us to be seated and, while the servant was preparing and serving a pot of very delicate green tea, we exchanged the inevitable Chinese preliminary courtesies – name, age, place of birth, profession, etc.; whereupon Pien Tao-shih, fearing that our host would be too modest to talk of his own achievements, intervened with a recital of some of the young man's austerities, which included never touching flesh or wine, never lying down but passing the nights seated upon his meditation cushion – during which he slept not more than two or three hours in an upright position – and undergoing rigorous physical yogas. Gradually the conversation drifted elsewhere, leaving me to enjoy the rôle of fascinated listener, and so I was able to study the youth at my leisure. His face was exceptionally pale and there were deep shadows under his eyes, but these marks of his austerities added to rather than detracted from his beauty. The more I gazed, the more I came under his spell and was dismayed by the prospect of having to part from him. Being in his company was more than a pleasure; it was a source of warmth and joy. Presently Pien observed :

'Here in the presence of the Fairy of the Mysterious Portal, does the goal of immortality seem so utterly unattainable?'

The question was embarrassing because I did not grasp the connection and, in any case, had by no means changed my mind about the folly of seeking transmogrification. The youth sat regarding me with lively interest as though eager to hear my views. Though Pien had given him no explanation, I felt sure that this strange young man fully understood my state of mind.

'Frankly, yes, Pien Tao-shih. You cannot mean that the – the, the Fairy of the Mysterious Portal is very ancient or has already achieved fleshly transmutation!'

Pien looked disappointed, but the youth laughed delightedly. 'No, no, dear friend from beyond the seas. I am exactly what I seem. Born in the Year of the Ox, I have still to reach my twentieth birthday. But I must not waste your time. You have come to consult the oracle.'

Completely at a loss, I stared at him blankly until Pien put in quickly: 'I have not told our visitor about your powers, but it happens he has need of them.' Glancing across at me he added: 'The Fairy of the Mysterious Portal is an infallible oracle. Unlike other oracles, his attainments are so high that our patron, Lü Tung-pin, communes with him directly. Since you were so remiss as to forget your dream, I decided to bring you here, although as a rule we avoid troubling the Fairy by allowing strangers to approach him. Were his powers generally known, he would be importuned by crowds night and day.'

'Please, please do not trouble,' I said anxiously. 'I would much rather not impose myself.'

The marvellously sweet smile expanded as the youth replied: 'You, a guest from a distant land, have been gracious in coming to this poor hut to afford me the pleasure of your company. Since I have no suitable gift to offer, I beg you to let me be of some service. What was the dream vouchsafed by the Immortal?'

It was as though he had read Pien's mind. The recluse now related the remembered fragment of my dream. The youth's smile faded.

'Dear friend, we cannot presume to inform the Immortal that his message has been *forgotten*! Such a thing could not happen once in a thousand years. It would be best for me to say you have come to express your gratitude for his condescension. It is possible his reply will enlighten us.'

So it was arranged. We took our leave immediately, promising to return after evening rice.

At the appointed time, Pien and I, donning thick robes, slipped out into the cold darkness. A gibbous moon riding high among the clouds gave but little light as we clambered up the rocky pathway; thorns tore at my legs and several times I slipped, sending a shower of earth and pebbles clattering down the slope. Coming to the place of monsters, I felt glad of Pien's company; in that faint light, the rocks seemed more than ever like fearsome creatures struggling to emerge from a cold grey mass. Instead of going to the pavilion, we climbed to the rim of a kind of rock-bowl situated some distance above it. In the centre lay a broad, flat stone surmounted by what I took to be an image of a deity depicted in an attitude of meditation; but it proved to be the Fairy of the Mysterious Portal himself, sitting motionless as the rock beneath him. Suddenly spots of fire appeared and something moved in the darkness beside me. Startled, I grasped Pien's arm, but it was only the old servant. Silently he pointed to a heavy bronze tripod placed in front of his master. Clearly we were expected to pay our respects. Respects to whom? The Fairy of the Mysterious Portal? Or the invisible being with whom he sought communion? It was an eerie thought.

Following my friend up to the tripod, I watched him plant the incense-sticks in a mound of ash and bow to the earth three times; then he stood aside, motioning me to do the same. Thanks to my long robe, I imagined I would look reasonably dignified as I performed this ancient rite, but its skirts almost caused me to fall ignominiously on my face. Somehow I managed to do what was expected, struggling not to appear ridiculous. Afterwards, as I stood gazing at the motionless figure, a lovely serenity overwhelmed me. Not knowing what to expect, yet feeling it might well be moving, I did not regret having quitted the warmth and comparative comfort of the hermitage. When Pien took my hand and led me off behind some rocks, I felt bitterly disappointed and begged him to allow me watch whatever was going to happen; but, for some reason, my pleading inspired him to drag me still further away. Even so, we were still within earshot of the high, pure notes of a voice intoning an ancient hymn of impressive beauty. Never had I heard a voice or melody so sweet. Even the Fairy's servant, who must have been long accustomed to such lovely rites, shared our rapture. Peace and serenity shed their balm like moonlight flooding the landscape from a clear autumn sky. I had closed my eyes, the better to allow those exquisite sounds to float into my mind when, all of a sudden, I felt a pang of dread. A moment later the song was cut off amidst harsh, discordant laughter. A prolonged silence followed, during which my companions stood as though petrified. Presently a dialogue began, the youth's sweet voice alternating with the deep threatening tones of some intruder who seemed to be whipping himself into a fury. The marvellous peace had been swallowed up in an atmosphere murky with evil, and my being was invaded by an animal-like perception of danger.

'What is it?' I whispered, wondering why we had not tried to run to the youth's assistance. Instead, Pien and the servant, shouting to me to keep close to them, began running and leaping down the mountain, *away* from the rock-bowl and straight towards the young man's lonely dwelling. Soon I was breathless and stumbling at every step, whereas my Taoist companions seemed able to pick their way effortlessly past even the most difficult obstacles. For one sickening moment, I thought some dangerous pursuer was close upon us; but it proved to be the youth himself, running swiftly and smoothly, as though his feet were but skimming the ground. Somehow I sensed that, though an interruption as dreadful as it was unexpected had most certainly occurred and had perhaps endangered the young man's life, he alone was untouched by panic; that, far from fleeing whatever evil threatened, he had joined us to give the feeling of comfort and protection which his presence immediately conferred.

On reaching his pavilion, I made to follow him inside, but Pien was still in a state of consternation and, scarcely sparing time for some hurried farewells, he pulled me away. Once again, we were running and slithering downward as fast as he could make me go. It was not until we were safely through the hermitage gates that he regained reasonable composure and embarked on profuse apologies, begging me not to allow one dreadful incident to spoil the happy memories of my visit.

'You see, you – that is to say all of us – might have – but, forgive me, it is worse than imprudent to speak of such matters. Please, please put this evening out of mind before you leave tomorrow.'

Burning with curiosity, I begged in vain for an explanation; the harder I pressed him, the more his distress increased. Had I been able to prolong my stay, perhaps I should have received an answer in course of time. As it was, to this day I have no idea what caused our headlong flight. It would be easy to attribute it to the sudden appearance of a ruffian who posed a physical threat, but a conviction of our having been threatened by a much more terrible and impalpable evil remains vividly in my mind, though whole decades have passed since then. Besides, it is impossible to believe that fear of mere physical violence could have affected Pien as it did, to say nothing of the servant. Undoubtedly they would have rushed to aid the strange youth who inspired such love even in the hearts of newcomers. To my mind, the explanation is so fantastic as to invite ridicule; therefore I prefer to maintain a Taoistic silence.

The following morning, Pien Tao-shih kept a promise made on

the day of my arrival. Taking me into his cell, he pointed to the blank wall-scroll and described in great detail the painting with which he had now mentally endowed it. My white elephant had its back to him, but its head was turned as though watching him out of the corner of its eye. Its tail hung down disconsolately. I, its rider, was enveloped in a purple robe that descended to my ankles. Only the back of my head was visible beneath the wide black hat he had decided I should wear. An open fan fluttered in my hand and on its leaves were inscribed the words: 'Thousand-league distance, friendship illimitable.'

Pien Tao-shih looked sadly forlorn as, standing deferentially behind the senior recluses, he joined them in bidding me farewell. The rocky path leading down from the hermitage was now slippery and deeply puddled. Thinking fondly of the elephant, I wished it had been real.

Chapter 3

Demons, Fox-Spirits and the Realm of Magic: Popular Taoism

According to an ancient and once widespread tradition, the founder of Taoism was not Lao-tzû, but the Yellow Emperor who is believed to have reigned more than four-and-a-half millenia ago! Taoism's magical practices and, above all, its more exotic yogas were largely attributed to him and he was therefore venerated as much as Lao-tzû. In any case, by the third century B.C., it is certain that strange beliefs and practices already antique when Lao-tzû was born, had become co-mingled with that sage's teaching and that the reigning Emperor Shih Huang-ti was an ardent devotee of magic. That Taoism later became an organized religion with monasteries, temples, images, liturgies, rites and other features of the kind is, however, attributed in particular to the efforts of one Chang Tao-ling, known to posterity as the Heavenly Teacher. In the province of Kiangsi, amidst a landscape on which nature has lavished her finest brush-work and mastery of soft colours, stands the Dragon-Tiger Mountain on which Chang Tao-ling was born in the first or second century A.D. Tradition has it that the Venerable Sage Lao-tzû, appearing to him in spirit form, enjoined him to discover the formula for compounding the elixir of immortality. To all appearances, Chang was successful in that task, for he is credited with having ridden heavenwards on a tiger's back in his hundred-and-twenty-third year and with preserving his identity thereafter by successively reincarnating in the bodies of one after another of his own descendants. Each of his specially favoured progeny succeeded in turn to the name Chang Tao-ling, the process continuing until well into the present century. In the eighth century A.D., the Emperor Hsüan Tsung officially proclaimed Heavenly Teacher Chang's jurisdiction over 'all Taoist temples in the world'; and, though in fact there was never a time when that dignitary was accepted by *all* the Taoist monastic communities, his sect remained the largest and most popular up to the virtual end of Taoism's existence as an organized religion some twenty years ago.

Alas, the Heavenly Teacher is no more! Yet it scarcely seems possible that a line of pontiffs could endure for close on two thousand years, vanish in our lifetime without trace and, in so doing, cause not a ripple. True, from the founding of the Chinese Republic in 1911, the pontiff's power had waned from year to year; nevertheless, he had thousands upon thousands of devotees until the last. Exactly when and where he vanished are matters still disputed. Several authorities give different dates and varying accounts of the matter. According to one story, Chiang Kai-shek's government banished him prior to the nineteen-fifties and one Chinese writer claims that the former Heavenly Teacher is now living in Portuguese Macao where he solaces himself, dragon-wise, amidst dense, rolling clouds – of opium! No one seems to know for sure what has befallen. Personally I would like to think that the Heavenly Teacher managed to follow the rather disconcerting custom attributed to Taoists of vanishing without trace or, better still, that he was successfully transmogrified.

How colourful was the empire ruled by this spiritual potentate – a world of alchemy, divination, magic nostrums, conjurers, oracles, miraculously endowed swordsmen, masters of rain-making, and exorcists skilled in the humbling of fierce demons! To my lasting regret, I had no opportunity to visit Dragon-Tiger Mountain and pay my respects to that extraordinary figure before he and his mysterious realm had passed beyond human ken. Even so, I was privileged to see many pockets of that realm at a time when most parts of China, especially in the centre and the south, were thickly sprinkled with shrines and temples whose devotees practised the ancient arts, and acknowledged Chang Tao-ling's supremacy. Today only the merest traces of those arts linger, even on the outermost fringes of the Chinese world – such as Taiwan Island (to an insignificant extent) and the overseas Chinese settlements in south-east Asia.

Scholars, both Chinese and Western, have long regarded Taoism either as a down-to-earth philosophy aimed at living to a ripe old age in comfortable harmony with one's surroundings or, alternatively, as an exalted form of mysticism. Such people are eager to deny – sometimes quite heatedly – that popular Taoism has more than the most tenuous connections with the teachings of its founder sages, Lao and Chuang. Readers who share this view are invited to skip the rest of this chapter lest they grow indignant at my failure to pour scorn on practices often castigated as 'a medley of charlatanism and gross superstition'. For, with sincere apologies to the partisans of 'pure Taoism', I propose to deal kindly and at some length with the so-called aberrations of the Heavenly Teacher's sect. My purpose is to describe Taoism, not in an idealized form but exactly as I found it during what may well prove to have been the last few decades of its corporate existence. The very antiquity of its magical doctrines is a sufficient reason for according them some respect. Then, again, it happens that I generally encountered Taoism in its more popular forms long before being granted any real understanding of its higher mysteries. Besides, I must confess that I thoroughly enjoyed the colourfulness and occasional grimness of its 'magical' aspects. I hope that many readers, whether or not I can persuade them to believe in demons and fox-spirits, will find the stories of them entertaining.

Whereas the mountain hermitages of Taoist quietists and philosophers were mostly small, the monasteries containing temples dedicated to the popular divinities of that faith were often large and splendid, though generally located in remote spots chosen for their natural beauty. To avoid too many personal details, such as tedious descriptions of why and how I came to be in places whose very names may be found unpronounceable, I have decided to thread together several episodes involving contact with magical and ghostly Taoist practices. This I shall do by relating them to a single monastery which is really a composite of all the popular Taoist centres I visited in widely separated parts of China. It shall be called the Abode of Mysterious Origination (Miao-yüan Tao-kuan) and its principal component temple or shrine-hall, the Hall of the Three Pure Ones (San Ch'ing Tien).

Once I travelled up a river flowing swiftly, but broad enough for the water to seem almost still. Its rugged banks rose steeply, sometimes forming the base of hills or mountains. Close to the top of one of them grew dense thickets of bamboo with fronds so intensely green that the curving roofs of the monastery, except when sunlight was reflected by their emerald tiles, could barely be distinguished even by an observer eagerly scanning the hilltops from the prow of an approaching junk. From a wooden jetty built for the use of pilgrims, a path led upwards, curving round folds of the hills in a manner so contrived that, each time its steepness began to seem unbearable, I came upon a level stretch long enough to allow me to regain my breath. In less than three hours, a man in his twenties (or an old one, if he had acquired the effortless gait that comes with Taoist training) could reach the monastery's outermost gateway. This was a solitary, elaborately roofed arch standing athwart the path with no walls to bar my progress. If for some reason I had chosen to walk around instead of through it, there would have been no obstacle. Its function was to inform pilgrims that they were now to set foot on sacred ground. Attached to its roof was a horizontal gilded tablet some three feet long which bore the words: 'Portal to Heaven's Southern Region' (Nan T'ien Mên). Beyond this gateway, the wilderness of trees and undergrowth gave place to thickets of feathery bamboo that had doubtless been planted to give the monastery's green-roofed buildings a suitably Taoistic air of not being quite surely where one would expect to find them, or perhaps not anywhere at all. A sudden turn and there, with its back close against the mountain, stood the monastery, looking quite solid and stationary after all, though on other occasions I was to see it present the aspect of a fairy palace floating in a sea of clouds. Unlike a Buddhist monastery, it had been deliberately made asymmetrical. Its outer wall, topped with glazed green tiles, rose and fell with dragon-like undulations to accord with the natural contours of the mountain-side. Beyond the gatehouse rose the roofs of many buildings, some small, some very large, arranged in what struck me as picturesque disorder until I perceived how cunningly a subtle orderliness underlay their seeming disarray. Between the gatehouse and the first of these buildings lay a rock-garden simulating natural scenery; this had counterparts in several of the inner courtyards, but each was constructed in a style so individual as to come as a surprise. By way of contrast, most of the larger courtyards contained somewhat formal arrangements of curiously gnarled trees or flowers and shrubs in porcelain containers. The various residential quarters consisted of rather squat buildings dwarfed by overhanging roofs, whereas the main shrine-hall and the great library beyond were so tall that even the shrine-hall's triple roof with its widespread, fantastically contoured eaves seemed to sit lightly on its walls and pillars. The only displeasing feature was the brightness of the gold and crimson lacquer adorning that huge building (doubtless in imitation of the richly ornamented shrine-halls of Buddhist monasteries, whose splendour was more pleasing to the eye because a strict symmetry and certain other features lent them the appearance of imperial palaces; whereas, in a Taoist setting, magnificence seemed out of place). However, all the other buildings, including the hall which housed the library, had a subdued charm that was all the more noticeable on account of that single imperfection.

I need not describe the general appearance of the inhabitants of the Abode of Mysterious Origination or the welcome they accorded me, for all over China Taoist recluses had in common the high-piled hair, curious headgear, long robes and courtly manners of those I had encountered on Mount Nan Yeo. Instead, I shall plunge straight into an account of my first meeting with the Abbot, a fine-looking man with penetrating gaze, silky white beard and cheeks as red as apple-blossom.

After prostrating myself as courtesy demanded, I chose a chair standing close to the door of his cell and affected overwhelming diffidence when he invited me to come closer.

'Your Immortality, I would not dare. I am quite unworthy.'

Smiling his pleasure at beholding a barbarian grounded in at least the rudiments of civilized behaviour, he disconcerted me by a backward leap on to his bed, drawing up his legs so swiftly as to produce the effect of an illusion. It was extraordinary. One moment he was standing indolently upright; the next, despite his considerable bulk, he was restfully seated cross-legged and poised. Ignoring my surprise, he began to make dignified weaving motions with a horse-tail fly-whisk. No doubt this display had been intended to impress me not so much with his personal prowess as with the remarkable efficacy of Taoist training.

At that time, I knew almost nothing of Taoism as a formal religion, for Pien Tao-shih and the hermit of the Western Hills had scarcely mentioned the subject; so I decided to begin to repair my ignorance.

'I have noticed, Your Immortality, that your esteemed monastery has a magnificent shrine-hall containing three great images. To what deities is it dedicated?'

'The Three Pure Ones! Enthroned in the centre is the Jade Emperor, embodiment of the First Principle, that is to say of the formless Tao Itself. On one side is a sacred being known as Heaven's Marvellously Responsive Jewel, who represents the harmonious working of the Tao's positive and negative components. On the other side you surely recognized a representation of the Venerable Sage Lao-tzû. You must understand that poorly educated people, unable to comprehend the formless, prefer to pay respect to easily recognizable forms. It is but right to express mysteries in a way they can grasp without too much exertion, otherwise they would fail to pay homage to the Sacred Source and its endless manifestations. Naturally they cannot appreciate the subtle teachings of our great sages; nevertheless, they venerate Lao-tzû for other reasons, such as his having been born white-bearded and deeply wrinkled as a consequence of passing eighty-two years in his mother's womb, or his success in attaining to an immeasurable age. Even though the truth of these matters is disputable, such beliefs help such people to see him as a very mysterious and miraculous person, which is exactly what he was; so they arrive at the inner core of truth despite their unfortunate ignorance. We followers of Chang Tao-ling use methods to suit all kinds of men. If you stay here long enough, you will see for yourself.'

Raising a teacup to his lips, the Abbot thus indicated that my first audience was at an end, presumably because there were duties requiring his attention. His reference to Chang Tao-ling told me that the Abode of Mysterious Origination was likely to house some sorcerers or men believed to wrestle with authentic demons. Perhaps I should witness examples of conjuring and exorcism. This prospect proved so fascinating that I promptly abandoned my new-found interest in Taoist religious iconography; for I had read that the Taoist Trinity, like the shrine-halls, liturgies and rites, had been introduced mainly to enable the monasteries to compete with their Buddhist counterparts; whereas magic and demonology were, in a certain sense, authentic components of the ancient Taoist tradition. So it happens that to this day, even my knowledge of the Western Royal Mother is largely confined to that one small detail of her biography which tells us that a thousand youths yielded up their lives to provide her with the means to immortality by expending upon her lovely body their entire stock of vital energy. I suppose, that, like Niang Niang (another Taoist Goddess) and Kuan Yin (a Buddhist Bodhisattva depicted in China as female), she was really a form of the Mother Goddess worshipped under many names throughout the ancient world until, in the West, she was supplanted by – or transmuted into – the Virgin Mary. Depictions of divinity in female form are surely a response to a deep, though sometimes unperceived, human longing.

At the time of my first visit to the Abode of Mysterious Origination, my attitude to Taoist magic and demonology was one of frank scepticism coupled with a whimsical half-desire to believe. It was only gradually that certain awe-inspiring occurrences convinced me that benign and evil psychic forces really do exist, though not necessarily in the anthropomorphic forms in which they are generally depicted; and that it is possible, if highly inadvisable, to enter into wary relations with them. Some of the stories that follow are meant not merely to entertain but also to demonstrate that Taoist recluses did manage to penetrate to an eerie realm beyond the confines of most modern people's experience.

Following my courtesy call upon the Abbot, whose abrupt dismissal still rankled slightly, I began wandering about the monastery to survey its courtyards and buildings, most of which had features at once charming and fantastic. Unexpectedly I came upon a sight that, by contrast, struck me as utterly revolting. In a deserted corner of the precincts not far from the elegant main gatehouse stood a building which, since it was too large to be a recluse's dwelling, must surely be put to some public use, in which case no one would mind if I walked in without permission, just to see what it contained. The picturesquely latticed windows were of painted wood spread with translucent rice-paper, so that I could not peer inside; the door was secured from without by a heavy wooden bar that could easily be removed; so, looking round half-guiltily to make sure that I was not observed, or alternatively to see if there was anyone from whom I could ask leave to enter, I slipped the bar from its sockets and laid it quietly on the ground. The heavy brass-hinged door consisted of two leaves which opened inward; as neither yielded to a gentle exploratory pressure, I pushed one of them rather hard, causing it to revolve on its hinges with a dreadfully loud groan, precipitating me all too abruptly into the gloomy interior. For gloomy it was, and in more senses than one. As my eyes became accustomed to the dim light, I realized that my curiosity had plunged me into a veritable chamber of horrors – three of its four walls were fronted with life-sized plaster demons of baleful aspect, busily engaged in punishing the ghosts of errant humans. The tongues of former scandal-mongers had been lanced and split with metal prongs; other delinquents, guilty during their lifetime of crimes specified on labels tied to their ghostly necks, were being sawn in half, pressed against metal spikes, tossed into a lake of fire, forced to sit naked on needle-sharp icicles, or subjected to one or several similarly ingenious tortures, most of them recognizably related to the nature of the poor wretches' crimes. Enthroned in the place of honour opposite the doorway loomed Yen Lo Wang, the dark-visaged Lord of Death, of whom the only kind thing that could be said was that he was not leering like the demons but performing his task as judge with an expression of stern impartiality. Whether the shivering, naked ghost before him had accumulated a stock of virtue that did or did not outweigh its former sins was a matter for mathematical investigation. Calm-faced, rather handsome accountants were seated on either side, totting up the credits and debits, and hell's ferocious, red-eyed lictors stood opposite, ready to pounce upon each ghost found wanting in virtue. The whole scene looked like a grim parody of proceedings in an old-style Chinese courtroom in the days when successive Sons of Heaven ruled the empire from their Purple Palace in Peking in accordance with a code of laws specifying the exact penalty to be attached to each offence. Standing in that murky chamber surrounded by such gruesome reminders of man's devilish inventiveness in devising means of inflicting pain, I found myself temporarily in sympathy with those scholars in whose breasts the Heavenly Teacher's followers aroused feelings of scorn; but, upon reflection, I recalled that Christians, both Catholic and Protestant, and even Buddhists, were wont to depict hell in guises just as revolting, though seldom by means of life-sized statues. Thoughtfully, I walked back towards the pale-gold ray of sunlight sweeping in through the open doorway.

I had just slammed the bar back into place when an elderly recluse, whose small head and thin neck brought to mind a tortoise, bore down as if to scold me for my prying.

'That place is better kept locked,' he remarked. 'It might give our honoured guest nightmares.'

'No fear of that, Your Reverence. All the same, permit me to say that I did find the place out of harmony with what little I have heard of your exalted faith.'

This seemed to please him, for a radiant smile lit his wrinkled face. 'Quite right,' he said. 'But then, you see, the pilgrims expect that sort of thing, and it is an efficient way of teaching them which offences are especially grave. If you study the figures carefully, you will see that some offences not listed as crimes in this world, such as malevolent gossip, acquisitiveness, arrogance and so forth are rated as being more serious than mere thefts of property. So there *is* a certain logic in it. Still, we do not like that place and keep it shut except during festivals when the pilgrims come. You may suppose that the bar is there to keep the demons in; in fact the door is secured because we do not like to be reminded of such a blemish to the beauty of our monastery.'

'But you do believe in hell?'

'Do we?' he answered. 'Yes, I suppose we do, officially. Our faith has inherited a good number of ancient beliefs. Those of us who speak out against the more absurd ones are unpopular with the pilgrims. They *love* to come to this building, you see. Most people have a high opinion of their own merits, don't you think, and can provide a whole list of extenuations to excuse their faults; so the sight of those torments, far from making them shiver, gives them the same sort of pleasure that a man seated beside a charcoal brazier in winter gets from contemplating his good fortune in being safe from the blizzard raging outside. You can scarcely imagine a man so conscious of his own shortcomings that he *expects* to go to hell. Such objectivity would be unnatural.'

Feeling more kindly towards the Taoists, I thanked the old man for his explanation and strolled into a courtyard where two elderly recluses were sitting in the sunshine playing a kind of chess for which three hundred and sixty black and white pebbles are required. Coming as it were straight from hell, I was reminded of those Taoist paintings which depict two bearded ancients engaged in playing chess with human lives; each time white secures an advantage, a life is saved; when black retaliates, some other life is lost. One of the joys of staying in a Taoist monastery was that one could see so many sights identical with what human eyes beheld over a thousand years ago – the same architecture, hair-dos, garments, gestures, manners, occupations and amusements.

That night, when my thoughts turned back to that ghastly chamber, I recalled two stories (not specifically Taoist) illustrating crassly materialistic notions of the after-life that must have dated back to the remotest antiquity. Strangely, they were still harboured by many Chinese – not all of them illiterates, as the tale concerning heaven will show. The first I had culled from a work of P'u Sung-ling, an eccentric scholar noted for compiling an anthology of bizarre anecdotes relating to supernatural matters. It ran as follows:

A gentleman returning from a visit to the country brought back some unusually fine water-melons which he placed in his bedroom for safe keeping; but it happened that, before he could enjoy them, death claimed him in the night. When Yen Lo Wang's demon lictors came to seize his ghost, its state of terror was so pitiful that even those stony-hearted, iron-beaked creatures were moved. Thoughtfully eyeing the melons, one of them advised the poor ghost to carry them down to the judgement hall as a means of smoothing things over. His Awful Majesty good-naturedly accepted the fragrant offering and made an imperceptible alteration in the records that enabled the ghost to re-enter its former body to enjoy seven more years of life. Thenceforth lively recollections of Yen Lo's horrid kingdom prompted the melon-fancier to such exemplary piety as to qualify for rebirth in congenial surroundings.

The other story, which illustrates a similarly crude notion of the after-life, but this time pertaining to the heavenly regions, had been told me in all seriousness by a Malayan Chinese student during our undergraduate days at Cambridge. While still too young to comprehend the fact of death, he was told by his parents that his grandfather had passed away. It was hard for him to understand why his daddy and mummy looked so upset; for death, whatever that might mean, had not changed Grandfather in any special way; he was often to be seen wandering about the house at night, looking grumpy just as usual. But when his daddy came to hear of this, he grew dreadfully pale and said something like: 'Alas, dear boy, your Gran must be in terrible distress, otherwise his restless spirit would have left this house forever. Next time you see him, be sure to ask.'

Unafraid, the innocent child questioned his grandfather at their very next encounter.

'My boy, you can have no idea,' replied the ghost. 'I can find no rest at all. The gate-keepers of the Chinese heavens chase me away, declaring there is no admission for people dressed in European-style clothes like this white drill suit in which your father so thoughtlessly clothed my corpse. At the Christian heaven, it is the same. The guards drive me off because someone once forgot to sprinkle holy water on my forehead. Now nothing is left for me but to wander unendingly among those unhappy shades who, being childless, have no descendants to offer sacrifices before their tombs, which is really quite unfair considering I begat no less than seven sons. They do offer sacrifice, but I never get a whiff because the essence of the food and drink is wafted straight to heaven.'

When the child reported this problem to his parents, the old man's body was hurriedly exhumed and the unsatisfactory white drill suit exchanged for a Chinese robe, whereafter the ghost was never seen again!

Stories of this kind are amusing in their way but, lacking the ingredient of grimness, they have little relevance to the real world of ghosts and demons. Among the recluses living permanently at the Abode of Mysterious Origination were two exorcists who, even before I had been told the nature of their dark profession, made me feel ill-at-ease in their presence. Both were men of commanding appearance with preternaturally bright eyes, whose gaze was discomforting and whose complexion was unprepossessingly pallid. They were said to spend much of their time in meditation and to regard the calls upon their special skill as exorcists as a tiresome inconvenience to which they submitted largely out of compassion for their patients. Moreover, the monastery's revenue and public image depended to some extent on displays of marvels. Whether truly high-minded or not, these two strange men were admired by the other recluses, who described them as 'freely expending great measures of their vital energy to relieve the sufferings of demon-tormented beings.' Mastering my instinctive distaste, I went out of my way to ingratiate myself with them in the hope of being allowed to observe the symptoms allegedly caused by demonic possession and to witness the rite of exorcism. This second object proved unattainable, for I learnt that an exorcist has to be left alone with his writhing patient, but those grim recluses did promise to let me see the next patient before one of them drove the demon forth. While waiting for this promise to be fulfilled, I was fortunate enough to hear from the lips of a pilgrim from Canton the nearest approach to an eye-witness account of exorcism that could be expected under the circumstances. This Mr Lee, though a canny trader, struck me as an upright person unlikely to tell tall stories just to create an effect. Cut down to its essentials, his tale was as follows:

'On Mount Lo-fu in my native province of Kwangtung, there is a famous Immortal known as the Cloud Wanderer. Not very long ago, the youngest daughter of my cousin, who is, by the way, a tea-merchant, fell victim to a malady that caused violent seizures. She sickened only months prior to the date fixed for her marriage to a wealthy Hong Kong lawyer, and so her parents naturally concealed her misfortune as far as possible, hoping to have her cured in time for the wedding. In vain they summoned practitioners of Western medicine and doctors skilled in our Chinese healing art. Two months were wasted before an intimate friend thought to call in the Cloud Wanderer, who instantly and with good reason diagnosed possession by a member of that particularly vicious type of demon which seeks to prolong its existence by battening on the bodies of healthy youths and maids. Thus they destroy their victims one after another. It is pitiful.

' "Be calm," the Immortal told her parents. "Illness might have had a lingering aftermath, whereas when I have compelled this demon to leave her she will be strong and well – unless fatal inroads have already been made on her stock of vital energy. You would have done well to summon me before."

'You know perhaps that exorcists are rather intimidating in appearance, but the Cloud Wanderer did not look the sort of person to cause a young lady to lose her wits on catching sight of him. Very well. I shall tell you. In between her fits, my cousin's daughter showed no symptoms of illness beyond a severe lassitude, and she had been reasonably well for several days when the Immortal came to diagnose her complaint. No sooner did her parents bring him to her chamber than a fit came upon her. Writhing like a girl put to torture, she screamed foul abuse, shouting words that no well-raised girl would know, much less employ.

' "Oh, so it's you again!" exclaimed the Immortal sternly. This caused some astonishment for he had never before set eyes on the girl, but in truth the remark was addressed to the demon, whom he had once had occasion to drive from the body of a young boy of the Auyang family in Tungshan.

' "How dare you claim acquaintance with *me*!" replied the demon haughtily. "Go and —— yourself in that ruin of a monastery. It's the only love you'll get, you idle Taoist bone!"

'Offended by such undignified abuse, the Immortal said sternly: "Unless King Yen Lo takes you back to his murky kingdom, I shall destroy you, you weak-minded devil!" So saying, he interlocked his fingers in a sign of great power, whereupon the poor girl shrieked as though stricken and lay cowering back against the wall. Turning to the parents, the Immortal remarked: "You will find there is nothing difficult about his case. In one night I can subdue this paltry demon and make him fly for his life. If by noon tomorrow it is still troubling her, I shall take even sterner measures but remit the fee for my services."

'Well knowing that malevolent demon's vindictiveness, he ordered a room to be cleared of furniture and adornments, commanding the servants to sweep it thoroughly so that, if the girl should happen to be dragged along the ground, her clothes would not be soiled. The following evening, having fasted a full day, he returned and set up an altar to his patron deity. Then, advising my cousin to shut his daughter in a room as far away as possible, lest the demon, hearing the sound of the preliminaries, should torment her with redoubled fury, he lit candles and incense in utensils of heavy pewter and performed the introductory rites behind closed doors. Alas, the clash of his cymbals penetrated to the furthest corners of the house, driving the afflicted girl into a frenzy; the women attending her had to bind her arms for fear she destroy herself. An hour before dawn, the Immortal called for a fine young cockerel and, beheading the bird, scattered its blood about the room as an offering to the spirits he had summoned to assist him. As for the flesh, it was intended to tempt the demon into allowing itself to be ejected from the maiden's body. When all was ready, the shrieking girl, whose arms the Immortal now caused to be unbound, was pushed into the room and the door locked behind her.

'What happened next can be imagined, though the Immortal never speaks of his art and one learns of what occurs only from what the patient's household make known when they come to the temple to give thanks to the gods. Hour after hour the frightened parents had to endure listening to the clash of cymbals, heavy footfalls, the clang of metal ritual objects being hurled about the room, laughter, screams and imprecations, and, at last, a struggling and panting as of strong men locked in combat. And the voices! The Immortal's, loud and challenging; the girl's harsh and pitiful by turn; the demon's, now ferociously defiant, now wailing like a wandering ghost's. The mother, believing her daughter was being tortured, was beside herself and tried to break her way into the locked room; her husband had to have her forcibly removed to a neighbour's house.

'Long before noon, the door was flung open and the Immortal, panting and shockingly dishevelled, cried, "It is done!" When the father and his servants ran in, they found a shambles. Twisted and broken remnants of the pewter incense-burner and candle-sticks lay among the splintered fragments of the marble-topped, black-wood altar. The floor, ritually sprinkled with chicken's blood, had been fouled with the bones and feathers of the bird, besides lumps of candle-wax and a quantity of ash from the over-turned incense-burner. The chicken bones had, of course, been sucked clean of every particle of flesh and marrow. After flinging open the door, the Immortal leant weakly against the wall, fatigued beyond all bearing. As for the poor girl, she lay slumped in a corner, unconscious and scarcely breathing. Tenderly she was carried to a bedroom where a careful examination by the women-folk disclosed no sign of violence. Her pale skin was neither scratched nor bruised, except for wounds where her own nails had torn at her cheeks. Her hair and garments were scarcely more disarranged than they had been at the time when she was pushed into the Immortal's presence. Clearly the main struggle had taken place *after* the Immortal had conjured the demon forth from her body. Later, the Immortal informed her parents that he could have vanquished the demon within less than an hour if the girl's weak state had not made it essential to coax it away from her before resorting to violence. When at last it had responded to his spells, the demon, spying the carcass of the chicken, had promised to go its way in peace; but no sooner had it devoured the bird than, with strength renewed, it made a treacherous attack that nearly cost the Immortal's life!

'The Immortal, having bathed, donned fresh garments and eaten a great breakfast, pocketed his fee without so much as glancing at the money and departed, saying to the parents: "You have nothing more to fear from the demon, but your honourable daughter's vitality has been drained almost to the point of death. Nourish her well."

'The girl, on regaining consciousness, recalled nothing of what had occurred. She had no more fits, and behaved to her parents with sweet docility, but her strength had been sucked away prior to the Immortal's coming; she was scarcely able to stroll in the garden, supported by the shoulders of her serving maids. Two months later, she fell into a coma and died. So you see, unlike most of the Cloud Wanderer's exploits, the story has a tragic ending, but it constitutes a classic case of exorcism free from abnormal or unlooked-for features.'

About a week after hearing Mr Lee's story, I was summoned to the cell occupied by Shên Tao-shih, the younger of the two exorcists residing at the Abode of Mysterious Origination. Motioning me to follow, he led the way to a courtyard surrounded by pilgrim dormitories which were rarely occupied at that time of year. In one of them a lonely figure lay upon a sleeping-platform – a middle-aged peasant woman who seemed to be in a daze, for she paid us no attention but kept pulling idly at her disordered hair and emitting bleating noises.

'She is fortunate enough to be possessed by nothing worse than a water-sprite. It seems that, while she was washing clothes at the margin of the river, it lodged itself in her body. Such sprites are really dangerous only when deep water lies nearby. Her husband brought her up here after spending three sleepless nights preventing her from running off towards the river. Apparently the sprite sleeps throughout most of the day, for the patient seldom shows signs of acute distress until evening approaches.'

'And how do you propose to cure her?' I asked, longing for an invitation to be present at the rite.

'With fire, naturally, since fire and water are the elements most often at variance with each other.'

'With fire!' I repeated. 'Will not the patient be hurt?'

'That is like asking me if I know my job as a doctor,' he answered with slight asperity. 'What you suggest is most improbable. Look!' He struck a match and, though it was broad daylight, the sight of the puny flame drew a piercing shriek from the woman, who sprang up and huddled back against the head of her bed moaning pitifully.

'You see how easily water-sprites are intimidated. Tonight, the creature will be taught to leave humans well alone.'

Though I pleaded earnestly to be allowed to watch, Shên Tao-shih was adamant. That night, while getting ready for bed in my little guest-cell on the opposite side of the monastery, I heard a distant clash of cymbals that continued for perhaps an hour. That was all. In the morning while I and two or three other guests were breakfasting off rice gruel flavoured with salted river-shrimps, the exorcist strode in with a beaming smile to invite me to see the woman before she left. Putting down my chopsticks, I followed him to where she was standing just outside the guest-refectory door. Her long hair was now neatly arranged in a bun and, though she looked tired and wan, it was obvious that she was altogether in much better shape than when I had seen her last. On being suddenly confronted by a barbarian from the Western Ocean, she instinctively made as if to run; but that, in a Chinese peasant woman, was a normal reaction and quite the reverse of her previous listlessness. By and large, I felt disappointed. I was strongly inclined to suspect that the wily exorcist had diagnosed some minor ailment and, having sought to impress me by alleging a case of possession, administered a suitable remedy before leaving her to get a good night's sleep. And yet? There had been her horrified shrinking from a match-flame and the noise of cymbals during the night. Casually I produced a cigarette and lit it, watching the woman for signs of fear, but her rather stolid expression did not change. The incident, if not impressive, had certainly been peculiar.

In the nineteen-thirties, Taoist exorcism was still widely practised and apparently with success; for, whether the patients were actually possessed by demons or were simply what we should call schizophrenics, there were reliable stories of successful cures being wrought. On the other hand, the more dangerous art of evoking spirits (other than as invisible presences speaking through the mouths of human oracles) had become extremely rare, so that, during my several visits to the Abode of Mysterious Origination, I tried in vain to obtain authentic information about evocation rites. The recluses took it for granted that demon evocation was well within the bounds of possibility, for they had heard or read a great many accounts of this mystery as practised by Taoists in days gone by; but none could quote a recent case supported by reliable testimony. At length a rather fat, good-natured recluse born in the neighbourhood of Peking, whose powers as a musician were much esteemed, decided to satisfy my curiosity by relating a story concerning a Mongol shaman who, so he assured me, had conjured up a demon in circumstances that pointed to a method similar to Taoist-style evocation.

'The story goes back some years, my friend, say ten or twelve years after the founding of the Republic, when Sun Yat-sen was still the people's idol – a tiresome, demagogic ranter, we Taoists thought him. At that time, I was a serving-lad in the Tung Yü Temple in Peking and knew several members of the family concerned. The chief protagonist was a skin-merchant named Chang I-lo, whose mother and third uncle had long been at loggerheads about a piece of landed property in Pao-ting Fu, their native home. The old lady happened to die rather suddenly of a mysterious ailment and Chang I-lo, convinced that his uncle had poisoned her, indiscreetly voiced this charge to all and sundry. The uncle was certainly an evil-hearted person besides belonging to the cult—a cult whose name it is unwise to mention even among trusted friends. Its followers perform abominable rites that have been illegal for centuries. Dangerous men! As a boy I kept out of the way of Chang's sinister relative each time he visited our temple.

'As a skin-merchant, Chang I-lo had to travel to Kalgan annually to buy furs and hides from Mongolian trappers who would call at his inn with their goods. In the year his mother died, when he was preparing to visit that city, an assistant working in the medicine-shop near the Tung An market went to see him as if on business and persuaded him to visit a certain Mongol shaman residing in Kalgan, a man renowned for conjuring up the spirits of the dead. By conversing with his departed mother, Chang could discover whether and how his uncle had poisoned her.

' "A man may not live beneath the same heaven as the slayer of his parent" remarked the seller of medicines. "If your suspicions are confirmed by so reliable a source, no honourable man will blame you for making away with your uncle. The Law is the Law, of course, and Sun Yat-sen's people have turned it topsy-turvy; so the authorities might take a harsh view of such an act, but people in general will esteem you as a filial son."

'When Chang I-lo reached Kalgan, he learnt that the shaman dwelt in a small *yurt* (felt tent) pitched near the top of an escarpment a few miles north of the city wall. There was no road, so he hired a young lad to run beside his horse and show him the way. When they had topped a rise which brought them in sight of the *yurt*, the lad asked for his money, declaring he was afraid to approach it more closely; so Chang paid him off, perhaps glad that it was still early enough for him to be safely back within the city walls before sundown.

'At the entrance to the *yurt* – a wooden door set in the canvas – he met a smutty-faced Mongol child who motioned him to go straight in. It was dark inside but not too dark to see. On the further side of the stove sat an elderly Mongol lolling back on a pile of old rugs. No less grimy than the boy, he was clad in a tattered yellow ochre robe covered with grease-stains – he probably wiped his chopsticks on it after every meal. The whole place smelled offensively. To the odours of dirt and poverty was added that of rancid butter emanating from some silver lamps burning before the usual sort of Buddhist wall-shrine. Chang felt thoroughly upset. Surely a successful demon-conjurer would be able to afford surroundings of greater elegance? As it was, there was nothing in the room besides the shrine, the pile of old rugs and a battered bronze tea-kettle bubbling on the stove.

'The shaman greeted him in Mongol, a language all Peking skin-merchants have to know for business reasons. Chang spoke it fluently, whereas the shaman could probably speak very little Chinese, if any. His next words gave Chang a shock.

' "You have come on a grave affair and would speak with your mother."

'Who could remain calm in the face of such prescience? And Chang, I remember, was a rather timid man. But then, it was encouraging to discover that the shaman really did possess unusual powers.

' "Ten silver dollars," was the next pronouncement. My friend, if you know our thrifty Peking merchants, you will understand the working of Chang's mind. Had the Mongol been clad in silks and his *yurt* furnished with fine rugs and other luxuries, he might easily have extorted forty or even fifty dollars. As it was, observing signs of poverty all around him, Chang foolishly decided to give him less than had been demanded. Calmly he laid just five silver dollars on the edge of the pile of carpets, shamefacedly adding a sixth when he saw the shaman's look of anger. Such miserliness would have set anyone against him, but it cannot have made any real difference. Later on, the Mongol punished him cruelly, but one can scarcely suppose that petty meanness was the real cause. In my humble opinion, Chang would have needed a very large sum indeed to escape what was in store for him.

'Placing the miserable fee in his sleeve, the Mongol folded his legs as for meditation, carefully tucking in the skirts of his gown to keep his feet from the draught. Chang said later that this surprised him, for the tent was so stuffy that he himself was sweating. Next, the Mongol picked up a hand-drum with metal pellets attached to it by thongs and, twirling it with such strength that the sound resembled hail pelting on a thinly tiled roof, began to chant.

' "*Durra-durra-drrrrh!*" went the drum. "*Ooooah aieyee yaaauu*" intoned the Mongol in a deep bass voice. You know the sort of thing. Presently his body began to jerk and sway, arms flailing, and now and then his gestures were so menacing that Chang, who was seated on the floor, slid hastily backwards, almost singeing his back against the stove. Suddenly there came a rush of wind. The Mongol emitted piercing yells and the canvas walls of the *yurt* began straining and trembling – yet the sunlit rents in the material remained as bright as ever and Chang was aware that, though a cold wind raged within the *yurt*, the steppe outside remained as windless and peaceful as before! Soon he noticed that the darkness inside had increased; for, though he could still make out the Mongol's violent movements, such details as the grease-stains on his robe were no longer visible. True merchant that he was, Chang's first thought was that an attempt would soon be made to rob him!

'Noise, noise, noise, then mind-shattering silence! The wind died as abruptly as the rattling of the drum. No sound to be heard, but the tea-kettle's gentle hiss. A long, long silence. So this was the moment! His departed mother's shade was about to manifest itself. He would hear her voice, perhaps even see her well-loved features! Holding his breath he grew tense. Tears started to his eyes.

' "Incestuous turtle! Sister-raping dog! Stinking lump of human dung! How dare you impugn the crime of murder to your honoured uncle, impious Chang I-lo!"

'Chang shrank back appalled. How could the unseen owner of that high-pitched, metallic, sneering voice know his name or the accusations he had made in far-away Peking? It was not the voice of anyone known to him, whether now alive or dead, and most certainly not his mother's. Nor could it be the Mongol's, for the abuse had been delivered in impeccable Chinese, the very accents of his home-town, Pao-ting Fu. What manner of person could read his inmost thoughts and parody his intonation? To save his sanity, he seized upon the notion that the foul abuse had after all been hurled at him by the shaman, who had somewhere acquired a perfect knowledge of Chinese. It was all a plot aimed at securing the bag of silver he carried beneath his robe. That was it! Fear gave way to rage and he was about to set about the tricksters, when a renewed bout of terror intervened; for now he discerned a second and taller figure seated upon the pile of rugs in such a manner that parts of the shaman's face and body should have been hidden. But they were not! Two figures overlapping and yet both entirely visible? How could that be? His mind must be afflicted by an illusion due to the poor light. Whatever comfort he drew from this conclusion did not last long, for he soon saw the hitherto shadowy form acquire the more solid aspect of a burly fellow seated cross-legged, the white soles of his felt Chinese slippers glimmering against the dark material of his robe. Chang's belief that he was the victim of hallucination had already begun to waver when some pieces of ill-cured charcoal in the stove behind him burst into flame, causing a lurid light to shine upon the stranger's face. No comforting doubts remained. Such horribly ill-favoured features set in an expression of such inhuman malevolence could belong only to a fiend!

'The shaman had performed his task so well that our filial skin-merchant ran shrieking from the *yurt*, stumbled upon the door-sill and crashed face-down on the dusty earth outside. Scrambling to his feet, he heard amidst bursts of high-pitched laughter the awful words: "No man flees his shadow. No matter where he goes, it follows!" Flinging himself astride his horse, he dug his heels into its flanks before remembering to unhitch the rein from the tethering post. The hateful Mongol child's laughter was now added to the fiend's.

'One can well imagine poor Chang I-lo urging his horse to gallop ever faster, blinding the passers-by with clouds of sand. A day or two later, back in Peking with his load of hides and furs, he poured out the story to his family, including a young cousin from whose lips we were soon to hear it in the Tung Yü Temple. In a way it was laughable; not so, the sequel. Everyone tried to comfort Chang by insisting that he had been deceived in some cruel way for his meanness to the shaman; but Chang I-lo, obsessed by the words "No man flees his shadow", could talk of nothing but arrangements for his funeral. A few days later he fell ill; the physician diagnosed a preponderance of the fire element in the region of his liver, but it is doubtful if he properly understood the nature of the malady. Presently it became known that Chang's wife no longer dared to pass the nights with him, for she would wake up time and time again to find her husband talking loudly to himself between fits of weeping and laughter. What frightened her most was that he seemed to have *two* voices, one that argued, wept and pleaded in familiar tones; another that shouted threats and obscenities or laughed and murmured in high-pitched accents that seemed to belong to a stranger!

'Advised to summon a Taoist exorcist, the lady obstinately refused, declaring that Taoists gave people nothing but worthless paper charms in return for good money. On this account, Chang I-lo soon passed away, but not as a result of illness. Early one morning, his wife and servant, coming in to attend to him as usual, found the bed-clothes soaked in blood which had gushed from what the authorities were to describe as self-inflicted knife wounds. You can guess the truth of it. At the funeral there was, of course, much talk of demonic possession until his sinister third uncle, looking decorously mournful, put a stop to it by declaring such superstitious nonsense a disgrace.'

On reaching this point, my chubby Taoist friend fell silent, foreseeing no need for further explanation. When I pressed for one, he looked surprised, but complied in his usual genial way.

'Naturally the uncle was at the bottom of all that happened. On learning that I-lo quite rightly suspected him of murder, he must have hastened to Kalgan by train and paid the shaman handsomely to evoke a demon powerful enough to destroy his nephew. The seller of medicines may have been bribed or innocently led into directing Chang I-lo to visit the shaman.'

'But why choose so bizarre and complicated a means of silencing poor Chang?'

'What better alternative had he? To have poisoned two members of his family within the space of a year would have been dangerous, don't you think? Whereas, since our modern laws take no cognizance of demons, his method was flawless. Chang's family might persuade some individual police-constables to accept the truth, but the police would have been laughed out of court had they attempted to base a murder case on demonic possession!'

'How true! Thank you for the story, but I do wish you had one about specifically Taoist methods of demon-conjuring.'

'Dear friend, dear friend', exclaimed the recluse amidst hearty laughter, 'you surely do not believe there can be several ways of evoking demons! Shaman or Taoist, what difference can it make?'

'But you have not told me *how* the shaman went about it.'

'Ah,' he replied, shaking his head. 'I wish I knew. Yes, I very much wish I had studied that fascinating art, but where in these days would one find a teacher! All I can tell you is that some demons are self-existing entities that must be summoned by means of spells and cajolery, whereas others are mental creations of the one who sends them forth. The latter are the more dangerous unless an intended victim, recognizing his tormentor for a mere phantom, boldly slashes at it with a weapon of iron or steel; for then its power departs and the victor is left with a mangled paper doll no longer animated by the magician's psychic breath. Such phantoms are especially dangerous because, unlike natural demons, they cannot be bought off by promises of succulent corpses, jars of fresh blood or similar delicacies. No one would take the trouble to create a phantom by power of mind unless to wreak harm on somebody and, since it draws its existence from its creator, it has no purpose, no aim except to destroy its destined victim. If Chang I-lo's wife had called in a competent Taoist, the type of demon afflicting him would have been determined and suitable measures taken. One does not like to *destroy* genuine demons except as a last resort. They love their lives as much as we do and have the same rights to existence. Only in the case of a mentally created phantom would a Taoist use violence without giving it the option of departing in peace, for a demon of that class has no life to lose, being a mere extension of the magician's mind; it may therefore be destroyed without compunction, but the sword-stroke must be powerful, swift and effective; were one merely to wound such a phantom, it might rush back and avenge itself by destroying its creator. You may say that the Mongol shaman deserved to die, but to my way of thinking that would have been an unjustifiably drastic punishment. Probably he bore Chang I-lo no ill will, but created the phantom merely to oblige Chang's uncle, just as a swordsmith would forge you a good sword if you paid him well enough. No one punishes the swordsmith for a murder committed with a weapon he was paid to fashion.

'In the case of demons which draw life from the emanations of putrefying corpses, mouldering brooms, rotting rope and so on, it is enough to destroy the objects from which they took their being, whereupon such demons vanish. There are also, of course, were-tigers and vampire-demons that are so destructive of human life and so greedy for the tender flesh of children that people consider it necessary to destroy them. Even so I feel less drastic measures would meet the case, such as confining them in sealed caves. There are several well-authenticated accounts of were-tigers in the form of women making devoted wives and mothers when they have, for one reason or another, married human husbands. When their true identity is discovered, as is bound to happen sooner or later in the course of a long marriage, they usually slip away into some forest or mountain fastness to escape being slaughtered, without having to resort to devouring their husbands and children as a means of keeping matters secret from the neighbours.

'Men, animals, ghosts, demons – all deserve sympathetic consideration. Formed from the great Tao, Matrix of the Universe, all are equally necessary to nature's purposes. If we destroy any being without good cause, how can we expect our fellows to treat us less belligerently? Let live, leave well alone, abstain from exaggerated reactions and one may be sure of remaining on good terms with all the hosts of heaven, earth and hell. Even corpse-devouring demons are capable of gratitude. In my youth, I befriended such a fiend who at that time inhabited a dry well in the Tung Yü Temple. Ever since, it has constituted itself my protector. Now and then it goes astray and devours somebody's chickens, but its sense of loyalty is too strong for it to permit its fellow demons to molest me or my friends. Once when I was passing the night in a bower close to the mountain peak where I sometimes go to gather medicinal herbs, a famished tree-spirit pressed upon me and began to suck my vital energy. Fascinated by its burning gaze, I could make no movement to save myself. The creature would have drained me of blood, breath and semen, leaving me dead, had not my guardian fiend intervened by recounting my poor little virtues in such terms that the tree-spirit, greatly abashed, begged my pardon and went off to hide its shame.'

It is pleasant to turn from demons to a more poetic, though sometimes equally dangerous, class of supernatural beings known as fox-spirits. All over China there used to be small fox-towers, a reflection of the widespread belief that certain foxes are playful, fairy creatures able to take on human form and perpetrate practical jokes, both humourous and upsetting. There were also the dreaded *hu-li ching* – foxes that took the form of lovely maidens so as to suck from their infatuated human lovers great stores of vital energy. Since their victims were apt to pine away and die, the epitaph 'poetic' may seem inappropriate; however, the *hu-li ching* were said to be so ravishingly beautiful that many a young man thought his life a cheap price to pay for the months of exquisite pleasure that preceded his decease. Anecdotes about fox-spirits, both playful and malevolent, are innumerable. In the nineteen-thirties, I came across a factual newspaper report of a fox-spirit harassing a policeman by daylight on one of Peking's largest thoroughfares. Another story, related by the victim's youngest brother, a Taoist recluse surnamed T'ang, ran as follows:

'When we were young,' began T'ang Tao-shih, waving a silken fan on which he had executed the likeness of a shoal of prawns with a deft economy of brush-strokes, 'I lived with my parents and elder brothers not far from Si-an. The brother nearest me in age had such a fondness for reading ancient stories that my father was obliged to beat him for failing his school examination. The next day he ran away and, some time later, was reported to have joined a community of Taoist recluses on Mount Hua. My father sent for him at once, but he did not return either then or later. Within less than a year he was dead, for a reason I shall now make clear.

'One evening while he was taking a stroll in the neighbourhood of his hermitage, a party of female pilgrims happened to come in sight at a moment when he felt a powerful urge to urinate. Embarrassed, he looked round for a secluded spot and chose a vacant space between the mountain-side and a ruined fox-tower. Being careless, he urinated in such a manner that some of the urine trickled over the sun-baked soil down on to the base of the fox-tower! On returning to the hermitage, he remarked jokingly that he had committed sacrilege against the fox-spirits. His fellow recluses, thinking it no light matter, advised him to take incense, candles and roast chicken to make amends to the foxes, but this he neglected to do, thus compounding his dangerous folly.

'Thereafter, whenever my brother had occasion to pass that tower, he would hear mocking laughter and once a voice reviled him by name, hailing him as the "Loose-Penis Immortal" – an inelegant expression, as you will certainly agree—and Fourth Brother, assuming that a younger colleague was playing pranks on him, retorted with a curse. Nothing notable followed until well into the autumn, when it suddenly turned cold and the mountain-side recluses drew forth from their clothes-chests thickly wadded garments. It was the sort of weather to huddle over a brazier, drinking hot tea or roasting chestnuts; meals were served in pewter chafing-dishes heated by boiling water or burning charcoal. No one cared to go out of doors in those icy winds; but, one very cold day, my brother was obliged to go down into the city to arrange for additional winter supplies.

'On his return, he missed his way in a dense cold mist laced with gusts of driving sleet. You know how it is on Mount Hua when seas of cloud cut off the hermitages from the world of men. Drenched and shivering, he looked round for shelter. Presently he saw a light glimmering through the mist. Greatly relieved, he buffeted his way to the source of this brightness and, to his amazement, came upon a cluster of buildings he could not recall having seen; but Mount Hua is huge and no one can be sure how many hermitages and monasteries nestle among its folds. Though he banged his fists on the gate, no one came; but a leaf of the gate yielded and he stepped into the outer courtyard of a monastery that lay in ruins. It seemed deserted, except for one set of rooms with paper windows brilliantly illuminated. Drawing nearer, he caught the soft notes of silken lute-strings brushed by the fingers of an expert. Pounding on the door, he shouted to those within and a Taoist serving-lad appeared. Bowing deeply, the boy invited him to enter a lighted room beyond. There my brother came upon a startling scene. Instead of a little band of recluses discussing philosophy over a bowl or two of mulled wine, he beheld an old gentleman, elegantly dressed in long gown and ceremonial black silk over-jacket of a kind seldom seen today, who sat listening with rapt attention to the lute-player, a sweet young girl in her middle teens.

'The musician was dressed simply but charmingly in peach-coloured jacket and white silk trousers embroidered with silver thread. Neither of them so much as glanced round at my brother, but the old gentleman impatiently motioned to him to be seated. Just then the girl began to sing in a voice so melodious and melancholy that Fourth Brother was close to tears. It was as though all the sorrows of the world had gathered to confront him. Presently a new song began, one full of amorous longing, and the beautiful singer's eyes now rested on my brother's face. He was entranced. Long before the lilting song with its undertones of passion reached its end, he had incautiously lost his heart. When the music stopped, the dignified elder remarked:

' "Youthful Immortal, my humble surname is Hu. We have been eagerly awaiting a visitor. Please come closer to the table and do us the honour of accepting a cup of inferior wine quite unworthy of your distinguished palate."

'So saying, he gestured towards a table set out with drinking-cups, a pewter wine-pot and some dishes of savoury titbits. Just as he was about to introduce the young lady, the serving-lad brought him a written message which caused him to exclaim: "A thousand pardons. I must leave you, oh pure-hearted youth. An affair of consequence demands my attention. Pray do not stand on ceremony. My insignificant daughter will attend to your esteemed requirements. Your noble bearing assures me that I may leave you together without impropriety."

'So my brother, blushing and stammering, was left in the company of a pale-faced beauty as cool and lovely as the Moon Maiden, whose glittering snow-palace is a symbol of her eternal virginity.

'The titbits were delicious enough to have graced a provincial governor's table. The serving-lad remained outside, appearing only briefly to bring in a new wine-jar or to hand them perfumed towels. The lady seemed engagingly self-possessed, but my hermit brother's embarrassment precluded much conversation; until, by a somewhat unexpected freedom of manner, she led him to suppose that she could scarcely be a spotless maiden reared in the strict seclusion of the innermost courtyards of her home; perhaps, after all, she was one of those musicians who can be hired to entertain male guests in more ways than one – with music, elegant conversation and, if so disposed, by engaging in the sport of mandarin ducks. Viewing her thus, his own manner became more free and he did not shrink from creating occasions for their hands to touch as she filled his cup or urged him to sample some new delicacy. Each time this happened, a flood of liquid fire ran through his body, racing up to his crown and down to the very tips of his toes. His infatuation grew beyond all bounds: and when, while the third wine-jar was being replaced by a pot of fragrant tea, she smilingly gave instructions to the lad not to disturb them unless summoned, my brother felt an irresistible longing to indulge in a contest of clouds and rain.

'When, with exploratory boldness, he placed his hand lightly upon her shoulder, she accepted the caress with such coy delight that his last doubts vanished. With such a girl, a denizen of the world of wind and willows, bashfulness on his part would have been out of place and he was too young to recognize the importance of conserving his vital powers. Soon she was lying in his arms on a low, thickly carpeted divan which might well have been placed there for the purpose, though he was disturbed by a vague recollection of not having seen it up to the moment when a pressing need to recline had arisen in his wine-heated mind. Far into the night they sported; nor, when the candles guttered and expired, did they trouble to call for replacements. Fourth Brother was overwhelmed by a bliss hitherto unknown to him, although he was a youth not altogether inexperienced in the art of conjuring clouds and rain. Whenever renewed doubts or fears assailed him, he had only to say, "But what if your august parent were to———" for a slender finger to be laid upon his lips and soft laughter to invite him to further ecstasies.

'Before the first light of a cold winter dawn, the lady whispered:

' "Dearest Elder Brother, you must leave me. It would not do for strangers to arrive and find us so. Go back to your hermitage, dearest and most vigorous of Immortals, but be sure to come and visit me very, very soon."

'She instructed him never to call on her by day and not to betray to others her presence on the mountain. As to why she had taken up residence in a remote monastery so long abandoned that all but the one set of rooms had fallen into ruins, she laughingly explained that she had prayed earnestly for the joy of being favoured by a gifted young Immortal and that, as a result of her pious austerities, her wish had at last been granted. She turned aside all questions as to her father's whereabouts, assuring him that all would become clear in good time. One of the strangest aspects of the prolonged association that now began between them was that, back in his hermitage, he could never recall where exactly the monastery she inhabited was situated and yet his feet never failed to take him there by the shortest route in spite of his having to approach it always by night. On leaving, he would scan the great name-board above the ruined gatehouse, but the pre-dawn darkness, intensified by the shadow of overhanging eaves, obscured the huge gold characters.

'For months their rapturous meetings continued. Back at the hermitage, his fellow recluses found it strange that their young colleague was so often absent from evening rice in the refectory and that his bed remained unslept in, for the cold had intensified and, even at midday, nobody cared to leave the warmth of the charcoal braziers except in a case of dire necessity. But these were recluses who had taken no monastic vows and the Abbot was too good a Taoist to resort to punishment or interference, which meant that good order arose spontaneously, since every recluse was free to follow his own regimen; to have asked questions or attempted to restrict my brother's movement would have been the very negation of Lao-tzû's exalted philosophy. Alas,-near the close of the First Month (some time in March), the Abbot, happening to send for my brother and finding him now pale and sickly, inferred by means of his esoteric powers that the ill-fated youth had fallen victim to a dangerous fox-spirit! Addressing him with compassion and serenity, he said:

' "My dear young disciple, if you persist in this folly, your life will have run its course before it has properly begun. It would be surprising if the Autumn Festival this year (about October) were to find you still in the land of mortals."

'Though recognizing the correctness of the Abbot's diagnosis of his fast-increasing debility, Fourth Brother obstinately continued to go his way, deeming that life without his adorable partner would not be worth living. Yet he wept at the thought of dying so young and of having to embark upon the after-life with his two souls (*hun* and *p'o*) so undeveloped that total dissolution must be his fate. On divining the young man's state of mind by means of his occult powers, the Abbot, in defiance of his own high principles, reluctantly gave orders that my brother be locked in his cell from dusk to dawn, except during the evening-rice hour, when he was to be brought to the refectory in the custody of a colleague. Once or twice, Fourth Brother managed to evade his gaolers by leaving the monastery an hour before dusk, but this ruse was soon countered by his being ordered to keep to his cell night and day. There he remained alone, his heart consumed with fiery longing. Then, one night, the watchman while making a round of the hermitage heard unexpected sounds coming from my brother's cell. Mingled with a youth's soft laughter were silvery accents that told their own story.

'On receiving the watchman's report, the Abbot was forced to conclude that the fox-spirit had grown so shameless as to indulge in lewd pranks right under the pious community's noses! This was in its way a satisfying development, however, as it now seemed possible that the audacious vixen could be driven off in time to save my brother's life. Several recluses were ordered to fashion sacred swords from ancient coins threaded together to form both hilt and blade. Such weapons, effective but not deadly, would serve to teach the fox-spirit – which was invulnerable to fire or steel – a well-merited lesson in decorum. By some unknown means, however, the vixen came to know of these plans; thenceforth, during its visits, the lovers conversed in whispers inaudible to the listeners stationed in the courtyard outside.

'One night, acting upon the Abbot's order, six or eight recluses armed with magic swords burst into his cell, only to find him alone and sleeping peacefully. But his wan and skeletal appearance warned them that their friend was rapidly approaching his end, so closely had he come to resemble someone in the last stages of a fatal malady. Doubtless the fox-spirit, having sucked almost the last drops of my poor brother's vitality into its alluring body, was now looking even lovelier and more aglow with health than ever. The preparations for putting an end to its visits were intensified. The Abbot, though not unaware of the danger to the entire community that would result from arousing the implacable hatred of a whole brood of fox-spirits, felt bound to exert himself to save the poor youth's life. Short of actually killing the treacherous vixen, he was prepared to go to any lengths in order to destroy its power over my brother. (Naturally, to have killed the creature would have been too gross a betrayal of his principles, since foxes no less than men have the right to live out their lives to the full. To have murdered the one in order to save the life of the other would have amounted to wilful interference with nature's creations.)

'Alas for the good man's intentions! On the eve of the Jade Emperor's birthday, when the recluses and serving-lads were busying themselves with preparations for a large influx of pilgrims, my brother slipped away unnoticed during the hour before midday rice. Nothing more was seen of him until the morning of the festival itself, when some children playing among the ruins of a long-abandoned monastery close to the foot of Mount Hua stumbled upon a terrifyingly gruesome sight.

'Their ball had sailed into the western courtyard, an especially gloomy place which people instinctively avoided; hurrying in to retrieve it they found themselves among low buildings with gaping doorways and latticed windows from which the remaining window-paper hung in tatters; great sections of the roof had fallen in, leaving the largest room open to the sky. Thinking the ball might have fallen there, the little boy who chanced to be in the lead crossed the door-sill at a run and there stopped short with a scream that brought the others crowding in behind him. On the floor, close to the mouldering remnants of a once prettily lacquered lute, lay the blood-soaked body of a Taoist recluse. Who he was and whether young or old, they could not say, for the eyes and fleshier parts of his face and body had been ripped away from the bones, presumably by famished dogs or wild animals. The children's wails of terror brought peasants running in, and these horror-striken men noticed that the surrounding dust was pitted by pad-marks so numerous as to suggest that a whole colony of foxes had come to feast off the dead man's flesh. I need not tell you that I am speaking of my unfortunate brother.

'I have often thought,' T'ang Tao-shih continued, 'that Fourth Brother's fate was infinitely harsher than he deserved. After all, his defilement of the fox-tower had been due to nothing worse than carelessness and he would scarcely have answered that taunting voice by cursing had he not supposed that the taunt emanated from a colleague playfully amusing himself. My brother was far from being a stupid man and no one in his senses would knowingly be discourteous to a fox-spirit! Such perfidious creatures are invariably treated with deep respect. One keeps as far from them as possible and, when a confrontation is unavoidable, uses fair words, however vilely they seek to provoke an insulting retort. It is my belief that the vixen made my brother's carelessness and subsequent rudeness a mere excuse for robbing a lusty youth of his vitality. If ever you chance to encounter a fox acquainted with human speech, I implore you to guard your tongue; your very life will depend upon your skill in exercising self-restraint.'

These tales of demons and fox-spirits, however far-fetched they may seem, well illustrate the atmosphere prevailing in many a Taoist monastery. The recluses and their followers accepted the reality of the spirits much as we Westerners accept the menace of the millions of invisible germs filling the earth's atmosphere. In those days, I believed that such tales must have at their core some relatively unusual occurrences which the over-credulous Taoists misinterpreted as being of a supernatural character. Since then, I have come to revise that estimate, partly as a result of seeing with my own eyes – if not the forms of devils or fox-spirits, then other manifestations just as inexplicable except in terms of supernatural forces. For example, it was difficult to dismiss the *visible* exploits of some Taoist adepts in making themselves invulnerable to flame and steel. Throughout the history of China and neighbouring countries there have been many accounts of this art, starting with those Chinese master-swordsmen, who by the use of Taoist charms, made themselves invulnerable in conflict. It is true that during the Boxer uprising of 1900, hundreds of peasants supposedly rendered invulnerable by the power of a minor deity, the monkey-god, were mown down by the guns of foreign soldiers, but they were ignorant men who depended for their invulnerability solely on magical incantations instead of seeking surer methods of attaining it.

During the great annual fair at the Abode of Mysterious Origination, when such hosts of pilgrims streamed up the mountain-side that the large dormitories could accommodate only a fraction of their number, leaving hundreds to make use of sleeping-mats spread out on the courtyard flagstones, the recluses put on many demonstrations of abnormal powers for their visitors' benefit, such as almost bloodless piercing of the flesh, and fire-walking, to say nothing of divination, seemingly miraculous healing, and so forth. As to the genuinness of the flesh-piercing and fire-walking, there could be no doubt. After watching what went forward, I came to credit the devotees with the attainment of at least a limited degree of invulnerability. Two possibilities presented themselves: first, temporary invulnerablility acquired during a state of trance, perhaps to be explained as the result of an entranced person's being able to make swiftly co-ordinated muscular movements and to take right decisions instantaneously; second, invulnerability acquired by yogic practices leading to an advanced state of consciousness in which the mind assumes direct control over normally involuntary physical activities such as breathing, blood-flow and the self-healing processes with which nature has endowed us.

To give at least some weight to my opinion, I propose a short digression that illustrates how belief in the attainment of invulnerability persists among people at all levels of education in the countries close to China's frontiers. The first anecdote, which concerns a group of Shans (Burmese subjects of Thai origin) involved in rebellion against the Burmese authorities, pertains, I believe, to the year 1969. A Burmese military detachment had threatened a whole village with destruction unless all the men under thirty-five gave themselves up. This condition could not be fulfilled as the younger villagers had slipped away months before to join the partisans. To the amazement of the women, the remaining menfolk, instead of helping their families to escape into the jungle under cover of darkness, spent most of the night of grace preceding the punitive attack in visiting a Buddhist monk with a reputation for great sanctity, who dwelt alone in a hill-top temple some miles away. Towards dawn, they returned and armed themselves with *das* (jungle knives), rusty swords, ancient guns and the like, preparing to do battle with soldiers! It seemed sheer madness, but the women's protests met with obstinate silence. When the sun rose, the men sallied forth into a hail of rifle-fire issuing from the fringe of the surrounding jungle where the Burmese soldiers were encamped. The women and children, crouching close to the ground, watched horror-struck as the intrepid band of husbands and fathers disappeared among the trees, running towards the waiting foe. Ferocious shouts, the crackle of musketry and agonized screams filled the air in turn, until presently the sound of firing died away and, after a terrifying silence, there came into view – not angry soldiers bent on slaughter, but the husbands and brothers whom the women had given up for dead! The soldiers had fled, leaving several casualties behind, whereas the Shans, despite their inferior numbers and poor weapons, had lost but two men! The key to this extraordinary incident was supplied by the women of that village who were questioned by my informant only two days after the event. They described their men as having returned from the temple looking like people bewitched. Although they did not stumble or exhibit other familiar signs of intoxication, it was at first supposed that they had callously passed that fateful night in a mammoth drinking session. Silent and withdrawn, eyes seemingly ill-focused, they had ignored the women until sunrise and made their memorable sally while still in the same abnormal state; but, unlike sleepwalkers, they had run out with speed and grace, covering the rough ground unerringly without as much as glancing down. Though the women may not have realized it, they were clearly describing men in a state of trance. My informant, a Chinese trader, held, as I do, that warriors immersed in deep meditation-induced trance emerge unscathed from battle, simply because their reactions are in fact much faster and better co-ordinated than those of people in a more usual state of consciousness. The principle involved is not unlike that which enables archers trained in Zen to hit the target unerringly with a very minimum of effort. As to whether that fully explains how all but two of them weathered what the women described as a hail of fire, I really cannot say. Something even more mysterious may have lain behind their astonishing success.

In the early nineteen-fifties, an English-language Bangkok newspaper carried a terse report on a recent execution. The condemned man had received permission to go to his death chewing a comforting wad of betel nut. As was usual at the time, the mode of execution was for a single marksman to aim at a circle drawn upon a white cloth-screen, behind which the condemned man, holding flowers and incense in his manacled hands as an offering to the Buddha, had been placed on a low stool in such a manner that the painted circle exactly coincided with the part of his back through which a bullet would reach the heart. On this occasion, the gun misfired or failed three times in succession to hit him at almost point-blank range, whereupon the condemned man was requested to spit out the betel nut so as to avoid prolonging the executioner's unpleasant task still further. Scornfully he complied and was executed without further mishap. A point not made by the reporter, as though too obvious to require comment, was that the betel nut must have been endowed by an Acharya (holy man) with the power of conferring invulnerability. In Thailand, opportunities to test a man's alleged invulnerability are not very rare. To my lasting regret, I once declined to pay a Thai policeman one hundred *baht* (US $5) in return for the privilege of slashing his arm with a weapon of my own choosing. I was, of course, afraid of wounding him and getting both of us into trouble; yet he would scarcely have risked a severe wound for so small a sum, unless convinced that my weapon could not be made to pierce the skin. As it turned out, I probably chose the wiser course; for, towards the end of 1971, the Bangkok newspapers came out with the story of an educated man so sure of his newly won invulnerability that he persuaded a friend to test it with a gun. The friend complied and, unfortunately, shot him dead! Clearly adepts may be mistaken as to the extent of their attainment, but it does not follow that no such attainments are possible, as my experience during the annual fair at the Abode of Mysterious Origination will show.

Like all large temple-fairs in China, this one provided a delightfully varied and colourful scene. Incense-smoke rose in clouds before the altars of the gods whose gilded images and jewelled robes gleamed with the reflected light of innumerable candles, as pilgrim followed pilgrim into the great shrine-hall. In the score or so of courtyards, large and small, altars to less exalted but highly popular deities had been set up, and each was so crowded with worshippers as to leave them no space to prostrate themselves in the customary fashion. Not all these visitors, whether men or women, wore the blue cotton jacket and trousers of peasants; there was a fair sprinkling of people whose silken gowns or Western-style clothes indicated that the monastery had numerous supporters among the educated classes. There were, besides, scarlet-clad layfolk weighed down with heavy chains who had toiled up the mountain thus handicapped in fulfilment of penitential vows generally made for the benefit of sick parents or children. These penitents had progressed from the landing-stage below, prostrating themselves after every three paces. No less to be wondered at were the elderly ladies with tiny golden lilies (feet stunted to a mere three inches in length by being rigidly encased in sodden bandages since early childhood); with slow and faltering steps, they had accomplished the long, steep climb unaided and undaunted.

Imagine the disappointment of those old ladies if some scholarly sage had met them at the temple gateway, crying: 'You'll get no exhibitions of vulgar marvels here, for we are true followers of Lao-tzû and have no truck with superstition!' Happily, nothing of the sort happened; the pilgrims were able to feast their eyes on many, many wonders. There was, for example, a pond containing a small island where sat three recluses so rapt in meditation that they were not seen to stir during the festival's three days and two nights; there were displays of fantastic strength and agility by elderly recluses whose feats drew roars of delighted astonishment; and, of course, the two exorcists had been requested to put on a display. This last took the form of a pantomime in which, by means of incantations, a shrieking woman was delivered of a tall black demon with lolling tongue and eyes that shone with living flame, who, leaping menacingly towards the crowd, had to be driven back with ghost-swords fashioned out of ancient copper coins. Though well aware that this was a purely symbolic representation of demon-fighting, the pilgrims were impressed, for they did not doubt that the gaunt exorcists were capable of dealing just as effectually with real demons. In fact, one youth went into convulsions and those grim men, after making some show of curing him on the spot with menacing cries and gestures, carried him off to their quarters, from which he emerged a few hours later apparently in the best of health. Whether that, too, was part of the symbolic performance will appear later.

The fire-walking was scheduled to take place in the great courtyard fronting the shrine-hall on the second morning of the fair, and so the score or so of recluses and laymen destined to participate spent the night performing a special ritual to the music of flutes and drums. The pilgrims (husband, wife and little daughter) whom I had invited to unroll their sleeping-mats on the floor of my cell slept peacefully through this preparatory rite, whereas I lay awake for hours enraptured by that infinitely sweet, though disturbingly eerie music. Neither before nor since have I heard its like; the piercingly high notes conjured forth my soul or, to use a more modern expression, sent me on a fabulously joyful trip. Starting up from the deep sleep which had overwhelmed me a little before dawn, I found that the Abbot had sent over a plate of hot sesame-seed-topped buns with a savoury meat stuffing – no doubt a pious offering he had received from one of the pilgrims. Licking the last grains of sesame from my lips, I ran to where, being tall, I could see over the heads of the spectators crowded ten deep around three sides of the courtyard fronting the shrine-hall, the doors of which were closed.

As a prelude to an account of matters hard to credit, permit me to quote a passage from the article on fire-walking in the 1965 edition of the *Encyclopaedia Britannica*: 'While injuries do occur, they seem on the whole to be much less frequent than would be expected ... especially as the devotees do not apply any artificial preparation before the ordeal to protect their bodies.' Moreover, in countries such as Malaysia with large Chinese communities, fire-walking can occasionally be witnessed to this day during the annual or triennial displays put on by some of the Chinese temples. As to its purpose, whereas the priests or recluses concerned may justifiably be suspected of giving some thought to the temple revenues, the lay participants, being for the most part devotees of the deity invoked, are prompted to undergo the ordeal by eagerness for self-purification in a manner that will spectacularly demonstrate the sacred being's power.

As I have said, the rite that took place at the Abode of Mysterious Origination was witnessed from the courtyard fronting the terrace, where stood the shrine-hall flaunting in the early morning sunlight the splendour of its gilt and scarlet pillars, elaborately painted roof-beams, upward-curving eaves and green porcelain roof-tiles. For the first time, I saw it not as a gaudy building out of place in those surroundings, but as one possessing a certain magnificence. A flight of marble steps led down to where a wide space had been cleared by good-naturedly driving back the pilgrim throng. Presently a flock of serving-lads appeared carrying iron buckets with long bamboo handles. Bandying excited chatter with the crowd, they ladled red-hot coals on to the ground, thus forming a glowing bed that extended from the bottom step across six or seven yards of flagstones. No sooner had the last coal fallen into place and the boys run off to join the spectators than a thunderous roll issued from a gigantic drum within the shrine-hall; the lacquered doors flew open and a score of barefoot devotees, clad in white garments, appeared on the terrace chanting a refrain to an accompaniment of cymbals and drums. With but a moment's pause, they leapt down the steps straight on to the wide bed of coals; these they traversed at a jog-trot, their feet descending on the glowing mass a dozen times or more. Their pace was neither slow nor yet unduly hurried, as it surely would have been had their flesh been normally sensitive to heat; nor did they look down or pick their way from one to another of those coals whose blackness indicated some slight abatement of temperature. On reaching the bare flagstones beyond, they came to a ragged halt and sat down, lest the pilgrims topple them in their eagerness to examine their unblemished feet. Two or three of them displayed small patches of lightly scorched skin; the rest, supported by the sacred rites and the intensity of their faith, had come through the ordeal unscathed. Any wavering of their minds would have resulted in terrible burns and perhaps disaster; distraught by the fiery agony, they might have fallen on to the live coals. While most of the spectators were marvelling at the devotees' miraculously unscathed flesh, two cynics bent down with knowing smiles to test the heat of the coals. Their sharp ejaculations drew a good deal of laughter, for they had paid for their cynicism by painfully scorched fingers!

Immensely impressed, I revised my opinion of a French acquaintance's account of a spectacle he had witnessed in Shanghai. As he put it, a Taoist devotee had been publicly bathed in fire! Naked but for a cloth about his loins, the man had calmly revolved on his heels, making a complete circle while, to a dramatic accompaniment of drums, cymbals, bells and flutes, a fellow recluse stood slowly emptying a bucket of glowing coals over his head and shoulders! A great sigh had come from the crowd when they saw him step backward unharmed, except for a charred loin cloth; their excitement had, according to my friend, been in striking contrast to the devotee's relaxed stance and graceful poise. No wonder many of them had fallen to their knees, hands clasped in homage! After witnessing the fire-walking, I no longer felt inclined to doubt the Frenchman's story. After all, if fire-walking were possible – and I had seen that it was – then why not fire-bathing?

In comparison with so spectacular a demonstration of mind's power over flesh, what occurred on the third and last day of the monastery fair may be thought relatively tame; yet, it struck me, upon reflection, as even more bizarre. In the midst of a grand procession led by the Abbot, now clad in a splendid brocade robe of bronze and scarlet, came a band of tall-hatted musicians followed by six devotees stripped to the waist so that all could witness their demonstration of inhibiting normal physical processes and reactions. From their forearms hung iron weights suspended from butchers' hooks, of which the spiked ends were firmly embedded in their flesh! Since then I have discovered (in Thailand) a way of simulating an analogous feat by means of a half-band of metal, concealed on the inner side of the arm, to the top and bottom of which are separately welded the hilt and blade of a very broad dagger which appears to have been driven right through the arm. It may be thought that the Taoist devotees at the Abode of Mysterious Origination employed a rather similar device; personally, I am convinced they did not, if only because, at a later stage, when the weighted hooks were lifted from their arms and handed round for examination, the gaping holes torn in their flesh were clearly visible. There was, however, but little bleeding, though the hooks themselves were wet with blood. The wounds, we were assured, would heal in a few days, leaving no scar. Other writers, in describing those strange rites during which Moslem dervishes transfix their flesh with skewers, have similarly testified that blood-flow, if any, is minimal; that the wounds close rapidly, and that no scars remain visible. In the case of dervishes (such as those described in *The Way of the White Clouds*, by the

Lama Govinda, a writer whose veracity is certainly impeccable), it has been established that they stab themselves after dancing their way into a state of ecstasy. Perhaps the Taoist marvel I saw was accomplished during a state of trance induced by meditation; but, knowing little of such matters at the time, I did not particularly look for evidence of trance; I recall merely that the devotees were silent and wore grave expressions throughout their ordeal, and that they stalked off in silence to their quarters when the hooks had been removed.

How are such feats to be explained? There simply is no explanation unless one accepts that mind-control can be so powerful as to affect the behaviour and properties of the body's physical components. A unique feature of this yoga is the ability to inhibit the flow of blood to the wounded limb. Numerous Indian, Tibetan, and Chinese yogic texts propound methods of controlling thought, breath, semen, body-temperature and so forth, but I know of none that deals with mastering the blood-flow. This is a matter that should be studied while opportunities for direct observation still exist, whether at Chinese temples in south-east Asia or at dervish centres in the Islamic world. The pace of 'progress' is now so fast that all too many ancient arts and sciences are on the point of vanishing.

I myself once underwent an ordeal which bears a slight analogy to those described. As part of a Chinese Buddhist rite, I was one of a handful of people who each had twelve short sticks of lighted incense affixed to the left forearm from which they stood up like spikes. As the incense burnt down into our flesh, we concentrated with rapt attention on a sacred formula honouring the Buddha – 'Namo pên-shih Shih-chia-mo-ni Fu!' The pain was presumably no less intense than in the case of any slow flesh-burning of similar magnitude, but my mind was sufficiently detached for me to reflect: 'Yes, great pain is there; but, in a certain sense, it does not hurt.' This anecdote has, of course, only limited application to fire-walking (which left neither burns nor scars on most of the participants) or to the feat with weighted hooks (which caused wounds that did not bleed and were destined to leave no scars), for the twelve small scars from that burning can be seen on my arm even after the passage of thirty-five years! Transcending pain by mind-control is one thing; causing flesh and blood to be somewhat impervious to fire or steel is much less elementary.

Soon after the pilgrims had departed, I called upon one of the Assistant Abbots, a fairly young and erudite recluse surnamed Wu, who had often sought my company and seemed to enjoy our long discussions. On this occasion, after the inevitable exchanges of bows and compliments, we drank tea together in his cell, meanwhile gradually relaxing to the point where we could put aside formality and talk as friends. Asked for an explanation of the feats performed during the fair, he said:

'You see, dear friend from the Western Ocean, mind is all! Eliminate thought and the mind is no longer to be differentiated from the formless Tao, in which all things and processes originate, however ordinary or extraordinary. By meditating at a level transcending the duality of subject and object, and by cultivating an inflow of vital energy, a devotee can acquire many unusual powers.'

He went on to describe what he called the three inferior categories of power. The lowest of all embraced feats attainable by what Westerners would call normal means, though arbitrary distinctions between normal and supernormal are apt to blur in a yogic milieu which tends to encourage recognition of the fact that many apparently supernormal powers – telepathy, for example – are rare only in a society that has allowed some of the human body's latent powers to atrophy. What the Assistant Abbot had to say about purely physical accomplishments was destined to afford me an insight into the Taoist origin of several arts cultivated by the Japanese, such as the smashing of bricks and boards with the naked hand; the ability to withstand extremes of temperature which, for example, enables adepts to stand meditating beneath waterfalls in the depth of winter; and, of course, those methods of combat such as *judo* and *kendo* which accord with the principle of utilizing an opponent's strength in such a way that the weak effortlessly overcome the strong—a basic Taoist principle.

'Dearest Englishman,' continued my friend (who was fond of using such affectionate expressions, no doubt because he felt that the antiquated and over-elaborate compliments customarily paid by Taoist recluses to their guests had become too stylized to convey genuine warmth of feeling, especially to a foreigner), 'you must know that the lowest of the six categories of power can be attained by all those willing to undergo the severe training involved, without their having to immerse themselves in the mystical contemplation and mental exercises required for the higher yogas. However, you would be right to complain that some of these feats are a waste of time and energy, being only one step removed from vulgar demonstrations of ability to consume more jars of wine, eggs, chickens or roast sucking pigs at a sitting than one's neighbours.

'Next come the second lowest powers, such as those displayed during our recent festival. They, too, are of no real importance. I place them above the lowest category only because the rôle played by mind is somewhat more obvious. One whose mind is disturbed or wholly occupied by trivialities cannot successfully command his flesh to withstand the effects of fire or metal. Also in this category are the attainment of true invulnerability to sudden death or physical injury, the art of healing oneself or others by thought or touch, and such rare but relatively useless powers as levitation. None of them causes astonishment in one who has grasped the truth that mind is the only reality. All physical processes and objects have their being in mind, which can naturally modify their nature, suspend their action or cause them to vanish, just as a novice who has learnt to be aware that he is dreaming can control the content of his dreams at will.

'The highest of the three inferior categories of power is that of successfully establishing contact with gods and demons, but I doubt if you believe in such things; so it would be useless to elaborate.'

His assumption was more or less correct, though my disbelief could no longer be described as adamant, for the mysterious episodes I had witnessed had reminded me of what had occurred on that terrible night spent in the company of Pien Tao-shih and the beautiful youth who was so assiduously cultivating immortality. Perhaps, after all, I had just missed a direct encounter with a demon! Even so, I was a long way from having crystallized my present belief that invisible entities, both benevolent and hostile, do indeed exist. What reader of such perceptive men of science as William James or C. G. Jung can doubt the existence of a whole plurality of forces with much the same attributes as gods and demons? Explanations may vary, but that there are such forces, call them archetypes, archangels or fiends, now seems to me indisputable. Furthermore, I am at one with my Taoist and

Buddhist friends in believing that, at a more nearly ultimate level of experience, it is found that all matter, animate or otherwise, *is* mind. It is because we cling blindly to the seeming facts reported by our senses – despite all the denials of their ultimate validity voiced by scientists and mystics alike – that we fail to perceive, much less accept, this truth. Why, then, should an intelligent man boggle at the thought or sight of material processes being modified by sheer power of mind?

'Your Reverence,' I remarked at length, 'permit me to ask two questions. First, why do so many of your educated countrymen make mock of what they call Taoist superstition and hocus-pocus, in spite of being aware of the explanation you have so lucidly put forward? Second, what are the superior three categories of power?'

He smiled. 'The *Tao-chia* of old accused us recluses of cherishing beliefs and practices but tenuously connected with the teachings of the ancient sages they admired, whereas scholars with a background of modern education charge us with perpetrating frauds in the guise of magic as a means of augmenting the monastic revenues. The former charge does not stand up to scrutiny. The ancient sages planted seeds of knowledge which have grown into trees with a luxuriant array of branches, thereby according with the nature of healthy, potent seed. If Taoism had not developed innumerable branches, it would be said of the sages that the seed they planted was of poor quality. But look to the trunk and follow it down to the roots. Here, in this centre of strange rites and practices, you will find a strong, unbroken connection with the mystical illumination of our patron Chuang-tzû. There has been no separation from our roots, only luxuriance of growth. It is true that hocus-pocus is often perpetrated by unscupulous persons who, pretending to possess certain power, batten on the purses of the ignorant. But, while the so-called magical feats of avaricious cheats and frauds are mere trickery from start to finish, genuine feats are not uncommon. I tell you frankly, dear guest from a mysterious region, the truth generally lies in the middle.'

Shaking with mirth, he sustained my puzzled gaze.

'Put it this way, my friend. You have observed how it was at our great annual festival. What did you see? A vast deal of showmanship, for after all even Taoist communities have to eat; those of us who reach the stage of living upon nourishment drawn from the air are few! You saw, too, a number of staged effects – call them hocus-pocus if you will – which were necessary because our lay-supporters expect to behold marvels, being ignorant of the truth that genuine marvels occur only in response to actual need. For instance, since they brought us no patients possessed by demons, our exorcists had no opportunity to demonstrate their skill and, in any case, the cures must be performed in private, whereas what the pilgrims required was some sort of spectacle. That is why we arranged for a youth to simulate possession during the charade and went through the motions of curing him in public. Yet, because a show was expected of us and we gave it, that does not mean that our remedies for demonic possession and other ills are fraudulent. On the contrary, hundreds of once-sick people in this neighbourhood can testify to the rarely-failing efficacy of those remedies in curing all sorts of maladies, including demon-possession. Dearest guest, did you not also see genuine marvels? Admit then that, of the charges you mentioned, one is untenable and the second true of our monastery only in a sense that is excusable.'

I nodded, more or less convinced, and repeated my question about the superior categories of power.

'The superior powers are the fruits of three graduated stages. First comes the ability to prolong life and vigour to the extent of living to a healthy old age, sometimes well beyond the normal life-span. Of this, I have heard you speak before, so I know you are conversant with the general principles. Next comes the achievement of immortality, whatever that is taken to mean. Members of the sect represented by this monastery interpret it as meaning rebirth of the *hun*-soul in a spiritual body able to exist for aeons; privately, many of us are inclined to doubt that other possibility, fleshly transmutation, although deference to those sages of old who are said to have been transmogrified compels us to discretion in the matter. The highest power is of course, that of keeping the mind perpetually immersed in the Tao so that at death, the finite being merges with its source, thereby gaining the only true immortality.'

'Immortality as an individual?' I asked.

'How can that be? All entities, both physical and subtle, are subject to growth and decay. At most one can prolong one's existence by a few millenia. Can that be called immortality? Measured against time's immensity, aeons are but fleeting moments. Who would wish to cling to his individuality even as a god, if he knew the bliss of losing it in the Tao? The answer to your question is that total loss is the only lasting gain. The masters of all other achievements are doomed to watch them fade and vanish, whereas the total loser wins forever.'

The implications of this philosophy, which as yet I understood but dimly, must be left to a later chapter. In reporting my conversation with the Assistant Abbot Wu, I have willy-nilly strayed from the realm of popular Taoism; or to use my friend's own metaphor, his teaching was beginning to lead me from the branches to the trunk and down towards the roots. Before according with that centrifugal movement, I must describe an important psychic manifestation belonging to what the Assistant Abbot called the uppermost of the three inferior categories of power.

In another book, I have described the performance of one of those spirit-possessed mediums still employed as oracles in most overseas Chinese communities. Since then, I have had a rather similar experience, also at Bangkok; the story is worth telling as a prelude to what I shall have to say about the spirit-oracle at the Abode of Mysterious Origination, for all such manifestations have a fair amount in common. The medium is invariably an unconscious vehicle for communicating the pronouncements of the spirit or deity invoked. Some years ago my friend, Gerald Yorke, came to Bangkok and on behalf of my present publishers invited me to set about a new English translation of the *I Ching* (*Book of Change*), an ancient Chinese classic venerated by Taoists, Buddhists and Confucians alike. Though viewing the task of doing justice to so ancient and profound a work with deep misgiving, I finally went ahead, relying for guidance on the numerous Chinese commentaries and on the careful vetting promised by some Chinese scholars in Hong Kong. Soon after completing the typescript, I was taken to visit a spirit-oracle newly come from Taiwan. It so happened that my friends and I arrived rather later than expected, to find the deeply entranced oracle delivering pronouncements on behalf of the spirit whose vehicle he had now become. A bystander who had been present from the start whispered that, during the preliminary rites, a sainted recluse who had passed away towards the end of the Ming Dynasty (seventeenth century A.D.) in the district of Swatow had been invoked. The spirit-oracle, who had formerly been a fisherman, looked like a person of little or no education long buffeted by the winds of harsh circumstance; such a man could at best be barely literate and even that was doubtful. Being in a state of deep trance, he was clearly oblivious of what was going forward. Eyes glazed, he lolled back motionless in his chair like someone fast asleep; but no sooner had a question been propounded than his right arm would begin to jerk spasmodically; presently the gigantic writing-brush held awkwardly between his rigid fingers would descend on to a stone slab liberally covered with liquid black ink and, very forcefully, splash huge, crudely drawn Chinese characters on to an outsized sheet of clean white paper hurriedly whipped into place by one of the temple assistants. As far as one could judge, the arm was acting independently of its slumbrous owner, who never so much as glanced towards ink or paper, though his brush descended unerringly on each in turn. Prodded by my friends into asking a question, I went forward on my knees and said the first thing that came into my head:

'As to the book that troubles me, have I done ill?'

It will be noticed that my words gave no indication of the type of book, nor of the nature of my trouble. As writers are few and readers many, it would have been reasonable to conclude that I spoke as a reader.

When my Mandarin had been translated into Swatonese, the oracle's right arm instantly came to life. With powerful strokes of the brush it slapped down a reply in four ill-written characters, which were carefully transcribed by a member of his entourage. The transcription read: CHÜN-TZÛ HSI HSIEN which can be rendered 'Superior Man gratified (to be made) manifest.'

To one familiar with the *Book of Change*, this reply must seem startlingly apposite, for the entire work consists of pronouncements as to what the Chün-tzû, Superior Man or Holy Sage, would or would not do under varying combinations of circumstances. The four characters clearly meant: 'Yes, it is good that you have translated the book; the Superior Man is gratified by your making his conduct manifest to the peoples of the West.' It should be added that, although the term 'Superior Man' is common enough in ancient Chinese literature, whole years go by without its occurring in people's conversation unless in connection with the *Book of Change*; also that, among the petty merchants and shopkeepers who composed the audience that day, there can scarcely have been one whose thoughts often ran upon that ancient work, to say nothing of anyone's chancing to suppose that the foreigner on his knees before the oracle might conceivably have translated it! Whatever the explanation, attribution to mere coincidence would be ludicrously far-fetched, yet I am in a position to guarantee that even the friends who introduced me to the séance had no notion of my connection with the *Book of Change* as, being diffident about my talents, I wished to keep the matter dark until my rendering had been accepted by the publisher acting on expert advice.

At the Abode of Mysterious Origination, it was customary to consult the spirit-oracle only at times when important decisions had to be made regarding the community's welfare. As I never chanced to be present on such an occasion, I have based the following account on what I was told by the Assistant Abbot Wu. One day a letter from the district magistrate within whose jurisdiction the monastery lay was brought to the Abbot by special messenger. It contained a courteously worded demand that accommodation be prepared for a whole company of Nationalist soldiers who were to form part of a force soon to be dispatched against a recalcitrant provincial army which had advanced its headquarters eastward to a town only about thirty miles up-river from the monastery and sent the government-appointed officials fleeing for their lives. Naturally the letter caused consternation, for Taoists have ever regarded soldiers as the most tragically misguided of human beings and the recluses were aware that the district authorities held much the same opinion of Taoists! To yield would be disastrous; soldiers were quite capable of stabling their horses in the shrine-hall or the Abbot's private quarters and of driving the recluses with blows to perform military tasks that contravened their principles. On the other hand, not to yield would be to risk the community's dissolution on some such charge as giving passive assistance to the rebels! Clearly this was a moment to seek oracular advice.

The resident spirit-oracle was an unremarkable-looking, rather timid man in his middle thirties whose mediumistic powers had been discovered early and thenceforth assiduously nurtured. I had often seen him about and had put him down as a mild, unobtrusive recluse with no particular standing in the community until Wu revealed his identity. However, from the moment it became known that a consultation was to take place, the oracle emerged into temporary prominence. During the three days of rites that marked the preliminary stage of invoking the irascible deity Kuan Ti to enter the poor fellow's body, even the Abbot bowed to the ground before him as though the dread War God had already taken up his lowly habitation. That fierce divinity – a former general deified by posterity on account of his loyalty, sagacity and brilliant military career – had been selected from among the hosts of heaven as the being most likely to provide a strategy for countering the impiety and generally gross behaviour of soldiers! Day and night, incense and tall red candles burnt before the crimson-cheeked, green-robed, more than life-sized image, whose handsome beard adorned powerful features set in an expression so forbidding that no Roman emperor or Prussian junker can ever have looked half so intimidating. When the time came for the final rite of invocation, the entire community assembled to perform obeisance; no doubt most of them found it hard to conceal their trepidation, for oracles possessed by the War God had been known to run amok and slaughter several bystanders, whether because their demeanour had inadvertently caused the deity to take umbrage, or, as Wu Tao-shih was more inclined to suppose, because the rapport between deity and oracle-recluse had been marred by some unguessable imperfection.

The oracle was ceremoniously led forth in procession and ensconced upon a throne that stood in the great courtyard, with its back to the marble steps leading down from the shrine-hall. To one side, but as far removed from the throne as was consonant with their being within earshot, scribes sat at a table, moistening their brushes and arranging sheets of absorbent rice-paper. Wu Tao-shih remarked that the scholarly recluses chosen for this task were usually so frightened that their calligraphy was apt to be appalling. Flanking the throne at closer range were two wooden racks containing a whole armoury of medieval weapons, these being part of the insignia of imperial generals and also handy in case the War God decided to make an example of the impertinent mortals who had summoned him from the pleasures of his heavenly existence. Wu drew an amusing picture of the mild-eyed oracle who, though clad in the full panoply of a general of old and sitting in an arrogant attitude with booted feet planted wide apart, could hardly bring himself to hold the mighty saw-toothed spear which an attendant had just thrust into his trembling grasp. Next, the unhappy man's glance fell shudderingly upon the array of swords, spears and axes flanking his throne; the very sight of such pain-dealing implements must have filled him with shame and misgiving.

Wu himself officiated. Clad in a sombre robe embroidered with protective symbols, expression no doubt guardedly solemn, he stood to one side of the oracle, head politely inclined, hands folded and modestly concealed by his sleeves, stance motionless as an idol's except when he gave the signal for the awesome rite to begin.

In response to his high-pitched command, the assembly bowed to the ground, whereat a great tempest of sound swept from the shrine-hall where the temple musicians could be seen through the open doorways frenziedly clashing giant cymbals, thwacking gongs and drums, or blowing at their clarinets as though their cheeks would burst. Wu told me that on such occasions the noise rivalled the din of embattled gods and titans; yet the serried rows of recluses stood like deaf-mutes, not so much as glancing towards the source of that boisterous assault upon their ears. All were staring fixedly at the oracle, whose features now bore too grim and martial an expression to be recognizable as those of their gentle colleague. Even his stature had filled out, giving him the air of a muscular, battle-hardened veteran of a hundred wars. His face and body had begun to twitch, his limbs to jerk; these spasmodic movements, slight at first, rapidly gained momentum, and, leaping to his feet, the terrible figure pranced about, menacingly twirling his saw-toothed spear. Suddenly he clanged its iron butt against his breastplate, whereat the thunderous music ceased abruptly and the musicians faced about, craning their necks as though listening intently.

The medium, lost in tranced oblivion, had assumed a look of such malevolent ferocity that the recluses quailed before his dreadful gestures and grimaces, even though his eyes appeared to be focused upon some inner vision; at times only the whites were visible, the pupils having vanished beneath the lids. Presently, with a clash of accoutrements, the dreadful figure resumed its throne, where he crouched with the seeming indolence of a tiger ready to spring. Warily the officiant advanced towards him, timing his steps to the slow, sad melody that now issued from the terrace, where stood a youth bowed gracefully over a slender bamboo flute.

As the melody died away, the officiant, employing the theatrical diction proper to ceremonial usage, uttered a question couched in the language which courtiers and the more scholarly military officials were presumed to have spoken on formal occasions a thousand years ago. The oracle, though motionless and attentive, sat with lips drawn back in a smile of such cruel scorn that Wu almost committed the discourtesy of stammering; indeed, having posed his question, he leapt unceremoniously backwards, for the menacing figure had sprung to its feet as though infuriated beyond measure at the temerity of a mere mortal's venturing to approach him. However, instead of plunging his weapon into the offender's breast, he clashed its great blade against his own armour with a prodigious force that snapped the steel as though it had been a shoddy toy. Then, throwing down the haft and seizing a heavy broad-sword in its place, he poured forth a flood of speech in a voice so harsh and grating as to be scarcely recognizable as human. The brushes of the cowering scribes flew over the sheets of paper; to ensure that not a syllable was lost, the one embarked upon a new phrase while his fellow was still completing the phrase just uttered. In two minds as to whether to stick to their task or flee, they nevertheless managed to do as required, though in calligraphy so shaky that, afterwards, not even they could decipher every word.

The oracle's torrent of speech broke off, and again the officiant advanced in time to that slow, soft melody. His second question unleashed a further flood of barely intelligible eloquence; but already it was apparent that the divine Kuan Ti's vehicle was close to fainting; the voice had weakened and the gestures had lost much of their ferocity. The answer to the third question tailed off in mid-speech; the oracle slumped backwards against the cushioned throne, head lolling to one side, tears and saliva dribbling from eyes and lips. The strenuous efforts to revive him before the deity left his body having proved unavailing, some attendants ran forward with a couch on which they laid him like a corpse; but, presently emerging from his trance, the poor wretch sucked eagerly at the spout of a teapot someone pressed between his teeth. The strong, hot tea revived him so that he was able to sit up and languidly reach for a second teapot, which he drained at a gulp. Apart from some facial twitching and an air of near-exhaustion, he had resumed his normal appearance and seemed not too much the worse for his harrowing experience. That mild, kindly, rather shrinking soul had after all survived the ordeal of sharing its body with the spirit of the tempestuous War God!

When Wu reached the end of his story, I exclaimed breathlessly: 'How I should love to see the record of your enquiries and the answers delivered by the divinely inspired oracle!'

A glare of mock severity escaped the Assistant Abbot before he composed his features into the slow, warm smile I liked so well.

'Dearest barbarian, one would have thought that even you would be sufficiently acquainted with the decorum that governs these grave matters not to demand what cannot with propriety be given. My questions, prepared beforehand in conclave with our Venerable Abbot, have, as you surmised, been recorded for posterity together with the divine Kuan Ti's answers, and the interpretations placed upon them by the Monastery Council. If you wish to view the contents of the book which contains the oracular pronouncements of the last five hundred years, you must stay with us long enough to be offered a place on the Council yourself; for would it not be unwise to make public matters so closely affecting our community's welfare? Nevertheless, I can inform you in rather general terms of what transpired, for an announcement was made to the assembled recluses as soon as the interpretation of the oracle had been agreed upon. Rest assured, most dear and highly esteemed layman, that the divine Kuan Ti's answer was both favourable and in accordance with the events that followed. His advice was to accept the district magistrate's demand to station troops within our sacred precincts with every appearance of patriotic fervour, since it was certain that very few troops, if any, would actually be sent here and that they could easily be induced to remain on their best behaviour for the short duration of their stay. A week or so later – it was, by the way, towards the middle of the Tenth Month last year – a detachment of less than twenty foot-soldiers under the command of a battle-scarred lieutenant arrived. Their appearance was far from reassuring. Neither the officer nor his men looked at all the sort of people to make themselves agreeable to civilians or respect our religious calling. Nevertheless, we easily persuaded that hard-faced officer to enjoin upon his subordinates the strictest accord with our monastic regulations, on pain of being severely disciplined.' Again came the slow, warm smile as he added: 'You know how we Taoists admire that weak and yielding element which placidly reaches its goal despite all obstacles?'

'Certainly, but flint is not to be eroded in a day.'

'Just so. Therefore water finds its way round.' He made a scarcely perceptible gesture which perhaps signified that the soldiers' good behaviour and swift departure had been bought at a mutually agreeable price.

'Good!' I exclaimed, 'But what if other soldiers come?'

'They will not,' he answered with assurance. 'At least, not in the near future. The oracle's communication on that point was straightforward.' His smile faded as he remarked more pensively: 'Regarding the more distant future, say three or four years hence, the oracle's pronouncements offered no such comfort. Savage armies will drive the people from their homes along the river and we shall flee with them.'

'Chinese armies?'

'The oracle vouchsafed no indication of their nationality. Nor was that necessary. Already Japan has swallowed up our Manchurian provinces and encroached upon territory at no great distance from Peking. A tiger waits only to digest its meal before setting off to hunt new prey. War will break out within a year or so, but the enemy will not reach this part of the country until long afterwards.'

'Is that your own estimate of Japan's intentions, or did the divine Kuan Ti inform you of them in detail?'

'A little of both,' he answered gravely. 'Oracles must, of course, be interpreted in the light of prevailing circumstances. They are seldom altogether clear. Even gods are handicapped when we compel them to speak through the mouths of mortals. That accounts for their alarming response to our invocations. As you will have gathered, even their most favourable prognostications are delivered in a manner likely to discourage those who might otherwise invoke them more often than need be. A medium, unless his powers are rarely used, seldom lasts ten years. Our oracle, for example, is resigned to an early death. Each séance cuts a decade off his life. We honour him deeply for his selfless dedication.'

Struck by his use of the word 'compel', I asked: 'Do you mean that a god – a great and powerful divinity like Kuan Ti – can be compelled to enter the medium's body and submit to questioning?'

'Most certainly! Why else should deities trouble themselves with our affairs? Do not ask me how the compulsion is exerted. That pertains to the most secret part of the preliminary rites.'

'And are ordinary ghosts and spirits equally refractory?'

'Ghosts!' he answered contemptuously. 'Most of them are delighted to answer a summons. Often enough they come unbidden. But who believes what they say? As with human beings, there are pranksters, liars and fools among them. Summon a ghost who once bore the surname Li and the malevolent or prankish wraith of some departed Wang may arrive in his stead, answering to the name of Li for the sheer pleasure of sowing confusion. As like as not, they were enemies on earth or else have quarrelled in the spirit world, so one can understand how each would enjoy bringing discredit on the other. No oracle in a monastery of good standing depends upon information supplied by common ghosts. Only deities can be looked to for genuine revelations, but they are generally so incensed by our presumption that they make everything as difficult and dangerous as possible. Then again what deity could be expected to relish having to voice his august ideas through a puny mortal? Imagine yourself trying to communicate with me through the mouth of a toad or butterfly!'

This conversation struck me at the time as merely fanciful, for experiences of accurate revelations being delivered by mediums who could not possibly have known my circumstances or even my identity were yet to come. My present belief that, unless the often stupid-looking and illiterate spirit-oracles are in fact amazingly telepathic, they must really be the vehicles of invisible powers is reinforced by what I have read of Tibetan oracle-mediums. Several writers have observed that, during possession, their whole appearance changes – not merely their facial expressions but the very lineaments of their bodies undergo transformations which no actor could counterfeit, sometimes taking on physical proportions quite unlike their own. Such terrifying changes transform them into strangers, so that photographs taken before and during possession resemble those of wholly dissimilar persons. Then again, possession generally confers superhuman strength, enabling the possessed to crumble or snap metal objects which, normally, he could not so much as lift or bend. These fantastic occurrences, recently recorded by dependable witnesses in such places as Kalimpong and Sikkim, continue to this day; the facts are beyond dispute, leaving only their explanation open to argument. Among the possible alternatives to spirit-possession so far put forward, there is none that accounts satisfactorily for all the facts; those who have actually witnessed the workings of spirit-oracles are inclined to recognize them, however reluctantly, as awesome manifestations of occult power.

Probably there *are* fraudulent cases, though it is difficult to imagine how spirit-possession of this sort can be counterfeited convincingly. It is just possible that genuine spirit-oracles or their sponsors now and then resort to subterfuge in order to avoid fiascos when their invocations fail at embarrassing moments. Even so, evidence of fraud in some cases is scarcely ground for the assumption that all cases of possession are fraudulent; at most, proven charlatanism serves to thicken the fog of uncertainty that scientists, disregarding the limitation of their competence, have brought down upon the entire range of paranormal occurrences. It has of course to be accepted that the invocation of gods and spirits is extraneous to the essential requirements of Taoism or any other mystical religion. It seems that induced possession pertains to a whole cluster of beliefs and practices surviving from an era that antedates all recognized religions by two thousand years and more. The same can be said of many components of popular Taoism; far from being comparatively recent accretions upon the teaching of Lao and Chuang, as the scholars would have it, they possess even greater antiquity than the works of those 'founder sages'.

Though Taoism offered the world many precious teachings that were but mediocrely exemplified at the Abode of Mysterious Origination, I cherish affectionate memories of such monasteries. There was a spaciousness about the life there, the recluses being, as far as I could judge, completely free to believe and practise what seemed best to each. They could, if they wished, devote themselves to religious rites and to psychic or magic arts, or to acquiring the various categories of life-prolonging and healing powers; but equally they could become immersed in painting, poetry, music or defensive combat, or else in philosophic speculation, in mystical contemplation leading directly to man's highest goal, or in any combination of those diverse pursuits. Though chastity was admired and encouraged, those who found it hard to bear or thought it undesirable were free to return home to wives and sweethearts at certain seasons. There were no dietary restrictions, nor was wine despised, though I never saw it abused. The chief moral enjoinment upon the community was that its members be courteous, tolerant, peace-loving and relatively abstemious. Such rules as governed their lives were of a kind without which few communities could function smoothly – the Abbot or Monastery Council would direct what administrative or other chores must devolve upon the individuals concerned. The one overriding consideration was the preservation of harmony and decorum.

Naturally the monastery had to remain solvent, yet those concerned with augmenting the income derived from fast-shrinking endowments of landed property seemed not to attach undue importance to that task, as was the case with the demon-exorcists, who greatly preferred sitting in meditation to the practice of their lucrative art. Rent from endowments apart, the chief sources of revenue were offerings brought by pilgrims, the voluntary donations with which guests like myself repaid the recluses' generous hospitality, and payments in cash or kind for specific services, whether spiritual, medical or otherwise. For example, obsequies for the dead could at the request of the bereaved family be made both colourful and elaborate.

But where, cry the scholars, did the sages Lao and Chuang come into all this? Assuming that such communities lived as admirably as you say, why did they usurp the name Taoist? Had they chosen some other name for their so-called religion, we should have no quarrel with them.

Well, in my view, the principles enunciated by Lao and Chuang formed the very warp and woof of the monastic fabric. The recluses were men who lived apart from the world of politics and commerce, seeking neither power nor personal wealth. The wild and lonely setting of the monasteries was ideal for the contemplation of nature's rhythms and transformations. Those recluses who were capable of appreciating the subtle philosophy of the *Tao Tê Ching* made much of it; quotations from its pages and stories from Chuang-tzû were forever in their mouths. Even those of lower intellectual calibre were relatively well informed about the essentials of Taoist philosophy; the very serving-boys were familiar with the meaning of the Taoist symbols carved or painted on buildings, gateways and garden walls. The humblest kitchen-lad must have been more or less clearly aware of the significance of the Tao as the formless womb of forms, the changeless origin of nature's limitless transformations, and the passive source of all energy and activity, for these were matters proclaimed on every hand, whether by symbols, paintings, liturgies, sermons or informal conversations. Who, finding the word Tao on everybody's lips, could have failed to gain some conception of its meaning?

If this favourable account of popular Taoism causes me to forfeit what small measure of esteem my Buddhist works may have brought me in the world of scholars, I shall shed no tears. The fact is that a real or fabled entity called Lao-tzû has long existed in people's minds as the father of magic as well as of philosophy. This Lao-tzû, who will continue to be of some importance for as long as a belief persists in his having been both magician and philosopher, is anyway closer to being a living force than that other Lao-tzû whose very bones have vanished. The teachings *ascribed* to him have shaped men's minds and produced results, some picturesque, some salubrious in other ways, and most of them morally uplifting. What difference would it make if it were finally proved that he never existed or that he had no truck with magic! Faced with such 'proof', I should, like Chuang-tzû at his spouse's funeral, beat my drum and laugh!

Chapter 4

Living in Harmony with Nature's Rhythms: Taoist Arts and Yogas

My experiences in the Abode of Mysterious Origination, though deeply satisfying, left me with a longing to learn more of the enigmatic shadowy Tao, to seek out both contemplatives able to perceive the oneness permeating its multiplicity and yogins willing to explain the means employed for prolonging life or achieving personal immortality. As to that ultimate mystical experience known as Return to the Source, I assumed that, at such exalted heights, all paths must merge, so that whatever was specifically Taoist, as opposed to universal, in character must be sought not on the highest peaks but in the upland valleys they shadowed. In reality, the practices of the recluses were by no means as smoothly graduated as the headings to my chapters; the distinctions between yogas aimed at longevity, personal immortality and mystical union were blurred and it is simply for the sake of convenience that I have treated yogic philosophical and mystical Taoism as though there were three ascending tiers. Since 'yoga' means 'union', my placing philosophy in the middle may seem odd as, in the highest sense, yoga and mysticism belong together; nevertheless their separation can be justified on the grounds that relatively few of the Taoist adepts I met were engaged in a frontal assault upon that shadowy goal which, from the mystic's point of view, transcends all others. Though the yogas, which in this chapter follow closely upon some random remarks about arts similarly imbued with Taoist principles, had undoubtedly been originally devised as a means of achieving indivisible union with the Tao, for the most part they were being used to attain lesser goals, whether longevity, personal immortality or just a quietistic communion with the Source that fell short of total surrender of the individual identity.

This brings us to that important distinction between what I arbitrarily term Taoist quietism and Taoist mysticism. It may be that Lao-tzû (and possibly even Chuang-tzû) resembled many later generations of adepts in being content to live in accord with the nature of the Tao, eminent and transcendental, which they intuited by entering daily into a state of stillness wherein direct consciousness of its all-pervading unity supervened. It is possible that the full mystical practice of burning up the ego once and for all in the pure flame of non-dualistic reality was of later date, the result of Buddhist influence. Be that as it may, it is certain that virtually all Taoist practice – yogic, philosophical, quietist and mystical – was based on experiencing the reconciliation of opposites, on conscious unification of the seemingly disparate and multiple, on direct perception of the identity of being and non-being, action and non-action. To achieve worth-while progress, it was necessary to apprehend unity in diversity, to identify the particular with the universal and thus to penetrate to a mysterious state of spontaneity by direct intuition, direct experience – *never* by a merely intellectual exercise. The difference, then, between the quietist and mystical approach was a difference of degree.

This widespread preoccupation with the unity underlying multiplicity is vividly portrayed in the marvellously subtle arts and skills developed by Taoists and their spiritual progeny, Buddhists of the school of Ch'an or Zen. Taoist painting and poetry can be seen to reflect a direct perception and conscious experience of nature's functioning which has little in common with the analytical approach of geologists, botanists and other exponents of the natural sciences. The Taoists, like Wordsworth, perceived that the universe is a living organism, that its groves and streams are interfused with mysterious spirit, its rocks and mountains endowed with life-force.

I have decided to interweave my memories of hermitages where Taoist arts and yogas were practised, producing a composite environment analogous to the Abode of Mysterious Origination, so as

TAOIST ARTS AND YOGAS

to embody in one community what I encountered in many places and individuals scattered over the length and breadth of China. As this will involve ignoring differences between the Northern and Southern Schools of Taoism – which, in my time, had much more in common than is often supposed – perhaps a few words on the subject are needed here. Tracing its lineage back to Wang Chung-yang or Wang Chê of the twelfth century A.D., the Northern or Ch'üan-Chên School, with headquarters at Peking's White Cloud Monastery, is reported to have been naturalistic, to have emphasized the use of medicine and diet rather than occult practices for cultivating the vital force, to have eschewed sexual yogas and followed a strict monastic régime involving life-long chastity and vegetarianism. The Southern or Chêng-I School, which some regard as radiating from the Heavenly Teacher Chang's monastery on Dragon-Tiger Mountain in Kiangsi Province, though Liu Hai-shan was probably the real founder, is said to have placed greater reliance on quasi-magical practices and sexual yogas for the attainment of immortality, and to have freely permitted recluses to eat meat, drink wine and depart to their homes at certain seasons to cohabit with their wives; indeed, some of its followers, though clad in Taoist garb, actually lived at home like ordinary householders. In practice, however, these differences were not sharply defined. It is clear, for example, that the founder of the Northern School and not a few of his successors did in fact regard sexual yogas as a legitimate and potent means of cultivating vitality; conversely, many recluses of the Southern School were life-long celibates. The charge of superstition, of dabbling in occult practices has been levelled at both schools (but of course the whole question of what are or are not occult powers, as opposed to highly developed normal attainments, requires examination). In my view, differences of spiritual lineage played a less divisive rôle than individual or community preference. So my composite hermitage may be deemed to pertain to either school. Physically it resembles one I visited in a mountainous region of west China.

Let it be called K'u-shên Tao-ch'ang, the Valley Spirit Hermitage, for the Valley Spirit, known also as the Mysterious Female, is no other than the Tao, formless and yet not wholly invisible to those with eyes to see; but such is its subtlety that the wanderer seeks it among the brilliant sunlit peaks in vain; whereas, peering through the mists and shadows swirling in a dark ravine, he may now and then receive a thrilling intimation of its presence.

The Valley Spirit Hermitage was not an easy place to reach, but I had been told by a retired official and a keen practitioner of yoga who had first come upon it and thereafter discovered its excellence, because it lay within a rural district of which he had formerly been magistrate, that it was well worth a visit.

'Even by our Taoist standards it is remote,' he said with the sadness of an old man too frail to travel far. 'Though Taoists have generally shunned the courts of governors and princes and taken pains to avoid the bustle of great cities where artificiality stunts natural endowments, their preference has been for places not too inaccessible to congenial visitors, nor too far from some small townships able to supply their frugal wants. Nevertheless, in the reign of our great K'anghsi Emperor (some three centuries ago), a certain scholar-turned-recluse of the clan of Chao, disappointed by some set-back in his career, led a party of recluses – some still in the first flush of youth – into a rugged wilderness to build a retreat from the world that would be approachable neither by bridle-path nor by navigable stream. The story goes that, on their fifth day in the mountains, an Immortal appeared and led them to a peak so far from human habitation that it had no name. The recluses dubbed it Phoenix Peak, seeing in a cluster of rocks near the summit a miraculous resemblance to a brood of phoenixes, necks proudly arched, wings majestically outspread. Quarrying stone, fashioning bricks, hewing and shaping timber with their own hands, the Master and his disciples built an enduring refuge in which to pass their lives in contemplation of nature's rhythms. Striding among cloud-topped peaks and mist-shrouded valleys, or sitting as motionless as the crags overhanging their chosen vista of waterfall, rocky pools and wind-swept trees, they found this wild beauty more entrancing than the orderliness of orchards, fields and parklands. The verses cut into the rock by these hermits and their successors describe the dancing phoenix rocks as marvellously evocative of visions concerning the creation of diversity from undifferentiated unity. As you will see, the upper parts of the bodies of those creatures emerge from a solid base of rock, as though the act of primeval creation were taking place before one's eyes. How I wish I could go with you.'

Whether Mount Phoenix Peak had been thickly wooded in the K'anghsi Emperor's days, I do not know. Long before I saw it, it had been denuded of the last vestiges of primeval forest and, from a distance, revealed no special features to distinguish it from its smoothly contoured neighbours softly tinged with pink and coral where tall grasses stood massed against a background of green and grey. On closer acquaintance, however, the mountain presented a less uniform appearance, being unexpectedly rugged and well-endowed with impressive rocks and clumps of pine-trees. The steep path crawling up its western face followed the convolutions of a torrent winding through a series of dark chasms. Not far from where the hermitage clung to the steep rock-face, these miniature cataracts were fed by a high fall; a long slim column of opal-coloured water thundered into a churning pool obscured by rainbow-tinted spray. Here, where the path took a sharp turn towards a stone stairway leading to the main gate, it could be seen that the recluses' love of unspoiled beauty had not deterred them from lending nature a helping hand. The immediate environs of the Valley Spirit Hermitage gave the impression of a series of rocks and caverns, overhung by ferns and luxuriant plants, which just happened to emerge from the undergrowth in this vicinity, adding enormously to its picturesqueness. What aroused my suspicion was that no other section of the mountain, apart from the chasms and waterfall, looked so exactly like the original of a Taoist painting. There was, of course, no obvious symmetry, but yet a sense of underlying harmony that was just a shade too pronounced to be altogether natural. Whoever had been responsible for making the 'guided wildness' of the approach to the hermitage even lovelier than nature's untouched handiwork had surely been a master of subtlety, for there was not an object within sight of the stairway of which one could confidently affirm it had been tampered with. (A milieu at once Taoist and yet free from paradox is in any case unimaginable.)

Taoists, the ancient progenitors of several horticultural arts now widely associated with Zen, such as flower-arrangement, certain kinds of landscape gardening and the growing of dwarf trees, were wont to employ loving artistry in subtly modifying nature – the trimming of shrubs to resemble deer and birds is an extreme and untypical example. In landscaping, the underlying principle was to avoid artificiality, not by refraining from improving on natural forms, but by bringing out or highlighting shapes – beautiful, amusing or grotesque – already inherent in the objects worked upon. A square should not be rounded, but a rough sphere could be made rounder; a shrub should be made to resemble a stork only if the stork already existed potentially in the plant's natural shape; water might be diverted from one pile of rocks to another to heighten the beauty of a cataract, but only if there were nothing inherently unnatural in the resulting flow and fall. Nature could be assisted to achieve masterly effects, but the concept in the improver's mind must in itself be based on intimate knowledge of nature's manifestations. In short, the aim in most cases was to assist nature to do what it might under more favourable circumstances have done for itself. Rockeries assembled from rocks chosen mainly for sheer grotesquerie were, like shrubs trimmed to resemble animals or birds, characteristic enough to be considered genuinely Taoist, but still exceptions to the general rule.

Reflecting on these matters, I mounted the mossy stairway, in no hurry to arrive. Low grey walls undulated to left and right of a rustic gateway whose massive lichen-yellowed roof overhung two squat pillars. The buildings lying beyond had once been uniformly grey, but their walls and fantastically curved roofs were so heavily encrusted with mosses and creepers as to produce an effect marvellously in harmony with the surroundings, whereas brightly lacquered posts and beams inset with miniatures of birds and flowers, like those which characterized large Taoist and Buddhist monasteries, would have been quite out of place. The one patch of vivid colour was provided by the gates themselves, for these had recently received a fresh coat of crimson lacquer, as if to heighten by contrast the charming simplicity of grey bricks and tiles half-hidden beneath their living curtains of copper, bronze and green.

The first of the community to notice my approach showed no sign of surprise on beholding a large, oddly dressed stranger with blue eyes and other exotic features. An old man in a tattered, earth-stained robe, he was engaged in digging a miniature canal; its purpose, so he told me later, was to bring water conveniently near the denizens of an out-sized ant-hill whom the recluses esteemed as neighbours. Giving me a friendly nod, he leant on his spade and uttered a peculiarly sweet bird-like cry (in emulation of the local phoenixes?) which presently brought two of his colleagues hurrying out to meet me. These were more elegantly dressed; the openings at the crown of their black gauze hats revealed hair-pegs of some jade-like substance; one wore a full robe of plum-coloured cloth that made a glowing background for his snowy beard; his companion, a younger man, wore a gown of sky-blue cotton that afforded glimpses of under-jacket and floppy trousers of plain white linen. Clasping their hands and pumping them up and down in welcome, they strode forward, murmuring the usual antique formulas, eyes dancing with amused perplexity at the thought of having to entertain a Western Ocean demon likely to know nothing of their language or customs; so I hastened to reassure them, bowing low with clasped hands raised to my forehead and uttering stilted courtesies scarcely less elaborate than their own.

The realization that their visitor, albeit a demon, was comparatively civilized brought smiles of pleasure. Within minutes of our exchange of courtesies, they were treating me with the informality due to a young colleague returning after a long absence. Such a warmly affectionate manner was irresistible; there and then I dismissed the fear, instilled by the ex-magistrate, of failing to persuade them to answer questions on yogic matters seldom discussed with strangers. Leading me across the hermitage's only considerable courtyard, they paused to enjoy my admiration of the central rockery – a world within a world. Its fairy mountains, streams and pools had been fashioned with mysterious intuition and an unerring sense of nature's lines and rhythms. The fragrance of incense hanging upon the air made me glance across to where I expected to see a shrine-hall of some pretensions, but there was none. In the place of honour opposite the gateway stood a natural cave, its mouth embellished with a simple timber and tile façade that did no more than suggest a temple-building. Over the portal, in place of a gilded tablet, hung a simple unvarnished board inscribed in green calligraphy with the words 'Grotto of the Eight Immortals'. The row of buildings standing at a right angle to its western extremity was pierced by a low archway, shaped like an open fan, that led into an exceedingly small courtyard surrounded by two or three bedrooms for guests and a private refectory for their use.

'You will not be alone,' said the younger of my guides. 'Being responsible for entertaining visitors, I sleep in the room opposite yours. It will be my pleasure to attend to your comfort. First I shall fetch you clean bedding and other necessities.'

The 'other necessities' proved to be a comb, towel, tooth-brush and tongue-scraper, a teapot cosily embedded in a quilted basket, two small handleless cups, a vase containing a few pine-sprigs, an incense-burner and a crimson packet of incense-sticks. The inclusion of incense was a charming way of indicating that they accepted me as a fellow Taoist. The burner was placed before a wall-scroll depicting the hermitage's patron deities, the Eight Immortals, of whom most were portly, bearded figures, but there was a sweet-faced lad among them, Lan Ts'ai-ho, the flautist, and the charming Ho Hsien-ku, a lady Immortal reputed to live on an iridescent powder compounded of oyster-shell and moonbeams.

'Where,' I asked, pointing at random to another figure, 'is the Immortal Chang Kuo's donkey?' Though I knew the answer, I was vain enough to enjoy making a small display of my knowledge of Taoist mythology.

'Ah, it is a very special donkey. Except when travelling, the Immortal folds it up like paper and keeps it in his sleeve.'

This was said with a smile that conveyed a certain scepticism as to the reality of the folding donkey, but it would have been unwise to take for granted that this little community of accomplished yogins viewed the Eight Immortals as merely fanciful figures. Since those beings had been selected as divine patrons of the hermitage, they probably bore an esoteric significance very different from that ascribed to them by popular legend. Whether this was so proved impossible to discover; the recluses, for all their willingness to discuss most other subjects, smoothly turned away questions as to their religious beliefs. No doubt ruefully aware of the government-instigated scorn for popular Taoism, they shrank from admitting that the learning for which the Valley Spirit Hermitage was justly famed did not necessarily conflict with beliefs of a kind castigated in the school text-books as 'retrograde superstition, the prime source of our country's backwardness'.

Throughout my stay, some half-a-dozen among the seventeen resident recluses took it in turns to entertain me. If this task were a special assignment, they performed it with such subtlety that one or another always seemed to be just on the point of doing whatever I wished to do; I was often thanked for bearing someone company when in fact his sole purpose in going wherever we went was to give *me* pleasure. They would escort me on leisurely walks to places of interest, such as shrines to nature deities; certain peaks from which the view was particularly fine at dawn, sunset or by moon light as the case might be; rocks cherished for their curiously suggestive shapes or because some long-dead hermit had inscribed on their surface couplets or poems chiselled in exquisite calligraphy; glades propitious for listening to wind-in-pine music; or gorges that contained some lovely cool, cataract or grotto. Eyes and ears closely attuned to nature, the recluses and their predecessors had discovered a hundred rare beauties and enchantments. Our expeditions, besides affording me opportunities for conversing with tolerant, humourous companions steeped in nature's secrets, were strenuous enough to provoke a splendid appetite for the evening meal; the food, simple but flavoured with a wide range of local mushrooms, tree-fungus, herbs and wild plants, was accompanied by a few cupfuls of mulled wine that wooed the long, snug sleep which autumn nights inspire. Gradually I established myself as a person sincerely interested in learning what yogas they practised in the solitude of their cells, but they were in no hurry to instruct me, preferring to keep the discussion to such peripheral matters as gardening, painting, archery and other exoteric means of achieving tranquillity of mind and body.

The Abbot, a younger and less striking-looking man than the white-bearded recluse in plum-coloured robe whom I had thought might be that dignitary, was fond of calligraphy, painting and poetry; slyly he allowed me to suppose his only other interests were the callisthenics and stately sword-play with which his day began. Once, when showing me some of his paintings, he mentioned two principles advocated by his teacher – first, human figures, though a natural choice for painters who themselves are human, should be introduced sparingly and be made to appear as much a part of the landscape as rocks or trees, since all alike are interfused by the Tao's mysterious nature, none having more or less significance than the others; second, void is the painter's greatest asset, in that whatever is sharply defined is thereby limited, whereas what is merely hinted at or left void in a picture is infinitely suggestive.

'You have doubtless heard that aphorism of the Venerable Laotzû which runs: "Clay moulded into vessels serves by virtue of its hollowness"; and, again: "The doors and windows built into a house fulfil their function by being void." To form is to limit. The Tao, being limitless, is void. Therefore the painter, seeking to emulate its illimitable quality, delineates form sparsely, leaving spaces which the viewer's mind will people with a myriad contents. A tuft of grass, its frosted blades bending in the wind, and perhaps a line to delineate the horizon, will suggest the sweeping onset of autumn; a bedraggled heron amidst a waste of snow, needing at most six strokes of the painter's brush, evokes the whole poignancy of winter; a single spray of winter-plum blossom in early bud foretells the passing of the frost-bound present. This principle of voidness and passivity must be carried over into all affairs. As Lao-tzû says: "He who excels in combat is one who does not let himself be roused." That the warriors of old flocked to our peaceful hermitages to foster their martial skills is no paradox; they came to learn how to apply the secret of emptiness, how to ensure that the enemy's sword, though aimed at flesh, encounters void, and how to destroy the foe by striking with dispassion. Hatred arouses wrath; wrath breeds excitement; excitement leads to carelessness which, to a warrior, brings death. A master swordsman can slay ten enemies besetting him simultaneously, by virtue of such dispassion that he is able to judge to perfection how to dodge their thrusts. A swordsman or an archer's aim is surest when his mind, concentrated on the work in hand, is indifferent to failure or success. Stillness in the heart of movement is the secret of all power.

'How can this be? It is because, in a marvellous sense, all objects in nature interpenetrate one another, just as, when gleaming jewels are cast upon a table, each contains within itself perfect images of all the others. The artist is one who goes beyond forms to evoke this mystery in the beholder's mind, thus liberating the subtle from the gross. Our paintings and poems are not intended to express the merely beautiful, but to awaken perception of what lies beyond beauty; hence the economy of strokes or words. Each painting, each poem is simple in itself, its function being to point unerringly to what, forever eluding direct expression, can be subtly conveyed by hints. How many names of Taoist adepts, hermitages and sacred writings contain the character *hsüan* – dark, mysterious! Where mystery is absent, art is no more than prettiness, or else a mere depiction of an object's gross, tangible quality;

whereas, where mystery is sensed, reality is not far off. A mountain or a pine-tree can be delineated in from one to four or five brush strokes, but there is little merit in so doing unless, by that very simplicity, the artist succeeds in conveying a mystery that stabs us because something within our deepest consciousness responds. The works of great artists and poets bring forth flashes of intuition that penetrate to the very core of our being, illuminating what has always been there, but lost to sight. The artist, seeing beyond the forms of things, perceives their secret essence, recognizes it as his own, and portrays it so that we, too, recognize it within ourselves. It is for that reason that the rocks and trees portrayed have a movement, a perceptible life-force, that makes them seem on the brink of turning into living beings.'

The Abbot and his colleagues were inspiring teachers. While waiting to receive instruction in higher matters, I watched to see how they applied to all their undertakings the stillness they intuited at the heart of nature's wildest disorder. Their arts never degenerated into the over-stylized forms so characteristic of Japan. The hermitage's rock-gardens, more informal than their Zen-inspired counterparts, embodied the same principles with much less appearance of rigidity and effort. In ten thousand Japanese gardens, the relationships of certain stones to one another are manifestly uniform; in these Taoist gardens, seemingly less well ordered, the harmony between 'heaven, earth and man' was more subtly portrayed; it was necessary to delve more deeply to discover the mysterious correspondences that underlay their deceptively casual appearance. As for indoor decorations, cut flowers were rarely used, but whole branches complete with leaves or flowers; or else flowering plants rooted amidst arrangements of stones or pebbles in simple pots or shallow basins that were carried out for a daily sun-bath. Autumn is the season for chrysanthemums, and some of the finest I had ever seen were brought into the little guest-courtyard for my pleasure. Their variety astonished me; although the range of colour did not go beyond yellow, gold and bronze, the petals of each species had their special shape and size and hue. To either side of certain doorways, pots of these lovely plants were placed on trestles of varying height, forming a sort of fairy staircase. As one of the recluses said: 'To prefer chrysanthemums to peonies or orchids shows discriminating taste, for their beauty is rather quiet than flaunting; they do not catch your eye at every turn, but the more you gaze at them the more you perceive their mysterious enchantment. Peonies are over-dressed like imperial consorts; orchids resemble lovely courtesans; chrysanthemums are like youthful recluses or nuns whose beauty is subdued and comes from within.'

When it came to building, even Taoists had to go beyond helping nature to produce its own effects. Architecture can never be a child of nature. However, buildings – green, brown or grey – could be made to blend harmoniously with their surroundings and so arranged as to avoid strict symmetry; the stiffness of rectangular walls could be masked by heavy overhanging roofs at different levels, whose curves resembled those of clouds or waves, and surrounding walls could be made to rise and fall with the contours of the hillside. Moreover, windows and doors need not invariably be square or oblong; some were shaped like the full moon or like silhouettes of vases, temple-bells, or folding fans. There were ways, too, of exemplifying the Taoist adage 'in is out and out is in'; very large fans ornamented with painted landscapes could be used to suggest windows of that shape opening on to a distant view; conversely small fan-shaped windows revealing real vistas could be cut into the wall to resemble pictures.

Though the Abbot, in speaking of his paintings, had reminded me that all natural objects, including man, are of equal significance, it was clear that Taoists had their preferences among the myriad forms embodying the Tao. Of flowers they prized iris, winter-plum, peonies, lotus, chrysanthemums and all varieties of flowering shrub; of trees, cedars, pines, bamboo clumps, maples and most fruit-trees; of birds, pigeons, mandarin ducks, herons, storks and cranes, to say nothing of the gorgeous phoenix; of other creatures, prawns, fish, frogs, cicadas, butterflies and most small species, but also foxes, badgers, deer, horses, tigers and the resplendent *ch'i-lin* (Chinese unicorn), and dragons whether denizens of water or of cloud.

One of my happiest memories of the Cloud Valley Hermitage is of our celebration of the Mid-Autumn Festival. Under a full moon of extraordinary brilliance, the whole community assembled on a natural rock-terrace projecting from the peak that rose behind the hermitage. There, after performing a triple prostration towards the icy palace of the Moon Goddess to the thrilling accompaniment of a melody played upon long, slim bamboo flutes, we sat warmly clad in quilted robes, drinking a special wine reserved for celebrations and enjoying all kinds of contests from which I alone was debarred by lack of skill. Intoxicated by wine and moonlight, a gnarled old hermit plucked melodiously at his lute-strings with fingers that seemed to fly; another took his place and then a third, each vying to produce such virtuoso effects as the sound of insects chirping or the sudden soaring of a flock of birds. Poetry-capping contests followed, during which four- or eight-lined verses were improvised at speed, the contestants supplying lines to fit the rhythm, rhyme and meaning of what had gone before. The climax of the evening was a combat between two pairs of recluses armed with swords. Dark robes billowing in the wind, sleeves flapping like phoenix-wings, they ran and leapt, cut and thrust with such agility that their weapons darting in the moonlight produced spurts of liquid fire. The clash of steel on steel and the flurry of sparks proclaimed that the great swords were no toys; it seemed impossible that the contestants would emerge unwounded from an encounter fierce enough for me to expect to see heads and limbs sundered from their bodies. The blows were not feints, but dealt in earnest in the sure knowledge that the opposing adepts had the speed and skill to protect themselves by parrying or swift avoidance. The combat had the aspect of a frenzied ritual in which the contestants were determined to die beneath one another's swords. By the time it ended, I was sweating with anxiety and could scarcely believe my eyes when the four recluses walked towards the Abbot smiling and unscathed.

That night, mellowed by the wine and touched by my glowing appreciation of all that had transpired, the Abbot consented to satisfy my curiosity as to what went on all day in the silence of the recluses' cells, into which I had never ventured. During the last few days of my stay, he generously spent part of most mornings instructing me. What follows accords in very general terms with the tenor and sequence of his teaching. However, as his exposition of the more advanced yogas was beyond my comprehension and the sum of what I managed to grasp has since faded from my memory, I have had to supplement my recollections by studying the works of others, notably those of Lu K'uan Yü (Charles Luk), an experienced yogin whose *Secrets of Chinese Meditation* (which includes a Taoist section) and *Taoist Yoga* have made some precious materials available to English-speaking readers. Nevertheless, I have sought to avoid perpetrating a mere rehash of what I gathered from those and other works, except in the case of one particular practice analogous to *kundalini* yoga, of which my own knowledge is too fragmentary. In the main, where my recollections of the teachings which I received orally differ from those of the authorities consulted, I have deliberately and uncritically clung to the former in the interest of variety.

Originally the objective of all Taoist forms of contemplation and yoga had probably been identical – the union of opposites within oneself in order that the mysterious light of the indwelling Tao might be made manifest. It was held that the indivisibility of the One and the many and the identity of opposites could sometimes be experienced by unaided intuition, but that quietistic contemplation, helped by breath control and other physical yogas, was of great assistance. The breathing yogas, frequently mentioned by Chuang-tzû, were certainly of very ancient origin and, though virtually identical with those of the Buddhists, they had probably been arrived at independently. The works of both religions testify to similar results – sensations of pure light shining from within, or experiences as of thunder and lightning also coming from within, followed by direct perception of the hitherto veiled core of consciousness. For highly talented adepts, contemplation alone was held to be a means sufficient in itself, the various breathing and alchemic yogas being supplementary aids. However, it had come about that these yogas were often applied to the attainment of other purposes – 'supernormal powers', longevity, personal immortality, etc.

My lessons took place in the Abbot's private sanctum, where the only luxury was a redwood case containing a collection of ancient hair-pegs and archer's thumb-rings of delicately-incised jade – green, white or reddish brown. Otherwise the furnishings were austerely sparse. On the first day, the Abbot asked for a summary of the yogic knowledge I had acquired from Buddhist sources, so that he could judge from its extent where to begin. So I said in brief:

'Venerable, I have received some instruction in meditation, but possess only hearsay knowledge of Buddhist yogas, though I believe their general purpose is the same. First, one seeks to generate tranquillity, to control the passions and to vanquish inordinate desire. Next, one strives to purify one's consciousness and thus permit the inflow of intuitive knowledge that comes from within when the flux of conceptual thought is stilled. The ultimate goal is to negate the ego, an elusory entity built upon misleading sense-perceptions, thus liberating oneself from the round of birth and death to which the karmic results of unenlightened thought and action have bound us for incalculable aeons. This ego-negation, which is exceedingly difficult to achieve, permits entry into the unborn, unmade, undying, indestructible state of Nirvana – but not, as far as I can understand, as an individual entity. Presumably the destruction of the ego leaves no such entity to hinder reabsorption into pure, illimitable being. I am eager to learn how the methods and goals of your honourable religion compare with these.'

The Abbot smiled. 'Let us put aside conventional courtesy. "Honourable religion" is a term better suited to Confucians or Christians. Ours is not a religion but a way to the Way; nor is it honourable or otherwise, being free from ornament. Our yogas and meditations begin, like yours, with the generating of tranquillity, that in the stillness of our hearts we may apprehend the Tao within, around, above, below us. Second, we seek to nourish our vitality and prolong our lives in order to gain more time for the refinement of spirit needed for attaining the higher goals. Then comes the compounding of the golden pill which some misguided persons have sought to produce by alchemical processes, whereas in truth it can be compounded only within the body and is therefore known esoterically as the immortal foetus. We Taoists are generally agreed that its creation is the means to immortality, but at this point paths diverge. Some seek aeon-long immortality, the attainment of a god-like state, as an end in itself; others strive to Return to the Source, an apotheosis identical with the attainment of Nirvana, though conceptions of the inconceivable naturally differ.

'As to your inquiry, we must put first things first. I shall begin by describing a simple method of cultivating inner stillness. Concerning our more advanced practices, I shall but touch upon them in outline, as they cannot be properly explained to those who lack preliminary training. Of the highest goal, Return to the Source, I shall say nothing; should you wisely decide to pursue it, you must look to your Buddhist teachers; the destination is the same, so why go to the trouble of mastering a new vehicle?

'Concerning the simple cultivation of stillness, the venerable Chuang-tzû wrote: "You have heard of the knowledge that knows, but never of the knowledge that does not know. Look into the closed room, the empty chamber where brightness is born! (The sage was referring to the Mysterious Pass of the Square Inch soon to be explained to you.) Fortune and blessing gather where there is stillness. But if you do not keep still – that is what is called sitting (in meditation) but racing around (in thought). Let your ears and eyes communicate with what is inside; put thinking and knowledge on the outside (i.e. banish conceptual thought). This is the changing of the myriad objects (back into their original state of nondifferentiation)."

'The venerable Lao-tzû's directions for achieving tranquillity also emphasize the need to stem the flow of thought, to cultivate keen awareness that is free from an object, for this is what is meant by the knowledge or knowing that does not know. Lao-tzû instructs us to "concentrate the vital force, but gently, so that one may emulate a babe, to polish the mysterious mirror (of the mind) and thus rid oneself of stain". By stain is meant clinging to the objects of perception. In another passage the sage bids us "be as the nameless Uncarved Block, that freedom from desire may follow", adding that "desireless and still, the whole universe would achieve spontaneous tranquillity". To acquaint us with the method of achieving stillness, he exclaims: "Block the orifices, close the gates, blunt the sharpness, unravel the knots, dim the brightness, smooth the uneven – this is called (achieving) the mysterious sameness".

'These teachings point, do they not, to more than mere tranquillity? A corpse is tranquil, but lacks awareness; you and I are aware, but our awareness is frittered away on ten thousand sights, sounds and feelings. What has to be acquired is inner stillness, keen unwavering awareness free from objects of perception, free from thought – a bright mirror that takes in all, but clings to nothing. For only when awareness is freed from all objects can it intuit the no-object that lies at the heart of our being. Only then can you act with true dispassion, with the genuine spontaneity that comes from non-involvement, with no devious or complex motives staining whatever light action you take in response to circumstances. For example it is necessary to eat; even animals make provision against hunger, but to buy wheat at harvest time and sell it at a higher price when stocks are low – a despicable ploy of merchants – has no parallel in nature. However, freedom from involvement is the least of the gifts bestowed by inner stillness. Of much greater consequence is the refinement of spirit that ensues and the dazzling rewards that stem from that.

Meditation and Breathing

'As to the means of achieving stillness, which is called compounding spirit so as to return to the void, thought-control is best assisted by yogic breathing which, as you surely know, is no mere matter of inhaling fresh air, healthy as that may be, but of accumulating the precious *ch'i* (cosmic energy, identical with the Sanskrit *prāna*). Profound breathing, which lengthens the human life-span and refines the body's substance, goes together with thought-control whereby deepened consciousness leading to the inner mystery is won. Posture requires attention, as wrong posture may inhibit the flow of *ch'i*. Since very ancient times, when adepts knelt resting their bodies on their heels, the cross-legged posture has been preferred. One sits upon a large cushion with a smaller one beneath the buttocks so that the thighs may press down more lightly; the feet rest upon the thighs, soles facing upwards. Those unaccustomed to this posture may find it so difficult to maintain that stillness eludes them, for which reason my Master used to allow those who embarked upon the Way rather late in life to use a straight-backed chair on which to sit, legs slightly parted, feet firmly planted on the ground. Whether one sits upon a chair or cross-legged on a cushion, the trunk should be held erect, but never stiffly, and the hands, slightly clenched, should lie knuckles up side by side on one's lap, the left thumb embraced by the right palm. Garments should be loose, belt or sash unwound; in winter, the legs and feet must be covered to guard against the cold. The lips should be closed, the teeth should meet without forceful clenching, and the tip of the tongue should rest against the palate. The eyes should be shut or the lids very slightly parted as a precaution against falling asleep, but not so widely as to permit external distraction. Incense burning in a nearby censer, besides attracting benevolent spirits whose presence is auspicious, helps to gauge the passing of time.

'Now let thought be stilled; the breathing, barely perceptible, should accord with special instructions. As thoughts arise, cease to follow where they lead, treating them as flotsam easily dissipated by the wind of rapt attention. If the mind cannot forsake them, let it attend to the play of each slow inhalation and exhalation on the tips of the nostrils. For a beginner, regular, slow and silent breathing is all that is required.

'Now withdraw the mind from the play of breath upon the nostrils and direct it to the Mysterious Pass of the Precious Square Inch – a place behind the mid-point between the eyes. Do not *think* about this Pass, but attend to it as though your mind were a lantern shedding its beam upon an object lying in the snow, neither clinging to it nor feeling interested in its nature. If brilliant rays shine from the Mysterious Pass, though this is an auspicious sign, pay no attention, permit no feeling of elation. The mind must remain objectless. Should the rays flood your being or any other strange phenomena occur, maintain dispassion. Into the mind's stillness will come, drop by drop – sometimes in the form of light – wisdom-bearing consciousness stemming directly from the Tao; with mind and Tao in conscious union, you will return to the primeval state of the Uncarved Block.

'Coming back to the ordinary state of consciousness should be slow. Presently you will open your eyes and stretch your arms to their full extent – but slowly! Before rising, reflect for a while on the experience of having come so close to the Nameless.

'There are people so avid for restored youth, longevity and even immortality that they are eager to proceed at once to advanced breathing-exercises or to the secret alchemy, but what can they achieve without first gaining proficiency in stillness? In our tradition only experienced disciples are permitted to embark on truly yogic breathing-exercises whereby the *ch'i* is forced through the psychic channels, thus purifying the body of defilements and diseases, and used to fan the blaze needed for accomplishing the secret alchemy. First, the pupil must learn to use his lungs properly at all times. (During the Mid-Autumn Festival, you may have noticed that those four swordsmen emerged from energetic combat, not gasping for air, but breathing as softly as men newly risen from sleep. From this you can gauge the importance of learning to breathe as nature intended.) With practice one comes to see that there is no need to hiss and roar; breathing can be almost imperceptible even when the lungs are used to full capacity. Never should it be forced or audible. As the neophyte progresses, he is taught a second mode of breathing, wherein the belly expands with exhalation and contracts with inhalation, thus reversing the process to which he was previously accustomed. No words can describe the full benefit of such exercises; of themselves they make one immune to many ills; combined with meditation, they purify the body, promote accumulation and circulation of the *ch'i* and enable one to enter at will into a profound state of inner stillness, from which one emerges each time to find the irritations of the world ever less disturbing, because something of that stillness lingers, bringing serenity and dispassion.

'But be warned. The practice of thought-control, whether or not accompanied by special breathing, must be regular. Haphazard practice, now long now short, performed at varying intervals, leads nowhere. A beginner ought not to be too ambitious. A third of an hour in the morning when the air is pure and the mind at its clearest, and again in the evening, to bring refreshment after the turmoil of the day, is sufficient for a start, *provided it is regular.*

'Of unrivalled importance is confidence in the yoga's efficacy. Therefore, before commencing your morning and evening practice, reflect upon the all-pervading Tao which nourishes the universe, forever unimpeded, because supposed impediments are as much a part of it as the waves are part of the sea. The only true impediment is failure to recognize that no impediments exist! Yet because you habitually *suppose* the myriad objects to form a barrier between you and the immaculate Tao, you should provisionally visualize the Tao as flowing into you, until you perceive the flow to be unceasing, however intermittent your perception. There must be no self-delusion. Any stupid melon can persuade himself into imagining that he feels the Tao circulating in the body and perceives its light shining through the Mysterious Pass, whereas a successful pupil requires no self-persuasion; returning from the formless to the form-perceiving state, he is aware of having undergone the awe-inspiring yet blissful experience of coming face to face with the Really-Is! Who could attain to *that* perception and yet be unsure whether it had occurred? But just suppose it were possible to mistake one's own tasteless saliva for pure honey, there are other signs. Men who have consciously beheld the Tao in formless state are mirthful; circumstances that appear to others as dangerously formidable, *they* recognize as laughably absurd, which is why true sages are sometimes taken for half-witted fellows grinning at daydreams. Hand in hand with anxiety and fear, ugliness is put to flight. Gems sparkle on dusty roads; puddles appear as pools of lapis lazuli; tough weeds acquire fragile beauty; dung takes on the charm of delicately mottled amber. But I go too far. These perceptions are seldom within the capacity of beginners.'

The Secret Alchemy: 1 Sexual Yoga
A day or two later, the Abbot gave me a general description of dual cultivation, an advanced yoga so abhorrent to the puritannical Confucian authorities as to bring great disrepute upon its Taoist adepts. Such opprobrium was scarcely deserved, for absence of lust and strict semenal continence were essential for the yoga's success. The purpose was to distill within the adept's body a golden liquid from which the elixir leading to longevity, immortality and mystical union with the Tao could be formed. As Yü Yen's famous commentary on the *Ts'an-t'ung-ch'i* puts it: 'At each copulation of heaven and earth draw to yourself the secret sources of *yin* and *yang*', in other words 'When you and your partner come together, combine the two vital fluids and draw them into your body.'

'The practices I have taught you,' began the Abbot, 'can sometimes be in themselves sufficient for achieving communion with the Tao; yet, since nobody can be sure what happens after death, it is well to seek longevity and, if some degree of immortality results, so much the better, as the opportunity to attain Return to the Source will be prolonged.

'Today I shall speak of the yoga of dual cultivation, the cause of our having unjustly incurred defamation. The alchemic manuals, such as the *Ts'an-t'ung-ch'i* which your friend Pien Tao-shih showed you, can often be interpreted as pertaining to three levels: first, the transmutation of cinnabar and lead into the miraculous elixir of immortality; second, the creation within the crucible in one's own body of a golden pill or foetus, as a means of cheating age and death; third, a similar form of internal alchemy depending on an ingredient derived from sexual intercourse. The second and third are governed by the same principles, rooted in the Tao, which also apply to political activities, military strategy and an individual's attainment of tranquillity, since all things large and small function in accordance with the same series of patterns and rhythms. Our mysterious classic, the *I Ching (Book of Change)*, stands squarely on this basis; the future, though not fixed, can be divined by relating a sequence of events to the cycle to which it belongs.

'The practice of creating an immortal foetus or internally compounded elixir by means of sexual intercourse is no cause for pious or prudish horror, for no one can engage in it successfully unless lust has been banished from his mind. Furthermore, this yoga was instituted by the Yellow Emperor, who received instruction from the three lady Immortals – the Simple Maid, the Mysterious Maid and the Chosen Maid – fragments of whose treatises still survive. Very properly all manuals of this kind are written in a language that does not reveal its secrets to the merely curious and profane; even so, their improper employment has led to revolting aberrations such as the administration to pregnant women of poisonous substances that cause them to give birth to lumps of flesh from which a stimulating male tonic can allegedly be fashioned. In my own province of Shantung, century after century the Government has engaged in punitive actions against organized groups of people alleged to have made the yoga of dual cultivation an excuse for lascivious behaviour. This charge may as often as not have been sheer calumny, however. For example the followers of Chang Chi-chung, who enthusiastically practised the sexual yoga night and day, burned themselves to death by the hundred sooner then yield to the government forces – such a sense of outrage indicates a stern purity of motive.

'For dual cultivation, the most essential requirement is conservation of the sexual fluid, which must on no account be expended. If the adept be a male, he must select a female partner in the best of health who lacks, however, the charms most likely to inspire lust or inordinate affection. While performing the yoga, he must keep lustful feelings at bay by contemplating the undifferentiated oneness of the Tao and, if uncertain of his ability to withhold emission, he may constrict the base of his organ with a ring of ivory or jade so tightly fitting as to permit him to continue practising the yoga all night long without risking the loss of his precious substance. That such a device is sometimes necessary disproves the old saying that an experienced adept can add twelve years to his life-span at each plundering of his partner's *yin*-fluid; for, if that were so, night-long activity would scarcely be required.

'Next in importance to strict conservation comes the ability to make the partner repeatedly expend her *yin*-fluid, draw it into one's body and concentrate it in the Chamber of Six Combinations, where the mingled fluid, united with spirit and *ch'i*, becomes a compact mass, which can be made to rise between the kidneys, following two courses parallel to the spine, and come to rest in the *ni-wan* centre near the top of the head. As in all high yogas, manipulation of physical processes must be accompanied by a manipulation of the consciousness. The blended essence is forced upwards by the power of visualization assisted by certain physical movements and by the pressure exerted by correct breathing. Some authorities, pointing to the Yellow Emperor's achievement of immortality by absorbing the vital fluid of no less than twelve hundred women, hold that very frequent intercourse with many partners is the most rapid and efficacious method; but this is not so, since a women's vital force unlike a man's, is inexhaustible. As Lao-tzû says : "The spirit of the valley is undying; it is called the mysterious female, whose portal is known as the fundament of heaven and earth. Though (its essence) if preserved, is delicate, use cannot exhaust it."

'Ideally speaking, this practice should be embarked upon in one's sixteenth year, for it is then – provided one has never suffered an emission – that one's vitality is fully developed yet unimpaired. Loss of semen involves a fatal expenditure of *yang*-force, which can however be repaired by skilful gathering of the *yin*-force in the manner just explained. As to the female partner, there is a saying : "Silver weighing fourteen ounces is desirable; it should never have been subject to smelting." This points to a girl of fourteen who has hitherto been a virgin. Girls of fifteen or sixteen will do very well, but in these days they are not easily procured, unless by marriage, which is inconvenient for dedicated recluses. Therefore is it said : "For dual cultivation, there are four prerequisites – place, method, financial means and partner." If the adept is a woman, all that has been said hitherto applies in reverse, but she will inevitably require many partners, for the male essence is easily exhausted.

'Third, treatises on alchemy expound the fusion of white lead and red cinnabar to produce the golden pill. By exponents of the sexual yoga, white lead is taken to mean the *yang*-fluid, and red cinnabar the *yin*-fluid; the golden pill is, of course, no other than the immortal foetus which results from their blending. Furthermore, the sexual act is compared to the union of water and fire; the over-lavish expenditure of these elements is noted as a prime cause of early death; whereas, skilfully blended, they become a potent life-force. Alchemy of this sort was certainly familiar to King Wên (1150 B.C.) whose wisdom is enshrined in the Book of Change, wherein the sixty-third hexagram known as *Chi-Chi* (completion) and written thus ☵☲ , consists of the trigram K'an ☵ , symbolizing water, placed above the trigram *Li* ☲ , representing fire. This brings to mind a cauldron placed upon a stove and therefore pictures alchemic fusion.

'Though antiquity provides numerous examples of humans attaining physical immortality and a divine status in the upper realms by means of this alchemic process, in recent centuries it has been employed chiefly as a means of promoting vigour and longevity. No one familiar with the facts can question its efficacy, provided the yogic instructions are observed in full – they include such matters as the mental concentration needed to bring about the alchemic fusion; the times and seasons at which the yoga must be practised assiduously or totally avoided; the 3-5-7-9 rhythm and the variety of strokes (strong, weak and almost imperceptible) to be followed by the male partner in stirring the sexual fire, as well as many other matters more or less secret and abstruse. The proof of their effectiveness is the successful adept's extraordinary strength and vitality which remain unimpaired or even wax in intensity over many decades. In my native province, I could introduce you to a handsome youth in his seventies or eighties. Nevertheless, for fear that you, dear friend, should be led to forsake the chaste approach to eternal bliss taught by your Buddhist masters, I assure you that the same effects are noticeable in the bodies of recluses who interpret the manuals in the sense that the alchemic process should be promoted and take place entirely within one's own body, no partner being required. Furthermore, the divine Ko Hung (circa 300 A.D.?) asserts that the Yellow Emperor owed his achievement of immortality not solely to the twelve hundred women whose vital fluid was used for compounding the golden pill. It was not until he had distilled and partaken of the Nine-Ingredient Drug that he ascended to heaven riding on a dragon. Master Ko Hung taught that a wise combination of several methods is best; to rely on the sexual alchemy alone would, in his view, give rise to the probability of failure.

'It is far from my intention to deride that chaste approach on which Buddhists lay such stress or to cause you to suppose that chastity is rare among Taoist adepts; for example, all the recluses in the poor hermitage you now honour with your presence have maintained strict chastity ever since first embarking on the Way. I wish only that you should have the breadth of vision to perceive that the path of the green dragon and white tiger and the path of chastity run parallel. Those who engage in dual cultivation with deep sincerity are no less pure in heart than life-long celibates, for both have abandoned the trivial preoccupations of worldly men to seek an exalted goal. You Buddhists, on losing hope of attaining the highest goal in this very life, seek to prolong your opportunities for progress by aiming at a propitious rebirth; we Taoists seek prolongation of this present life or, in rare cases, the achievement of an aeon of immortality for precisely the same reason. Both are overwhelmed with reverence for That Which Has No Name and, like lost children, have no other thought than to return swiftly to their Mother's arms. Beware of making facile distinctions. As Lao-tzû teaches, the thought of beauty is the root of ugliness; without the one, how could there be the other? A monk may be chaste but yet nourish lustful thoughts. An adept of dual cultivation cannot take one step forward until lust has been rooted from his mind. Therefore a good monk and a dedicated sexual alchemist are equally free from stain. What is more, for those who are troubled and distracted by lust, dual cultivation is purifying in that by this means lust is subdued to the mind's great benefit, and the precious generative fluid conserved to the immeasurable advantage of the body. Why then, throughout successive dynasties and to this very day, have the state authorities treated communities of sexual alchemists as monsters of depravity? It is because governments can be depended upon to do whatever is contrary to reason and to human welfare. No one knows how many conquerors of lust have received savage sentences for alleged debauchery! Had it been otherwise I would direct you to a secret hermitage where you would see for yourself the glowing health, well-nigh imperishable youthfulness, and saintly conduct of successful adepts.

'On Mount T'ai in my native province, we Taoists used to entertain visitors with a legend that well illustrates the greed and blindness in these matters of even the highest authorities. In the reign of the Bright Emperor (Hsüan Tsung, 847 A.D.), a certain influential physician of the Lu Family persuaded the magistrate of P'ing Tung County to release a wandering pedlar arrested on some groundless charge, who was suffering cruelly under the bamboo strokes intended to extort confession. Soon afterwards the pedlar visited his benefactor in secret and, before going on his way, presented him with a formula for distilling the elixir of immortality. Recognizing that fate had ordained for him a brilliant career as a Taoist recluse, Mr Lu forsook the world to dwell upon Mount T'ai, where he gradually achieved fame. Known far and wide as the Pine-kernel Fairy, he gathered a flock of disciples whom he instructed in the healing arts, encouraging them with a promise to transmit the secret formula to whichever of them showed the greatest devotion to their medical calling. Unhappily, some evilly-disposed person lodged a complaint against him with the T'ai-an authorities, alleging that the Pine-kernel Fairy practised medicine chiefly as a means of achieving a lecherous intimacy with female pilgrims to the sacred places on Mount T'ai. The local magistrate, appalled at the thought of proceeding against a recluse whose admirers included persons of the highest eminence, ordered the complainant to receive seventy strokes of the light bamboo as a punishment for wilful defamation. Nevertheless, to guard against eventualities, he secretly forwarded a list of allegations and other details of the case to his superiors, an act of worldly prudence which produced an unlooked-for consequence.

'One day a eunuch came posting from the capital, Ch'ang-an, bearing an imperial rescript. The magistrate was ordered to despatch the Pine-kernel Fairy, with all due honour and at state expense, to Ch'ang-an, where an imperial audience would be granted him. So it was done and the audience took place. The outcome was that the Fairy received a dwelling, a flock of servants and handsome emoluments in return for which he was required to compound the elixir of immortality for the Emperor's own use. In vain he pleaded that the elixir was not something that could be passed from hand to hand.

' "You are either too modest or regrettably selfish," exclaimed the Emperor who, supposing that the magic drug could be stored in a suitable vessel, had already bestowed upon the Taoist a commodious bottle of flawless green jade. "You will bring me the perfected elixir in time for my birthday. Meanwhile, whatever ingredients you require, however costly, will be instantly procured."

'The Pine-kernel Fairy entered his new dwelling in a mood of despair. He could neither obey the imperial command nor excuse himself by disclosing the true method of compounding the elixir, for in the latter case the charge of debauchery would surely be sustained and the Son of Heaven, in his dragon-wrath, could be expected to impose a penalty of the utmost rigour. However, presently a solution occurred to the unfortunate Taoist, who immediately regained his usual spirits. The Emperor's birthday being as yet seven months away, he set to work with right good will, causing grave doubts as to his sanity among the illiterate mutes by whom he had now, as a necessary precaution, replaced his servants. They observed that the Fairy, leaving dust to gather on the books and alchemical equipment so lavishly provided by the imperial bounty, spent all his days and nights in the company of the dozen or so young ladies he had discreetly acquired for his household within days of entering the imperial service.

'The Emperor's birthday arrived. The Pine-kernel Fairy, ordered to appear before the August Presence and hand over the vial of elixir on pain of grave penalties, took to his bed as if on the point of death, but not before submitting the following appeal :

"This slave is no impostor.
The imperial munificence has not been thrown away.
But the substance now bubbling in the crucible of the four elements requires more time to perfect.
Though the lead and the cinnabar have begun to blend,
thirty days are yet needed for their total fusion.
The golden pill is slowly taking form
and the furnace is being tended night and day."

'So the Fairy was granted a reprieve. The palace eunuchs, smiling into their sleeves, expected him to hasten to his laboratory and fan the furnace like a man possessed. Instead, by using the imperial mandate directing that all his needs be instantly supplied, he swiftly acquired temporary possession of all the inmates of the capital's most fashionable house of pleasure and set to work to gather their *yin*-force by his mastery of the 3-5-7-9 method (which, for as long as emission is avoided, can be performed night and day unendingly). Meanwhile, his door stayed closed to visitors, no matter what their rank.

'When the day came for his final audience, lictors stood waiting outside the doorway of the smaller throne-room with chains and shackles ready for his neck and limbs. Much to their amazement he preceded his escort into the August Presence with carefree gait and countenance so brilliant that it seemed a divinity now strode among them.

' "We are waiting," said the Emperor, bending his stern dragon-gaze upon that bright countenance. "Where is the vial?"

' "Lord of Ten Thousand Years," replied the Fairy smiling, "I bring with me the golden pill in perfected form. The crucible of the four elements of which I wrote in my worthless submission is no other than the human body which kneels before you. Therefore did I once memorialize Your Majesty that the elixir is not something that can be passed from hand to hand. Nevertheless, I can acquaint Your Majesty with the formula and it is only to be expected that Your Majesty, being a hundred times better provided with the vital ingredients than was this slave, will compound the golden pill more swiftly than a humble recluse could hope to do."

' "How dare you submit such paltry excuses!" roared the Emperor. "Did We not direct that all your needs be instantly supplied? With what ingredients are We a hundred times better provided?"

' "I was referring," replied the Fairy gently, "to the – to the – ah – relatively insignificant number of my wives."

' "Away with him!" commanded the Emperor, misliking the Taoist's lordly demeanour no less than his crude allusion to the prodigious number of imperial consorts. "This dog-meat monk is an imposter for whom a hundred blows with a heavy bamboo and banishment to a malarial region would be too light a sentence!"

'Thus, by being over-hasty, did the Bright Emperor lose a rare opportunity to acquire the precious formula; for, as the eunuch guards rushed forward, the Pine-kernel Fairy, who, on the previous evening had at last perfected the golden pill and achieved transmogrification, rose from the ground. Saluting the Emperor in dignified farewell, he sailed through the doorway and winged his way to the upper realms where cloud-riding Immortals pass their days in rapt contemplation of the Tao.'

The anecdote struck me as so funny that I burst out laughing. Even the Abbot smiled but he went on:

'Yes, the story is amusing and, of course, it is only a legend, although, as it happens, there are people on Mount T'ai who can direct you to the very place where, in the T'ang Dynasty, a certain Pine-kernel Fairy of the Lu clan used to instruct disciples in the healing art. We may be permitted to suppose that essentially the account is a true one, though certainly exaggerated. There is, for example, one quite incredible incident; it is impossible to suppose that an accomplished adept who had already aquired a dozen or so ladies for his household would have commandeered a bevy of fashionable courtesans. In the first place, women's vital energy being inexhaustible, there is no need to employ great numbers; in the second, professional girls make the least suitable partners as their emotions are too jaded to permit them to yield their precious store as easily as other women. My purpose in relating the story was to illustrate the folly of those in high places. How often has an emperor or great minister spent a fortune on achieving some object and, at the very moment when it lay within his grasp, lost it from sheer stupidity.'

The Secret Alchemy: 2 Internal (Kundalini-type) Yoga
The Abbot, himself a great adept at the non-dual internal alchemy, was not good at explaining to a novice how to produce a golden pill or immortal foetus within one's own body without the assistance of a sexual partner. To him the esoteric alchemic terms were so familiar that he seemed to take other people's understanding of them for granted. That I gleaned anything at all from his exposition was due to my having some knowledge of Indian *kundalini* yoga, a closely analogous system. Both are based on the

conviction that the body is permeated by a network of psychic channels radiating from the median channel which rises up the spine to the brain, and both demand the fusion of energies falling from above and rising from below as the means to achieving the goal. The part played by cosmic energy (*ch'i* in Chinese, *prāna* in Sanskrit) is identical. The similarity is great enough to have convinced many people that the two yogas are derived from a common source; but to a mystic, there is no inherent improbability in the notion of two communities arriving independently at a valid means of spiritual cultivation, just as skills in hunting, husbandry and so forth were independently developed in different parts of the world.

As *kundalini* yoga is now fairly well known in the West, a short digression may be helpful. It is said that God in the form of Dattatreya, being urged by Durga (Kali) to proclaim the secret knowledge, reluctantly consented to impart two allied forms of yoga from which he foretold that great weal or woe would result, namely tantric yoga (union achieved by dual cultivation) and *kundalini* yoga (union of the male and female forces within the adept's own body). He declared that the human body contains three great psychic channels (*nadi*) joined at the base, of which the median channel rises from genitals to crown, whereas the others have extensions to the nostrils. From them radiates an intricate network of minor channels by means of which cosmic energy (*prāna*) can be transmitted throughout the body, being activated principally by yogic breathing. Physical health, mental equilibrium, and life itself are thereby intensified. Much of this cosmic energy is stored in the *medulla oblongata* at the back of the brain; some is contained in each psychic centre (*chakra*) situated vertically along the median channel in the spine. The nondual yoga requires that the cosmic energy stored in the crown *chakra* be forced down until it strikes the *kundalini* or serpent energy coiled near the base of the spine, causing it to rise to the *chakra* close to the navel, whereat the *prāna* (upward breath) and *apana* (downward breath), having reversed their directions, will generate psychic heat (cf., the Tibetan *tummo* yoga). When this heat is experienced, the yogin can be assured that the serpent energy is rising up the channel in the spine on its way to unite with the cosmic energy residing in the centre near the crown. Their union results in an exalted state of yogic consciousness which, if several times repeated, ensures liberation in this life.

The psychic centres are thus:

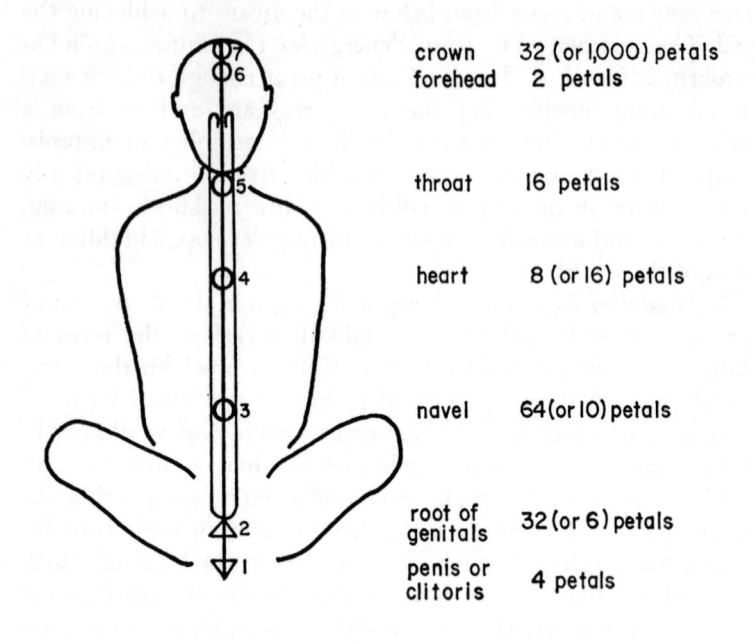

	crown	32 (or 1,000) petals
	forehead	2 petals
	throat	16 petals
	heart	8 (or 16) petals
	navel	64 (or 10) petals
	root of genitals	32 (or 6) petals
	penis or clitoris	4 petals

The heart *chakra* represents water; the navel *chakra*, fire. The forehead *chakra* corresponds exactly to the Taoist Mysterious Pass of the Precious Square Inch between and behind the eyes and is the place where, according to Hindu yogins, the Guru's instructions can be received during sleep, and light thereby be created from darkness. (The correspondence here between the two systems becomes more obvious when it is understood that the Chinese term, Mysterious Pass, can also be translated Dark Pass, and that this is the very place where the meditator perceives streams of light.) Moreover, there are Hindu expositions in which the dualism to be resolved by alchemic fusion agrees in most respects with the dualism detailed in Taoist manuals; according to the former moon = water = ova = mica = *shakti* has to be fused with sun = fire = semen = mercury = *shiva*. Substitute cinnabar for mica and lead for mercury; *ching* (generative fluid and the subtle energy pertaining to it) for *shakti*, and *shên* (spirit, higher consciousness) for *shiva*, and a perfect correspondence is established.

Another interesting correspondence is revealed in the following: In Hindu yoga, although man embodies sun and fire and woman moon and water, the *chakras* at the tip of the penis and clitoris pertain to water and fire respectively; similarly, in the Taoist depiction of the *yang* (male) and *yin* (female) principles, a seed of each is contained within the other.

The fruit of fusing the male and female energies residing in the adept's body is described in a Hindu work in these terms – 'a godlike unity is attained; the world of phenomena is transcended and the highest non-duality achieved in the form of supreme bliss; pure existence characterized by objectless consciousness is experienced; and so we speak of this union as Sat-Chit-Ananda, Being-Consciousness-Bliss!'

The Taoist internal alchemy, though having much in common with *kundalini* yoga, also has noticeable differences. They agree in utilizing the psychic channels for gathering and distributing cosmic energy, but the Hindu concept of two great channels to right and left of the median has no exact Taoist equivalent. The Taoist trilogy of channels consists of the median, known as the *ch'ung-mo* (thrusting), another to the rear known as the *tu mo* (control) which runs up the spine, and a third to the front called the *jên mo* (function). Taoist equivalents to most of the Hindu *chakras* are close. Speaking of them not as centres but as cavities, the Taoists hold the most important ones to be the *ni-wan* near the crown (which exactly corresponds, both in location and function, to the highest Hindu *chakra*), the Mysterious Pass between and behind the eyes, and the Upper and Lower Cinnabar Fields, situated at the solar plexus and below the navel respectively. The heart, the navel region, root of the genitals, and tip of the penis or clitoris also have yogic significance.

The inexactness of these correspondences does not invalidate either system, for we are dealing with a subtle anatomy unverifiable by the surgeon's scalpel. In both systems, the immediate object is to fuse the upper and lower energies by engendering psychic heat, which is done by proper control of the semen, breath and their subtle equivalents. Both result in notable invigoration and are conducive to the attainment of mystical perception.

Of the Abbot's description of this yoga, I could take in only his introductory remarks. He explained that it was based on three agents, each of which had a gross and subtle form; – *ching* (semen but also invisible generative force); *ch'i* (breath but also cosmic energy); and *shên* of two kinds, one inherent in man, the other cosmic). Of these he said that one must compound the subtle *ching* (essence) and transform it into the subtle *ch'i* (cosmic vitality); compound the subtle *ch'i* and transform it to the *shên* (cosmic spirit). This process makes three demands on the adept: maintenance of internal and external purity, keeping spirit and cosmic energy in a state of perfect quiescence, and strict conservation of the semen. 'If no emission takes place for three years, an inferior pill may be formed; for six, a medium pill; for nine, a great pill. For the rest, I have received Mr Lu's permission to draw upon the introduction to his invaluable work, *Taoist Yoga*, and to reproduce (in slightly simplified form) one of his diagrams.

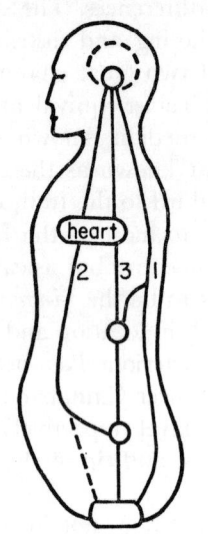

1 channel of control (tu mo)
2 channel of function (jên mo)
3 channel of thrusting (ch'ung mo)

solar plexus
(Middle Cinnabar Field)

Lower Cinnabar Field

root of the genitals

My understanding of Mr Lu's exposition is as follows:

This yoga is based on the principle of preventing the generative force, which is produced in conjunction with the semen, from being dissipated. As soon as it moves towards its usual outlet, it is turned back and driven, by means of inner fire kindled by regulated breathing, into microscopic orbit for sublimation. This orbit begins at the gateway situated at the base of the spine, rises up the spine along the channel of control to the gateway between the kidneys, passes through a third gateway at the back of the head, enters the *ni-wan* cavity in the brain and then descends by the channel of function to its starting point. This is accomplished by deep breathing to arouse the inner fire and bring pressure on the generative force (*ching*) so that, together with the fire, it rises by the channel of control to the head. With exhalation, the lower abdomen relaxes, allowing both fire and generative force to complete their orbit via the channel of function. Breathing slowly and deeply, in and out, one causes them to rotate in their orbit, thus cleansing the generative force, which thereafter is held in the Lower Cinnabar Field ready to be transmuted into vitality. Thus, when the generative force moves in accord with its worldly inclination, it is drawn into the Lower Cinnabar Field, which acts as a lighted stove supporting a cauldron of generative force ready for transmutation into vitality.

The purified force is carried to the Middle Cinnabar Field located in the solar plexus and there transmuted by psychic heat arising from the Lower Field into vitality, which now rises to the *ni-wan* cavity near the crown where, stirred by well-regulated breathing, it will concentrate. Thus, though the stove or source of psychic heat remains stationary, the cauldron containing the precious generative force transmuted into vitality rises to the crown; there, further transmutation follows, converting the vitality into spirit. All of this is accomplished by means of special breathing-exercises accompanied by vigorous movements of the eyes. As the vitality, driven by breathing and inner fire soars up and down, the cosmic energy in the brain causes spirit to develop and its bright light to become manifest. The internal copulation of the positive and negative principles developed by movements of the eyes and breathing respectively results in the distillation of the golden elixir. Next the pre-natal spirit, thus made manifest, is driven down to the Lower Cinnabar Field and there stored, while the adept concentrates his mind, causing the vital essence to vibrate and ascend and descend rapidly between the heart (seat of fire) and lower abdomen (seat of water). The spirit stored in the Lower Cinnabar Field, being thus enveloped by the vitality, unites with it to produce the immortal foetus in a state of complete serenity.

Thereafter follows the practice of breathing cosmic energy via two channels running respectively via the two channels of control and function, but starting from the heels and abdomen to the *ni-wan* near the crown. Thereby pre-natal vitality can be transmuted into milky-white ambrosia which falls upon and nurtures the immortal foetus contained in the Lower Cinnabar Field (abdomen). Intense concentration upon the foetus will result in a golden light appearing within the white light that shines through the Mysterious Pass. On perceiving the union of these lights, the adept should cease fanning the blaze of inner psychic heat and concentrate in the *ni-wan* the cosmic energy from other organs of the body. Now, uniting the two energies of vitality and spirit, the adept causes the foetus to produce a being that is truly immortal. Visualizing himself as leaping into the great void, he causes a gate to open in the top of the head, through which this being can pass freely and appear in countless bodies in space.

After an exposition somewhat similar to the one I have borrowed from Mr Lu, the Abbot continued: 'Thus is true immortality achieved by uniting the two energies of mortal or generative vitality and spirit through the agency of cosmic energy. Therefore are these three revered as the Three Treasures. The Three Pure Ones whose statues adorn our temples are, in truth, personifications of or correspondences to these three. But beware of supposing that this yoga is readily achievable. An excellent teacher, steadfast serenity of mind and the extinction of passion are essential. And, even with these, the average recluse can at best hope to prolong his life-span for a few decades. Any higher achievement is rare. In the ordinary course, after death the *p'o*-soul sinks into the realm of shades and there disintegrates, and the *hun*-soul, rising into the upper air, tends to disperse, though filial sacrifices may nourish it awhile. Only by phenomenal success in fusing the vital essence and spirit into one can the higher consciousness (*hsing*) and life-force (*ming*) be united and thus create an indestructible diamond-body.'

Questioned as to the meaning of 'indestructible diamond-body', since I did not know whether to take the term literally or allegorically, the Abbot grew evasive.

'Why do you suppose I favour one view more than another? Whom am I to speak with authority of what lies beyond mortal conception? And why should there not be many kinds and degrees of immortality? Seeds give birth to plants, eggs to birds. What is gained from the practice depends on what one puts into it. Had I devoted myself to swordsmanship, I should now be a soldier; by sticking to my books and becoming quarrelsome and self-opinionated, I could have made myself a scholar. As it is, I am an old wooden-head of a recluse, having developed but one of my natural potentialities. I am what I am because of what I have thought and done. By setting my heart on becoming a wandering ghost, I should probably succeed; by concentrating one-pointedly on transmuting myself into a fox-spirit or an immortal deity, fox or god I should probably become in one way or another. First there must be a conception of the state desired, then unfaltering endeavour to translate the concept into reality.

'There are adepts who assert that immortality is but a poetic synonym for longevity. You must have seen recluses long past their hundredth birthday who are still in full possession of their vital powers. Whether they are celibate or not, you may be sure they retain their reproductive energy, for semen is one of the crude elements from which are derived the subtle ingredients essential to the internal alchemy. An aged man able to perform feats of strength and endurance is generally termed an Immortal. More loosely the term is applied to young adepts who show promise of emulating those ancients. For recluses who share your Buddhist concept of a well-nigh endless cycle of rebirth, immortality is no doubt synonymous with winning a life-span within the higher tiers of a spiritual hierarchy embracing worlds both tangible and formless, though one knows very well that even gods do not exist forever. A more classical Taoist concept is that of achieving divine state either by fashioning a spirit-body or else by transmogrification. History, unfortunately, affords but few indisputable examples of the latter. However, we do know that the divine Ko Hung vanished from human ken, thoughtfully leaving a pile of discarded garments lest it be supposed he had wandered off into the mountains and lost his way home. Moreover, the *Book of Chuang-tzû* tells of a sage of Mount Ku Shê with a skin smooth as ice and white as snow, gentle and shy as a virgin, who nourished himself on wind and dew, rambled among the clouds, rode astride a dragon and, by concentrating his supernatural power, saved men from disease and want. Neither flood nor scorching drought could harm him. His very dust and leavings would have been enough to mould the greatest sage or emperor ever seen. Elsewhere

Chuang-tzû describes such Immortals as being impervious to fire and ice, lightning and storm. Riding the clouds and mist, bestraddling sun and moon, they wander at will beyond the four oceans, unmoved by life or death. One is free to take such descriptions literally or not. Ah, you smile! Yet I have read somewhere that, in the West, a doctrine affirming the resurrection of this fleshly body is widely preached. Have I been misinformed?'

'What,' I asked, grinning wryly at his thrust, 'does Your Reverence consider the highest goal attainable?'

'The highest! That is something else again. To proclaim that inner doctrine to the world would invite scorn in the ignorant and fruitless longing in the incapable. However, since you have raised the question, I shall take you to see a being who may conceivably decide to enlighten you. Come to my cell at dawn two days from tomorrow.'

Puzzled but excited, I presented myself to the Abbot just as the first light appeared in the eastern sky. Outside his door stood a youth carrying a light basket, who eyed me with immense surprise as though my arrival were unexpected and to some degree unwelcome; but just then the Abbot emerged and, greeting me with a smile, remarked to the novice: 'Do not worry. I have made myself responsible.' With these strange words he led us to the cavern which did duty as a shrine-room and, after lighting incense before the statues of the Eight Immortals, walked briskly forward to a narrow opening concealed behind the figure of Han Hsiang, that resplendently bearded sage who carries a basket of peaches. I would not have guessed that this opening existed and was even more astonished to find beyond it a very long natural passage which finally brought us to a rock-chamber open to what must have been the east face of the mountain, for the sky beyond was already bright with the rosy clouds of dawn.

In the centre of this chamber was a pile of old cushions upon which, rapt in meditation, sat a wrinkled ancient whose white locks fell about his shoulders in disorder and whose beard, albeit rather sparse and wispy, reached down to where his hands were resting, lightly clasped, upon his lap. His dark yellow-ochre robe was worse than shabby. All three of us bowed to the ground before him, but the ancient offered no acknowledgment and seemed not to be aware of our presence. To his left was an empty plate of fine porcelain embossed with a magnificent representation of the

Chinese unicorn in variegated colours, a padded wicker basket containing a teapot, a dirty-looking cup (also of fine quality but cracked and chipped) and an earthenware water-jar. The novice replaced the teapot by another that fitted the basket just as snugly and, rubbing the plate with a cloth, ladled on to it two bowlfuls of sweet glutinous rice. Next to these, he placed an offering of eight *sha-li* pears in various stages of ripeness, a bundle of red candles, two packets of incense-sticks and a box of matches. Meanwhile the Abbot, lips close to my ear, whispered:

'The Immortal has not quite reached the stage of living on air and dew, but two bowlfuls of sweetened rice and a little fruit last him for seven or eight days. The tea we bring is often left untouched. There is always clean, fresh water in the jar but no one knows when or where he fills it. We come with offerings only on the days that coincide with the four stages of the moon. This rock-chamber is inaccessible from outside, being set in the face of a deep precipice, but I have heard that it is connected by a sloping shaft with a similar chamber into which no one within living memory (unless the Immortal) has entered. Said to be the abode of a mountain spirit, it may contain a small spring, but I have seen from that hill-top facing us that, like this chamber, it is inaccessible from without; therefore the Immortal can never be disturbed by human visitors without my permission. I had hoped to find him resting from his meditations and in a mood to answer your question. You may be sure he knows we are here; his silence implies that he does not wish to be disturbed.'

We were about to slip away when the Abbot touched my arm. The Immortal had opened his eyes and was observing me with benevolent curiosity. Presently the beard fluttered and the old lips moved. The voice was surprisingly clear and melodious, though not raised above the level of a murmur.

'*Hui shuo jên-hua-ma*? (Are you capable of human speech?)'

Taken aback by such unexpected rudeness, I answered shortly: 'This person is familiar with three or four varieties of human speech, *Chinese included*!'

The Abbot sucked in his breath, distressed by my discourtesy. The novice looked as close to anger as a Taoist may well be, but the ancient merely smiled.

'There is heat in you,' he answered equably, 'rather more than the circumstances require. Can it be that a being familiar with human speech has yet to acquaint himself with human propriety? Here in this lonely place, few of my visitors are human, so it is reasonable for me to inquire what manner of communication suits each best.'

The expressions of my companions afforded no clue as to whether the ancient was being deliberately unkind or just very, very simple. Though foreigners in China are commonly known as devils, courtesy forbids their being thus addressed, and so his remarks could bear a highly offensive interpretation. On the other hand, since he had survived from a generation most of whom had never set eyes on a Westerner, if he really were, or believed himself to be, in contact with demons, he might reasonably have mistaken me for one, the more so as a quilted Taoist robe hid my outlandish garments. Therefore, speaking with greater deference and with some attempt at humour, I replied:

'This person comes from a country in the Western Ocean whose inhabitants sincerely believe themselves to be human, although our appearance and odd notions of decorum have sometimes led your honourable countrymen to suppose otherwise.'

'Ah, a foreign devil!' he exclaimed with such obvious pleasure that I could not take offence. Now that he recognized me for what I was, his use of the unflattering term could, in view of his great age and long seclusion, be due to his having never heard any other way of referring to Westerners. Recalling that, during the last century, the British Minister to Peking had received a letter addressed to him in all innocence as 'His Excellency the Principal Foreign Devil Envoy', I said blandly:

'That is so, Your Immortality. His Reverence has brought this person here chiefly to pay his profound respects, but incidentally to importune you with a question as to the nature of the highest state of immortality.'

'Ha-ha-ha!' laughed the ancient softly with a glance of puckish amusement that made him look years younger. 'What a question to propound to an ignorant old hermit! The Venerable Abbot, so wise and learned in exalted matters, is the very person to give you a satisfying answer. As for this lump of useless flesh, I shall answer a more down-to-earth question – namely, why should mortals concern themselves with immortality? It forever eludes our powers of conception; as to those who exert themselves to attain it, they are most likely to end up as immortal demons!'

As his voice died away, his old eyes closed to signify that the audience was at an end. Quietly we rose and left him to his meditations.

Back with the Abbot in his tiny courtyard, where he offered me tea and pork-dumplings for breakfast, we sat in the late autumn sunshine, comfortably sheltered from the wind. I questioned him eagerly about the old sage, but could discover little. It seemed he had been installed in his rock-chamber so long that no one could recollect having heard of a time before his coming. The only difference made by the passing years had been a gradual diminution of his diet. From eating a bowl of sweetened glutinous rice and some fruit every day, he had reached a point of requiring that two bowls be served to him once in seven days, so that he need not be disturbed more often. Where he had come from, his age, surname in lay life and so forth were all mysteries, but it could be judged from his speech that he had passed his early life in the province of Honan. Popular legend credited him with being three hundred years old, but the Abbot thought this an exaggeration.

'The Immortal rarely speaks of personal matters, but he once described to me an event he had witnessed as a child in the reign of the Chiach'ing Emperor. We may therefore suppose that his life has but recently entered upon its third sixty-year cycle. It is a pity he would not answer your question. No doubt he considers you young for such sacred knowledge.'

The Abbot's own reluctance to describe the highest goal puzzled me, for he knew I was already aware that it involved union with the Tao, that is to say true immortality, though perhaps not as an individual.

Some years were to pass before my curiosity was satisfied by another teacher. Only then did I come to know that the Taoist concept of this union was so dazzling as to baffle the imagination.

Chapter 5

To Know and Not Be Knowing: Taoist Philosophy and Kindred Matters

Though Taoist philosophers pure and simple – in the sense of having no truck with ritual, spiritism or magic, nor yet with yogic meditation – may always have been almost as rare in China as fox-spirits in London or New York, most Taoist adepts, whatever their connection with the realms of demons, magic and mystical experience, were also keen exponents of the philosophical teachings of Lao and Chuang. The aphorisms of those sages on the art of government, military affairs, economics, education and general conduct have influenced the thinking not only of Taoists but of the whole Chinese people throughout the ages, and they can now be seen as highly relevant to the modern world, especially as Western thinkers have learnt to question their own traditional values and to study the cultures of other regions in a spirit of sincere inquiry. Nevertheless, it should be borne in mind that even those aphorisms dealing with political and educational theory were rooted in the mystical principle of reconciling opposites; for the sages recognized that no peace is to be found in minds plagued by dualistic thought, since the undifferentiated Tao imbues all objects alike and contains in latent form all those that could possibly come into existence.

Cool, calm and deep, and permeated with sincerity was the teaching of Lao and Chuang. In studying what they had to say on specific issues, we are never far away from the underlying harmony in which, for them, all issues merged and were resolved.

The Taoist sages, with their abhorrence of interference in all its forms, wrote much that will rejoice the hearts of those who recognize how our society has been warped by *mores* and rules of conduct at total variance with natural law. It is good to reflect on the necessity or otherwise of many circumstances we have been taking for granted – war, taxation, penal measures, pontifical forms of education, and a system of morality which has come to such abject terms with greed for possession as to be riddled with cynical hypocrisy, to say nothing of being founded on some very strange categories of do and don't. (For example, I may not rob my neighbour of a loaf of bread; but if I can beggar him and ruin his whole family by unscrupulous practice which does not quite transgress the law, I am welcome to do so, and may even be praised for my business acumen!) Then, again, our whole society functions upon that balance of rewards and penalties of which Chuang-tzû, in speaking of the Emperor Yao (a ruler in the age of remote antiquity) declared: 'He handed out no rewards and yet the people worked hard; he imposed no punishments and yet the people were careful', adding that the subsequent institution of rewards and punishments had been responsible for the decay of natural virtue; therefore penalties had come to prevail and would be a cause of sad disorder to future ages. Or, as Lao-tzû put it: 'When prohibitory laws abound, the people grow poor ... When laws are numerous, there are many criminals!' This may seem utopian; but, in a society run on Taoist lines, which inculcated frugality and looked askance at the piling up of possessions and novelties, there would be enough for all and little incentive to act in a manner that would require restraint by penalties; as to rewards, who, being adequately clothed and fed, would have regard for them? Flocks of animals manage excellently without either rewards or penalties.

Ah, if the teachings of Lao and Chuang were taken as a universal guide, what stillness and what love! Not that they spoke much of love; it was their view that the Confucians' loud insistence on the need for benevolence and filial piety was a direct cause of the abeyance of those virtues. As Chuang-tzû pointed out, 'waving the flags of benevolence and righteousness' is a sure way of bringing confusion to man's nature. 'Then along comes the sage, huffing and puffing after benevolence, reaching on tiptoe for righteousness, and the world for the first time has doubts ... If the Way (Tao) and its Virtue (Tê) had not been cast aside, why should there be any call for benevolence and righteousness?'

In another passage, he says: 'The sage came along . . . with reaching-for-a-dangled prize of benevolence and righteousness, which was intended to comfort people's hearts. Then for the first time people learnt to stand on tiptoe and covet knowledge, to fight to the death over profit, and there was no stopping them.' The implication is that love of that spontaneous, unquestioning kind which very young and unspoiled children bestow without thought on all who treat them kindly is implicit in the Way; whereas frequent voicing of love is a sure sign and cause of its absence or decline. For close on two thousand years, we Westerners have paid lip-service to the injunction to love our neighbours as ourselves, but the sentimental attachment we still have to that ideal has not prevented us from using flame-throwers, napalm, fragmentation bombs and the like to burn to death or lacerate the flesh of neighbours whose ideology affrights us. Even among dear ones, cultivated and consciously directed love often leads to unwarrantable interference in the lives of those most deeply cherished, whereas to a Taoist mind interference was unthinkable. Then again, how many priests, politicians and businessmen seek to demonstrate their benevolence with would-be cheerful smiles that constrict their features into painful grins! How embarrassed Taoists would have felt at being the recipients of such forced amiability!

If people were encouraged to be themselves and if violence and punishment were set aside, love would flourish as unnoticed as the air, for the chief impediments to spontaneous affection – interference and coercion – would be gone. Cultivation of the Taoist virtues, namely frugality, generosity, absence of desire for profit, and reluctance to be saddled with power or possessions, would remove so many sources of friction that kindness and affection would prevail as a matter of course. In the Taoist communities where I stayed, there was warm-heartedness on every hand, but no *talk* of love; just as beauty would arouse no comment in the absence of ugliness, so was affection taken for granted in the absence of intolerance.

As to large-scale violence, Lao-tzû, who described armies as 'implements of ill omen', pointed out that 'when weapons are sharpened, the state grows chaotic' and that 'great victories entail much mourning.' Recognizing that the rulers in his day could not be prevailed upon to renounce force altogether, he recommended the utmost restraint. The wise ruler 'having achieved the purpose (in hand) is hesitant to press on to conquest. Success does not go to his head, nor make him arrogant or boastful, nor cause him to long for more or indulge in (further) violence' and 'Those who assist the ruler by means of the Way do not employ might to gain the world's submission; such methods are apt to recoil; where an army has passed, brambles thrive; in the train of a great conflict comes famine.' Furthermore, 'The best warriors are not warlike; the best fighters are not carried away by excitement; the best winners are loath to give battle; the best rulers are humble men. That is what is meant by the virtue of non-contention and by ability to use men well. It is known as matching Heaven's sublimity.' Speaking of oppressive government, he said: 'Where there is corruption at the seat of government, when the fields are clothed in weeds, when the granaries stand empty, what can we call those men who wear fine clothes, carry sharp swords and gorge themselves on wine and food but robber chiefs?' and, speaking of all forms of government, he asserted: 'Seeking to rule by action seems to me a way to fail. The world, (like) a sacred vessel, should not be tampered with. Those who act upon it mar it; laying hands on it, they lose it.' In all these passages, the underlying teaching is restraint – victors should not push their conquests, nor their advisers advocate harsh measures likely to recoil; warriors should fight, if they must, with calm dispassion, and rulers govern with humility.

Chuang-tzû's advice to rulers was that they should seek to remain virtually anonymous (a doctrine whose observance would have made the rule of many an American president more effective, but one which can scarcely ever have entered the head of a candidate for that high office). He observes that the ruler should 'make absolutely certain that things can do what they are supposed to do and that is all.' Into the mouth of Lao Tan (Lao-tzû), he puts the words: 'The government of an enlightened king? His achievements blanket the world but appear not to be his own doing. His transforming influence touches the ten thousand things but the people do not depend on him. With him there is no promotion or praise – he lets everything find its own enjoyment. He takes his stand on what cannot be fathomed and wanders where there is nothing at all.' In another passage he points out that the ideal ruler does not think in dualistic terms, for 'where there is unacceptability there must be acceptability; where there is recognition of right there must be recognition of wrong' and vice versa; avoiding such arbitrary and confusing categories, 'he illumines all in the light of Heaven', that is to say he draws upon knowledge from the stillness that is in himself and all men, leading others to conform with their spontaneous intuitions. Knowing his 'this' may also be 'that'; his 'that' also 'this', and each of them be at once right and also wrong, he abandons such distinctions, thus conforming with the Way.

That even rulers bound by financial and other constraints to do less than is desirable for the people could at least make their government more acceptable by avoiding pig-headed insistence upon their own methods of distribution is illustrated by Chuang-tzû's fable about some monkeys. Their keeper, finding that these creatures became furious because he gave each of them three acorns in the morning and four at night, had the wisdom to switch over to distributing four in the morning and three at night. The monkeys were delighted. 'There was no change in the reality behind the words,' wrote Chuang-tzû, 'and yet the monkeys responded with joy and not anger. Why not, if that was what they wanted? So the sage harmonizes both right and wrong and rests in Heaven the Equalizer. This is what is called walking two roads.'

To those on whom a ruler leans for advice, Chuang-tzû remarks that speeches on benevolence and righteousness and on the measures and standards thereof are merely a means of using the bad points of others to parade one's own excellence and will probably get the adviser into hot water with his master, if not cause him to lose his head! A good ruler has no need for such advice; a bad one will not heed it, so why upset unnecessarily whoever it is, and cause trouble for oneself? This, no doubt, was a sly dig at Confucius, who never wearied of inflicting his advice on princes.

Regarding rulers fond of mouthing about tradition, Chuang-tzû observed: 'Paths are made by the shoes that walk them; they are by no means shoes in themselves.'

The two sages vehemently opposed the profit-motive, that bitter fruit of calculated endeavour and self-interest. Speaking of the Superior Man, Chuang-tzû exclaimed: 'He will leave gold hidden in the mountains, pearls concealed in the depths, seeing no advantage in money and goods, no enticement in eminence and wealth ... no shame in poverty ... for he knows that the myriad objects belong to the one storehouse.' As lovers of frugality, the sages deplored the employment of special skills to create unneeded novelties and luxuries, which served merely to increase the scope of popular desires, since they perceived that the very essence of tranquillity and satisfaction is to have few desires, none of them of a kind hard to gratify.

The modern world of advertising and go-getting salesmanship is the very antithesis of the serenely joyful world that could be built by a people dedicated to simplicity. The whole concept of development, of introducing into deprived societies the elements of conspicuous consumption so that they will want more and therefore strive harder, would have struck Taoists as shocking duplicity; for behind the prompters of such 'development' are merchants who callously increase their sales at the cost of destroying people's contentment with a way of life for which most necessities can be supplied from within their own small communities. (In Laos, until that pleasant, smiling land was sucked into the vortex of the American-Vietnamese war, most villages were largely self-sufficient. Once an English resident cajoled a Laotian carpenter into making him a tiresomely complicated door; having insisted that the artisan name his own price, he then agreed to pay the fantastic sum which the Laotian, meaning to put an end to the matter, had jokingly named. At this the carpenter, far from being jubilant, stood scowling at the thought of being saddled with an unnecessarily complicated task for a reward that was large, but neither needed nor desired. The Englishman used to tell this story as an example of the Laotian people's 'shocking lack of enterprise'. A Taoist, on the contrary, would have applauded and sympathized most deeply with the Laotian.) It should not be supposed that Lao and Chuang were puritans. Under a Taoist-style régime, colourfulness and individuality would flourish, for Taoists were nothing if not poetic, and colour and poetry have always gone together; but there would be an underlying simplicity – high fashions, expensive stones and extravagant materials would vanish. Neither puritan drabness nor luxury could be held to accord with the Way.

As to education, if men imbued with Taoist principles were in a position to run our schools, many a text-book would be thrown on the rubbish heap as being too superficial, too utterly irrelevant to the pupils' development as people happily integrated with nature's rhythms, at ease with themselves, serenely in harmony with their surroundings, tranquil, content, free from anxiety or covetousness, not eager to contend, and therefore likely to live long, endowed with health and youthful spirits to the end. Smart alecks among teachers and those puffed up with learning would, like rapacious businessmen, have to turn to simpler ways of earning a living, for their 'cleverness' would be recognized as stupidity or cunning. Not cleverness but natural wisdom would be the educator's goal – the wisdom that arises from sparing time to listen to the stillness and to observe how effortlessly plants and animals satisfy their needs in accordance with circumstances. Plants do not have to be taught how to drink the rain or bend towards the sun! Students would turn from professors with stale learning in order to seek wisdom from those able to direct them to its source. Concerning these matters, Lao-tzû observed:

'True words may not be fine, nor fine words honest. Good words may not persuade, nor persuasive words be good. Wise men may not be learned, nor learned men be wise.

'Those who know do not talk. Those who (are eager to) talk do not know.

'To know and not be knowing is best. To be ignorant but think one knows is a disaster. Knowing one's faults is the means to faultlessness.

'Therefore the sage desires to be without desire, does not value what is hard to come by and learns (the wisdom of) not learning, that he may be free from the faults of the multitude. He promotes the spontaneity of things, not venturing to interfere.

'When (knowledge of) the Sublime Tao declined, benevolence and righteousness were substituted. The arrival of (specious) wisdom and intelligence generated great hypocrisy. It is when family members are at odds that filial conduct and loving-kindness are emphasized. A country has to be in chaos, before the concept of loyal ministers arises.

'Banish the wise! Away with the learned! Then the people will benefit a hundredfold. Banish (the concept of) benevolence! Away with (talk of) righteousness! Then of their own accord people will return to filial conduct and loving-kindness. Discard ingenuity and desire to profit! Then thieves and bandits will cease to rob. These three categories, being false (measures of conduct), are useless. Lead people to attach themselves to the plain and unadored, to think but little of themselves and to narrow the range of their desires.'

The sage was decrying not true wisdom but the specious learning and useless accumulations of knowledge which pass for wisdom. Teachers living in accordance with the Way would have little to say and, when they did speak, it would be to drop a hint, to advise perhaps, but never arrogantly. They would be too well aware of their own limitations to take it for granted that the teacher is necessarily wiser than his pupil. Inculcating the wisdom of not learning what the world most values, they would set themselves to guide young people's powers of self-development. Were that development to follow unforeseen paths, they would be hesitant to interfere, or else bring to bear the greatest tact. What Lao-tzû wrote about benevolence, righteousness, filial conduct, loving-kindness, loyalty and so forth was in direct contrast to what the Confucians taught. Those great pedagogues believed in harping on the necessity for absolute obedience to the ruler, to official superiors, parents, husbands, elders, whom they regarded as having a divine right to the unfaltering submission of their subordinates and juniors, stipulating only that authority should be tempered with benevolence – thus, in a Confucian society, a father incensed against his son could slay him with virtual impunity, whereas a youngster who as much as raised a hand against parent or elder brother laid himself open to the penalty of decapitation! Lao-tzû's point was that, in the absence of threats, punishments and demands for obedience and loyalty, subordinates and juniors would generally be only too happy to assist their seniors; everyone knows what pride children take in doing something of their own accord 'for Mummy', but their spontaneous joy soon fades when such behaviour is represented to them as a duty.

It is because children tire of exhortations to honour and obey their parents that they are driven to revolt. If elders behaved reasonably, not thwarting the young people's spontaneous development along lines according best with their own natures, if there were no talk of duty to honour and obey, most youngsters would accord love and respect to parents and teachers as a matter of course. Who needs to speak of filial conduct and loving-kindness in a well-knit, happy, understanding family? Who needs to speak of loyalty in a state where the ruler has made himself universally beloved? Who needs to fear robbers in a society where the accumulation of wealth and property is not desired? What better way is there of assuring people's happiness than teaching them by example to be easily content? How pleasant it would be for the Joneses to keep up with the Browns if both were intent on making life more simple! Lao-tzû was naturally not opposed to filial conduct and loving-kindness in themselves; it was Confucian harping on those virtues that distressed him, for he believed in a form of society in which they would flourish spontaneously and unremarked, as does love between mare and foal, neither of which presumably gives it a thought, being content with the actuality. Chuang-tzû reinforces this attitude in the passage: 'When . . . words rely on vain show, we have the rights and wrongs of the Confucians and Mo-ists (these latter made a great parade of loving all men equally). What one calls right the other calls wrong; what one calls wrong the other calls right. But if we want to right their wrongs and wrong their rights, then the best thing to use is clarity.'

Chuang-tzû's advice to teachers is contained in a story about a certain sage who, having been appointed tutor to an unprincipled young prince, faced a dilemma; to have let the young man do as he liked would have been to endanger the state; to have sought to control him would have endangered the poor tutor's life! The sage's way out was for the tutor, having made quite sure he was in the right, to humour the prince without becoming too involved, meanwhile learning to understand him thoroughly so as to lead him subtly to the point where he would be without fault. What wisdom! Everybody knows that young people have their pride, and hate to be shown up when in the wrong; but they are also keen to learn how to be effective, and warmly welcome guidance given with no hurt to their pride. Even children labelled ungovernable, and expelled from successive schools, have been known to respond admirably to this kind of treatment.

As to general conduct, the *Tao Tê Ching* contains many telling aphorisms which lead us to picture its author as a man of unusual sweetness, mellowness and good humour. As though describing himself, Lao-tzû says: 'The sage does not hoard. Giving his all to others, he is the richer for it. Not vaunting himself, he attains to wisdom. Not justifying himself, he becomes illustrious. Not conceited, he is effective. Not bragging, he comes to be supreme.

It is just because he does not vie with men that no one in the world can vie with him. How truly it was said by the Ancients "The bowed becomes straight"!'

Elsewhere, he says: 'I have three treasures which I guard and cherish. The first is compassion; the second, frugality; the third, humility. Compassion begets courage; frugality begets a liberal spirit; humility begets supremacy. Courage without compassion, liberality without frugality, supremacy without humility – these spell death!'

How sincere, how restrained was this sage! To talk like Mo-tzû of loving everybody is to go too far; to the ordinary human being Mo-ist style undiscriminating love is just not possible. Compassion? Yes. Though someone irk us grievously, we may still feel compassion, seeing in him a victim of the human condition and perhaps of his own or others' folly, hard to love and therefore all the more deserving of sympathy and goodwill. Frugality one would expect of a sage who realizes that tranquillity is best achieved by setting bounds to desire. But humility in one who (whether or not the great Confucius really paid him homage) must surely have been highly esteemed by his contemporaries was quite exceptional; for that was an age when turbulent sages strode through the doors of princely dwellings demanding to be accepted as heaven-sent guides, an age when sages were treated with honour even by those rulers who backed away from taking their advice. It certainly escaped Confucius that humility begets true greatness. The final sentence of the passage quoted remains enigmatic. Does supremacy without humility spell death? Winston Churchill, who wielded something like supreme power with great success, can scarcely be said to have been humble! Perhaps what Lao-tzû meant was death of the spirit, for no one full of self-importance can hear the voice of the stillness.

To emphasize that pride and a sense of self-importance are not merely negative obstacles to progress but a source of inefficiency, even of danger, Lao-tzû wrote: 'He who stands on tiptoe, totters; striding does not take one far. He who vaunts himself is stupid; self-praise leads not to high repute. Conceited men are not effective; no braggart rises to the top.' Some writers have interpreted these sentiments as pertaining only to the period at which Lao-tzû lived – a time of perpetual warfare among neighbouring states governed by capricious princes swift to reward unpalatable advice with death or to send dagger-men to visit those who were serving their rivals too successfully. Personally, I am inclined to take a larger view; to one imbued with Lao-tzû's inner stillness, putting oneself forward in a swaggering, ostentatious manner would seem folly no matter what the circumstances. Standing on tiptoe implies pretending to greater stature than one has, which inevitably leads to dangerous instability. Striding means forcing the pace of things beyond what they can bear for long. Vaunting oneself is a sure way of incurring envy, mockery or hatred. Self-praise – 'self-justification' is a more literal rendering of the text – is unneeded by those whose effectiveness speaks for itself. In other words, behaving conceitedly is likely to have at least two serious consequences; on the one hand, it leads to becoming the object of anger or contempt; on the other, it results in the stretching of one's (perhaps very real) ability to a point at which it can no longer be effective. So it is best to be modest and cautious, to avoid the limelight unless solid achievement brings one to the centre of the stage in spite of one's having no special wish to be there.

Lao-tzû paints a very endearing picture of true nobility in these words: 'Of old there were wise men possessed of subtle, mystic penetration so deep as to be unrecognized. Such was their unplumbable profundity that only their outward conduct can be described. Cautious as men crossing a river in the winter, hesitant as if shy of those around them, preserving the careful demeanour of guests, adaptable as melting ice, their conduct as simple as uncarved wood, their minds receptive as hollow valleys (they gave the impression of being) as murky as muddied water.'

This last simile is particularly striking. Only a man of deep profundity could enjoy seeming murky and dull. In other passages, the thought is carried even further: 'The multitude have plenty (of wit) to spare; I alone seem wanting. My mind is (taken for) that of a fool – muddled, blank! The common people shine; I alone seem dull . . . The multitude are purposeful; I alone seem worthless. I am different from all other men, because I value the sustenance fed to me by the Mother.' Seemingly vague, muddled, stupid even, the sage pursues an even course, careless of appearances, welcoming man's ignorance of his worth, for he knows that, in reality, worth derives not from himself but from the Tao which, unobstructed by grandiose thoughts of its own excellence, functions to perfection. People familiar with the works of the old Chinese

Zen Masters will be struck by the similarity of this passage to those in which the truly enlightened confess with some amusement that the world mistakes them for smiling half-wits. To quote Master Hui Hai:

> 'On meeting worldly men, I scarcely speak,
> and so they say that I am dull of wit.
> Without, I have what seems a dullard's stare;
> within, my crystal clarity of mind
> soundlessly tallies with that mystic hidden way
> which you worldly folk have yet to learn.'

Here, of course, we are slipping away from the practical philosophy with which this chapter deals into the realm of mysticism; but, even if the mystical substance of Lao-tzû's teaching is played down, how eminently sensible it is for a man to be cautious, hesitant, polite, adaptable, receptive in dealing with his unpredictable fellows, hiding his talents for use when needed. For who would wish to quarrel with or stand in the way of such a charmingly shy and receptive person? If he is sometimes taken for a fool, envy will be disarmed and merit applauded when it turns out that, in his quiet way, he has done just what was needed in a given crisis. Nor need others be afraid that such a man, having served his purpose, will preen himself, remain in the limelight, or demand rewards difficult or inconvenient to bestow, for Lao-tzû also says: 'Grasping at all you can get compares ill with stopping in good time. A point, however finely tempered, will not stay sharp forever. Filling your house with gold and jade, you cannot make them long secure. Priding yourself on wealth and position invites a fall. When success brings you fame, it is time to step down.'

Underlying all this is the great Taoist principle of not acting except in response to imperative need. When something has to be done, the wise man steps forward without fuss and deals with it as effectively as possible, but no sooner is the result ensured than he slips away to be free of unnecessary involvement. The true meaning of *wei-wu-wei* is not 'doing by not doing' but acting in a manner that entails the least involvement and proceeds from the inner stillness of the heart. As Lao-tzû says: 'The sage adheres to non-(involving)-action and practises the wordless doctrine' and again: 'Do what is free from (calculating or self-involving) action and disorder will vanish. Heaven and Earth endure because freedom from consciousness of self endows them with everlastingness. Therefore the sage, by putting himself last, comes first. Because he cares nothing for his person, it is preserved.' Or, to quote Chuang-tzû, 'Perfect speech is the abandonment of speech; perfect action is the abandonment of (self-involving) action. To be limited to understanding only what is understood – this is shallow indeed!' and 'You have only to rest in non-(involving) action and things will transform themselves.' Again, 'To rest in inaction and command respect – this is the Way of Heaven. To engage in (involving) action and become entangled in it – this is the way of man.'

Many are the advantages of abstaining from calculated and self-involving action in favour of action that is rooted in quiescence (or, as some would say, rooted in the Tao, the true Self underlying the petty illusory ego-entities responsible for all frailty and folly). Leaving aside the implications that follow from this mystical interpretation, the excellence of such action is still obvious; for, though whatever has to be done in response to the circumstances of each situation is performed as effectively as possible with the full amount of energy and dedication required, the doer need fear no stomach ulcers or nervous breakdowns, for the simple reason that no sooner has a decision been reached and the necessary action taken than he dismisses the matter from his mind forever. The best of his talents have been put to use without a trace of personal involvement, as is the case when an experienced driver, having applied brake and clutch to suit a momentary situation, continues on his way without giving his action a second thought – the greater his expertise, the less the thought required to make a suitable response to each emerging situation.

With action of this kind, however demanding, wear and tear on body and brain are minimal. As to the way such conduct strikes other people, what more could they desire of a man than that he carry out his tasks without boasting, without making stipulations and without prior or subsequent claims for credit or reward? Everyone welcomes a modest, retiring, thoroughly helpful person. A need arises; it is dealt with and, ceasing to be a need, it is forgotten. Lao-tzû's saying 'Therefore the sage, by putting himself last, comes first' does not imply that so wise a man *desires* to come first, only that he is the one to whom people will turn instinctively in a crisis. Chuang-tzû's frequent expressions of admiration for craftsmen so skilled as to achieve excellent results with a minimum of effort have a close bearing on our understanding of *wei-wu-wei*, the point being that Taoist emphasis on acting sparingly in no way implies belittlement of expertise. Men who act sparingly out of mere laziness naturally take no trouble to master particular skills, whereas Taoists who acted thus on principle recognized the extent to which a skill makes sparing action particularly effective.

The following dialogue demonstrates, however, that there is truth in the familiar criticism that Taoists carried the principle of non-involvement so far as to be unable to cope with problems affecting men in the mass – and this, in spite of their warm-heartedness, sure sympathy and helpfulness towards individuals. Once, on Mount Hua, a recluse presented me with a scroll on which his teacher had inscribed an oft-quoted sentence from the *Tao Tê Ching*: 'The highest virtue is like water which benefits the myriad creatures without contention.' Recluses were fond of murmuring homilies on water to visitors in search of instruction and this one was no exception. Pointing out that water, the most pliable and docile of all elements, is also the most powerful, he went on:

'No matter what the obstacles, water reaches its goal, whether by uniting with the air and getting a free ride, or by skirting round things or patiently eroding them. Consider how marvellously it bends all things to its purposes; voiceless, it generates sounds both musical and thunderous by contact with the other elements; tasteless, it conveys all tastes and odours; colourless, it reflects all hues. An exemplary embodiment of the Tao, it demonstrates that there are peaceful ways of solving all problems, accomplishing all ends. When puzzled by some conundrum, look to water for the key.'

'Well,' I replied, 'I have long meant to bring up a problem regarding the application of *wei-wu-wei* to the ordering of society. But first let me inquire whether Your Reverence considers that each of us has a certain responsibility towards the government and people of the country which is his home whether by right of birth or by virtue of long residence?'

The old gentleman nodded emphatically. 'Indeed, indeed. We Taoists, for example, seek to benefit society by leaving everything alone, by letting everybody go his own way unburdened by interference and yet holding ourselves ready to oblige people in case of need. If human society were always mutually unexacting, there would be few restraints from without upon individual freedom; those coming from the heart would be sufficient. As to our Chinese Government, it derides us in school text-books and by other means; sometimes it persecutes us, sequestrating our monasteries for profane use. How does one cope with rapacious officials other than by the herb-gatherer's method of dealing with wild beasts, which is to walk softly, offer no menace and draw no attention to his person? The ordering of society at large, if it were responsive to the Tao, would be so simple. Before governments learnt to meddle, society was organized to perfection. Bears have no government; I have not heard that they suffer from the lack of one. Governments, when out of conformity with the Tao, can function only by reliance upon coercion and fixed norms, though it is easy to see that, whatever a task may be, from cutting up a great fish for a banquet to the ordering of men's welfare, it can best be done by skirting the hard and finding the chinks. As I have explained, we hermits make no demands, keep out of people's way, and yet stand ready to offer hospitality, healing or advice to those who ask. Were the Governor of this small province to do the same, how great would be the people's esteem! Wherever there is water for human needs, there will be grain, vegetables and fish for dinner, and flax or cotton for weaving garments; therefore, since the earth freely supplies all kinds of materials for constructing shelter from sun and storm, there is but little a government can do to help people. Where rulers go beyond that little, they add nothing but sorrow and complication.'

'Very true,' I answered, 'but this touches upon the problem I mentioned. What is the Taoist prescription for men now living in cities whose vast numbers put them in no position to supply their wants from nature's store?'

'If people lived by the Tao, there would be no cities. Moderate in their desires, they would require no artifacts beyond those made at home by weaving, sewing, pottery and carpentry; not given to lust, they would sire children in numbers their communities could comfortably sustain.'

'Also true, Your Reverence, but the fact is that men, especially city-dwellers, are already too numerous to sustain themselves in a state of noble simplicity – hence those great sprawling cities with their miserable, undernourished hordes. What is to be done for them? Somehow they must be fed and clothed. Where could they go if it were decided to raze cities and reinstate the art of living in accordance with the Tao?'

This was not a question he had had occasion to consider. Watching his expression of suddenly aroused concern, I judged he had no immediate panacea for the grave problem of over-population.

'There must be a way,' he answered, casting about in his mind. 'No difficulty is insoluble, though remedies have often to be gradual. Cities, the fruit of centuries of growth, cannot be eliminated in a year. Wherever the solution for those crowds of unhappy people may lie, we Taoists, having played no part in bringing about their misery, would gladly help if we could. But would people so lost to stillness pay heed to our remedies? Would they listen? Would they be content to leave their property and fripperies behind and take to the simple life?'

'Well,' I replied, 'I think some of the younger ones would bless you if you could provide them with a workable alternative to living out the crabbed unnatural lives of slum-dwellers. Greed to acquire rich possessions is a disease not over-common among the young.'

I could see that the recluse was disturbed. Used to giving illuminating advice to individuals, he was shocked by the helplessness of his creed in the face of a problem so gigantic. As though thinking aloud, he went on: 'After all, city-dwellers do eat and wear the products of the country – meat and vegetables, cotton, flax and silk or wool, so it can be said that abandoning the cities would not lead to a sudden upsurge of pressure on the land for food and raiment. But where would the people go? Country landowners are only a degree less grasping than city merchants; they would not yield their excess fields without coercion, yet coercion can never, never be the way. You have set me a problem that requires much thought. We Taoists are used to providing remedies that work from within. Contemplating the Tao releases unparalleled creative power, bestowing spontaneity and serenity – in a word, unbounded freedom – but it is something each must find in the silence of his heart. Therefore a great sage would first be needed, someone able to arouse in city-dwellers a longing to be released from their bondage to brick and stone; but where in these days does one find sages great enough to command respectful attention? The change you have in mind would have to be gradual. First, a few wise young people would have to be persuaded of the wisdom of leaving the city to set up small farming communities of their own. In time, the trickle away from those grim walls would grow and, with the passing of years, become a flood. And why? Some of the pioneers would return on visits, laden with an enviable wealth of nature's endowments – health, vigour and the calm clear gaze of those who have left avarice and anxiety far behind.'

While he was speaking, the recluse's eyes had kindled, but suddenly there came a frown and he added mournfully: 'You need not remind me that setting the trickle in motion would be a task beyond an ordinary man's powers. Your question has so many profound implications. Perhaps when you come this way again . . .'

I was not destined to pass that way again. The long war with Japan and its attendant miseries so disrupted the whole country that the communist revolution inevitably followed fast upon its heels. I doubt whether that thoughtful hermit still dwells in seclusion upon Mount Hua, and I shall never know if his meditations gave birth to a less naïve solution to the evils of over-population and urbanization, which have since acquired disastrous proportions. Yet I still remember our inconclusive discussion for two reasons: it exemplified the extent to which the teachings of Lao and Chuang had remained a living force among Taoists recluses, while, on the other hand, it revealed the impotence of a quietist philosophy, however potent its effects on individuals, to allay the sorrows of man in the mass. A consolation one may permit oneself in this tragic context is that, even for men pent by circumstance within endless wastes of grimy brick and concrete, it is still possible to seek from within themselves total liberation from the tyranny of their surroundings.

Regarding the distinction so often made between 'popular' and 'pure' Taoism, almost all my contacts with Taoist recluses served to convince me of its non-validity. I do not understand why Western writers have clung to it with such persistence, especially in cases where, however intimate their acquaintance with the Taoist classics, they have never in their lives met exponents of living Taoism. (Until recently, Tibetan Buddhism was dismissed in much the same fashion as a tangled web of superstitions far from the main stream of Mahayana Buddhism. It is only since hundreds of refugee Tibetan monks fled their communist-occupied homeland and became more easily available to the outside world that recognition has begun to be accorded to the profundity and doctrinal purity of the Tibetan form of Mahayana. Alas, there can never be a large influx of Taoist devotees from mainland China to set the record straight!) By and large, Taoist recluses in the first half of this century were thoroughly imbued with the wisdom of the *Tao Tê Ching*, no matter how great or small their interest in other matters. Conversely, it is more than probable that the sages Lao and Chuang resembled the Buddha in recognizing that, while the universe is surely not the handiwork of a supreme deity, of a creator standing outside his creation, there are nevertheless various orders of invisible beings who, like humans, animals and plants, are an integral part of the universal order and subject to natural law. It is highly unlikely that, at a period when the existence of such beings was everywhere taken for granted, Lao and Chuang would have refrained from pouring their gentle scorn upon, or at least specifically refuting, such a notion, had they not subscribed to it themselves.

No one can speak with absolute certainty of the beliefs of Lao and Chuang, and so this last observation is a matter of inference. On the other hand, I can list from first-hand knowledge certain general characteristics of Taoist recluses as I found them in the nineteen-thirties and nineteen-forties; theses to my mind, reveal them irrefutably as having been – among other things – true exponents of classical Taoist philosophy. Those characteristics were :

1 A healthy impatience with tiresome and restricting conventions, but not necessarily with convention as such; for example, they clung to their distinctively antique garb, probably because it was loose, comfortable and exceedingly attractive without being fussy or expensive.

2 A taste for frugality which was by no means drab or puritanical, for they delighted in whatever simple pleasures their mountain retreats afforded.

3 A ready acceptance of life as it came, an absence of discontent that reminded me of Chuang-tzû's famous saying : 'Since the sage does not have the feelings of a man, right or wrong cannot get

at him ... When I talk of his having no such feelings, I mean he does not allow likes or dislikes to get in and do him harm. He just lets things be the way they are instead of trying to help life along.'

4 A preference for being inconspicuous, undemanding and uncombative, and the breadth of vision to submit gracefully to adverse circumstances when submit they must.

5 A care to avoid involvement in public affairs or civic duties, that was more than compensated for by their extreme hospitality and kindness both to travellers and to the local peasants.

6 A flair for running their communities with a bare minimum of regulations.

7 A readiness to laugh engagingly at mishaps as well as at what they took to be their own inadequacies and follies, so that grumbling and pomposity were scarcely to be found among them.

8 An inner stillness and a keen enjoyment of natural beauty, coupled with considerable powers of intuiting nature's processes and rhythms. Their reverence for natural phenomena, particularly rocks, water, wind and moon, was at once touching and poetic. Li T'ai-po's delightful poem, 'Three with the Moon and My Shadow' is so perfectly Taoistic in feeling as to reveal the poet's close kinship with Taoist sentiment. This was true of many of the greatest Chinese poets.

The one respect in which latter-day Taoist recluses seemed to differ markedly from the two sages, especially Chuang-tzû, was their preoccupation with prolonging life. Though Chuang-tzû's work does contain passages which can be construed as pointing to the possibility of attaining the god-like immortality envisaged by the recluses, and though some of his pronouncements on death suggest that he did not regard it as a final state, he displayed no inclination to prolong his own life beyond its natural span. For example, he wrote: 'How do I know that loving life is not a delusion? How do I know that in hating death I am not a man who, having left home in his youth, has forgotten the way back? Lady Li was the daughter of a border guard of Ai. When she was first taken captive (by the Duke) and brought to Chin, she wept until her tears drenched the collar of her robe. But later, when she went to live in the palace of that ruler, shared his couch and ate delicious meats at his table, she wondered why she had ever wept. How do I know that the dead do not wonder why they ever longed for life? . . . Some day there will be a great awakening when we shall know that this is all a dream.' Talking of the death of Lao-tzû, he put into the mouth of someone depicted as being amazed by the grief it caused: 'This is to hide from Heaven, turn your back on the true state of affairs, and forget what you were born with . . . Your Master happened to come because it was time, and he happened to leave because things follow along. If you are content with the time and willing to follow along, then grief and joy have no way to enter in.' His other pronouncements on death include: 'The True Man of ancient times knew nothing of loving life and hating death . . . He did not forget where he began; he did not try to find out where he would end'; 'What makes my life good makes my death good' and 'The sage wanders in the realm where things cannot get away from him and all are preserved. He delights in early death; he delights in old age; he delights in the beginning; he delights in the end.' On nearing his own death, Chuang-tzû tried to dissuade his disciples from giving him a sumptuous burial to preserve him from birds of prey, by saying: 'Above ground I'll be eaten by crows and kites; below ground, by mole-crickets and ants. Would it not be rather bigoted to deprive one group to feed the other?'

I imagine that a recluse, questioned about his eagerness to prolong life, might have replied: 'Acceptance of death at any time is all very well for a great sage; lesser people need more time in which to make full preparation for what follows.'

The quotations from Lao and Chuang sprinkling the foregoing pages are, in one sense, related only to peripheral matters, in that their pertinence to the mystical intuition that was at the very core of their belief has not been fully brought out. That is a subject requiring a chapter to itself; so far, my purpose has been to demonstrate how refreshingly the ancient teaching can be applied to the circumstances of *this* life, *this* world, whether in a mystical sense or not. For the sake of continuity, I have chosen as a modern protagonist of those aspects of Taoist philosophy which are not specifically mystical a certain Mr Jung Su-tuan, an old Pekingese gentleman of Manchu ancestry, who was fond of saying in the manner of someone murmuring a secret: 'The world knows me as a staunch Confucian. Who would guess that I am something of a Taoist in spite of myself?'

Pressed for an explanation, he once observed: 'For seven

generations we have been a family of officials, often of exalted station, and I once harboured an ambition to outshine my forebears; so my way has lain among those who would have burst out laughing had I voiced my secret longing to seek the company of pines and cedars and let the world go by. Being a Manchu, I could not rise high in the service of the Republic, but retained just enough loyalty to the family tradition to be shackled by it until too old to change my mode of living. Make no mistake, I never hankered after the austerities of a pious recluse; I should have liked best to be the owner of a garden-dwelling, peaceful yet not remote, where I would have devoted my days to tending plants and my evenings to composing a commentary on the *Book of Chuang-tzû*.'

'Not the *Tao Tê Ching*, Uncle?'

'No, indeed. Chuang-tzû develops Lao-tzû's best ideas and carries them further.'

'His *best* ideas? Do you mean those pertaining to ordinary life, or those hinting at Returning to the Source by means of contemplative practices?'

'Certainly the former. I am enough of a Confucian to think it unprofitable to speculate about unknowable matters. It is enough to learn how to cherish life by taking everything as it comes and experiencing both ups and downs with equanimity. As Lao-tzû says: "It is from man's recognition of (what is called beauty) as beautiful that ugliness arises; it is from man's recognition of (what is called) goodness as good that wickedness arises." So it is with all things, all qualities, all concepts. Wisdom lies in taking things as they are, not dubbing them pleasant or hurtful, moral or immoral, attractive or alarming. The world is the world; a man's life is as it is; longing for them to be other than they happen to be will not change them. Stop finding names for things. Some sensations give pleasure, others one would rather be without; but, since we are bound to undergo them turn by turn, why dread what is unalterable? If I die today or tomorrow, shall I be the only one to experience death? Think how many plants, insects, fish, animals, humans, ghouls and gods will breathe their last at the very moment my twin souls leave my body! Shall I cry for myself and not for them? Meanwhile, by keeping my head turtle-wise in my shell, I may hope to attract no more notice than a wayside stone; if I stick it out, be sure some loutish fellow will itch to chop it off! Also, there is nothing to be seen by looking high that is worthier of regard than what lies close to the skin of the earth.

'As a youth, I was one of a band of sworn brothers who vowed to grow powerful and wealthy. Of those who succeeded, not a few died before their time – Marshal Wu P'ei-fu had Nationalist hotheads dispatched with those old-fashioned broad-bladed swords; then along came Chiang Kai-shek's Nationalist Party, zealous to rid the world of both communists and reactionaries by means of automatic pistols. The Japanese followed and, for those who would not collaborate with them, it was swords again, but longer in the blade and thinner; for those who did collaborate, it was pistols when the Nationalists returned. As a political failure of modest means, I survived. How does this way of thinking strike you?'

'Well, Uncle,' I replied, 'I agree with you in the main, but I wonder if you have ever experienced the hellish existence that falls to so many people's lot? Neither rich nor famous, you escaped both broad-swords and pistols, and no Samurai practised the sacred Bushido art on your neck; but have you ever wanted for white rice or good wheat dumplings, or for well-cooked chicken washed down with fine green tea or Shaohsing wine? What of the peasants who have to make do with dumplings of coarse grain adulterated with ground peanut shells, and are lucky if they taste flesh as often as once a month?'

He was not disconcerted. Smiling at my lack of understanding, he remarked: 'When we Manchus ruled, the Lord of Ten Thousand Years never sat down to a meal of less than a hundred and eight dishes. Do you suppose his appetite was ever keen enough for him to distinguish shark's fin from ordinary beannoodles? The farmer who tastes flesh but once a month is less to be pitied. He eats with zest, though his food be just millet porridge. Unless men are so poor as to face starving or freezing to death – a prospect to which I admit no philosophy would easily reconcile me – the range of joy and sorrow does not vary greatly; the poor man munches an occasional treat of roast chestnuts with as much gusto as the rich man sets about some rare dish – say, bear's paws or camel's hump. In the absence of the worst degrees of pain and deprivation, acceptance of life's circumstances without distinction is a sure way to serenity; from serenity follows the harmonious balance of the body's elements on which perfect health depends.

'Pain accepted as inherent in the human lot becomes easier to bear. The leper who, though his arms be plunged in boiling water, feels no pain can take no joy in the softness of a horse's nose or the cool sleek texture of jade. Not for him the pleasure of running a hand up the nape of a schoolboy whose hair has been freshly cropped. The musician who can be roused to ecstasy by the melody of a lute plucked by a master-hand suffers when some child picks out a tune on a cheaply made Mongolian fiddle. I, with my indifferent ear for music, enjoy both. If equanimity is the best approach to sounds and feelings, how much more is it to be prized in relation to concepts. A youth, growing up as I did under an imperial tyranny, delights in the notion of popular government; in later years, when the gangsters have taken over, he recalls with tears the benevolence of the departed kings. Having lived through more revolutions and wars than I can remember, I speak on that matter with authority.

'Longing for things to be as they are not is needless self-torment. At the age of seventy-four, I can look back on scarcely half-a-dozen years of happiness. They began during the darkness of the Japanese occupation, that welter of brutality and of death both swift and slow which I abhorred until, of a sudden, I was set free by the realization that good and bad are names for two sides of the same coin, that they must be accepted or rejected together. In a flash I recovered from a life-long illness – the disease of categories – cured by the recognition that the bulk of our distress stems from labelling this or that desirable or loathsome. Those sorrows inherent in nature which remain even when labels have been discarded cease to be sorrows from the moment we decide to be realistic, to accept what is there or on the way as part of the must-be-so.'

He laughed with such gaiety that I had difficulty in composing myself to remark a trifle severely: 'At your age, Uncle, such serenity is enviable; in a younger man, it might be taken for selfishness.'

Still laughing, he shot me a keen glance. 'Yes, yes, there is a disease especially virulent among Englishmen – over-concern for society. The comfortably-off must help the poor and so on. Well, so they must and so do I (as far as my means allow), but that need arises because society itself is sick. If everyone observed natural law, the earth's teeming millions would all eat well and be warmly clad. We should live in villages each with land enough to furnish all necessities; no one would die of gluttony, and the man who accidentally came into possession of a second sheepskin-robe would be prompt to give it away; wearing two is uncomfortably hot and, with no sycophants to admire a best robe reserved for special occasions, having an extra one would simply mean cluttering the family cupboard. Even here in this province, Hopei, where close on forty million people are supported by less than a hundred and forty thousand square kilometres of arable land, there would be ample food for all if gluttony gave place to frugality. There are those who claim that for the whole population to live in harmony with nature is no longer possible. Why do they think so? During the long occupation, the Japanese dwarfs rarely penetrated far into the countryside and so most Chinese gave the cities a wide berth; for eight years, the great majority of people in Hopei lived close to the skin of the earth, growing their own food, dressing in garments of home-made cloth. In the great cities of Peking and Tientsin, though their populations were denuded, hunger was rife; in the country, people lived frugally and so there was enough of everything. You are not to believe that Taoist principles have no application to the present day. All that is needed to make them work is a change of heart on the part of merchants, officials and military men, who are the only ones to profit from the present artificial mode of life. You may perhaps remember what the sages had to say about the production of useless novelties wherewith foolish men are tantalized into becoming so envious or greedy that nature's balance is upset.

'I'll tell you another thing. No man can help another beyond feeding him when hungry or tending him when sick, unless by setting him in the way of thinking things out for himself, which can be done better by example than by words, and very often not at all. This means that a man's first duty is to himself; for, unless he has cultivated the Way, what can he have to say that is worth the listener's trouble and what sort of example is to be expected of him? He must learn how best to live; then others, envying his content and well-being, will come of themselves to ask questions; some may even heed his answers, especially if he gives them sparingly. Unfortunately the minds of men today are so rotted by contagions contracted at school that it is hard for them to see truth even when it lies, as usual, right before their eyes.'

'What is the remedy?' I asked, thinking sadly of the millions who live and die without ever being able to imagine the face of truth.

'The remedy is to find your own truth and live by it. In that way, you will save yourself trouble and perhaps draw a few others away from their senseless clawing at the slippery precipices of dualistic thought by convincing them that the sound of bamboos creaking in the wind is a wholesome substitute for concepts. When the wind blows, the bamboos creak; when it dies away, they grow silent without giving a moment's thought to the relative virtues of creaking or silence. Bamboos just respond to circumstances. If the wind becomes a gale, they readily bow their heads and thus avoid being broken. When you chose Chu-fêng (Bamboo Wind) as one of your Chinese names, you did well, for the bamboo, green even in old age, very strong and yet pliant, soft within and unashamed of bending, is symbolic of Taoist wisdom; and the wind, so free in its movement, so unexpected in its immediate action and yet predictable in terms of cycles, is the very breath of the Tao. Your having selected such a name marks you as being something of a Taoist, whether by choice or in spite of yourself.'

'I hope you are right, Uncle,' I answered. Ironically his flattering reference to my name is probably one of the reasons why the whole conversation remains so fresh in my memory – a very un-Taoist reason for recalling an exposition of Taoist philosophy.

I should perhaps explain that Mr Jung once remarked 'Insofar as I am a Taoist, I side with those scholars who look no further than the works of Lao and Chuang.' I had offended him by comparing him to another sage, Liu An, the author of a collection of philosophic utterances known as the *Huai-nan-tzû*, in which Confucian and Taoist wisdom are blended.

'I don't know why you should think that. From what I remember of the *Huai-nan-tzû*, it contains many things with which I disagree—something about achieving immortality in this very body by a fancy sort of breathing. When Chuang-tzû practised yogic meditation, it was surely not with *that* sort of end in view. Besides, the *Huai-nan-tzû* makes things too cut and dried. It describes the emergence of the Tao from void in such a way as to make one suppose that, prior to the birth of heaven and earth, there were *two* things—first the void and then the Tao; but the

Tao being unborn and eternal must always have been there, primordial formlessness being as much at one with it as the forms to which it gave birth. Then there is something about the *Huai-nan-tzû's* conception of the Tao which makes it ridiculously solid, a sort of all pervasive substance. The true sages were more subtle. Though Lao-tzû also describes the Tao as emerging from void, he did not mean that a distinction should be made between them. He meant that the Tao as form emerged from the Tao as void.'

I suppose that, among my Chinese acquaintances, 'Uncle Jung' came closest to being a 'pure Taoist' in the scholarly sense; so I laughed when I heard his granddaughter say that once, when something had prevented him from going to the White Cloud Monastery to take part in the New Year rites for warding off misfortune, he became so nervous that he scarcely put his nose out of doors until his wife hit upon a remedy. Rather grudgingly, she handed over her own precious talisman—a silken bag containing grains of earth from each of China's 'Seventy-Two Blessed Places!'

That acceptance of the philosophy of the sages usually went hand in hand with a profession more open than 'Uncle Jung's', of belief in a spiritual or at least pantheistic order becomes all the less surprising when we recall that Plato and a good many others who hold their places in history as philosophers were avowedly religious men. The usual Taoist view, already ancient in Lao-tzû's day, was that all objects are animate; and it may be that modern man will soon find cause to revise the rigid distinction now made between animate and inanimate. Holding that rocks, pools and trees are manifestations of spirit is no more nor less bizarre than supposing the same of human beings. While prepared to accept that the further a Taoist devotee advanced in wisdom, the less importance he attached to propitiating gods and nature spirits, I do not attribute this to a lessening of faith in the existence of such beings, but rather to the recognition that spiritual progress has to be achieved by self-endeavour for which supernatural aid is unavailing.

I have already observed that the nature of the religious beliefs of my Taoist friends was hard to fathom, as they were so shy about revealing them. They readily admitted, however, that their more elaborate rituals were performed primarily for the satisfaction of lay-supporters who valued colourful and spiritually uplifting ceremonies. Indeed, had this concession not been made, the laymen would have been lured away by the rival attractions offered by Buddhist monasteries where, in accordance with the Buddha's own teaching, skilful means (*upaya*) were employed to capture the interest of the laity prior to leading them gently to embrace more subtle concepts lying beyond the immediate scope of their comprehension. That the Taoist pantheon itself, the temple architecture, the rites and liturgies were more or less made to resemble Buddhist prototypes is often ascribed to a pecuniary motive, that of attracting enough visitors to make up deficits in the monastic expenditures; but the major consideration was the notion that catering to the religious aspirations of simple, often illiterate people in ways they could appreciate was a solemn duty. This I could understand, but I wish I had been more persistent in probing the religious beliefs of the educated recluses. All I could gather was that instruction was imparted to adepts stage by stage, each stage with its appropriate symbology.

A notable example of symbolism, with meanings within meanings, is furnished by the Three Pure Ones (*San Ch'ing*), whose statues graced the main shrine-hall in most of the larger monasteries. As one recluse put it: 'People say we invented the Three Pure Ones as a counterpart to the Three Jewels (*San Pao*).' (He was referring to the three great Buddha statues by which Chinese Buddhists symbolize the Buddha, his Doctrine and the Sacred Community.) 'In actual fact the Three Pure Ones were worshipped before our ancestors had so much as heard of Buddhism. Then again, they represent ideas unknown to Buddhists, for they embody many aspects of a trinity of primal forces that runs through all our teaching—the Three Powers (*San Ts'ai*), comprising Heaven, Earth and Man; the Three Positive Forms of Spirit (San Yang Shên), known as Original, Conscious and Real Spirit; the Three Virtues (*San Tê*), Compassion, Frugality and Humility; and the Three Principles (*San Yüan*), Essence, Cosmic Vitality and Spirit. How could these be separate?'

This was very interesting; for, if he were right, those outwardly anthropomorphic statues possessed not only mythological but also cosmological, mystical, ethical and yogic significance. It is possible that other symbols sometimes ignorantly decried as 'magical mumbo-jumbo' had similar depths of meaning. Unfortunately, I did not chance to receive this explanation of the Three Pure

Ones until a little while before the march of political events made me decide to leave China rather abruptly; by failing to pursue the matter then, I lost a final opportunity to delve into the esoteric meanings of Taoist iconography.

It is a pity that Confucian condemnation of institutional Taoism was so readily accepted at its face value. That many Taoist recluses attached importance to the yogas for attaining longevity and transmogrification, or to ritualistic and magical practices which aroused scholarly disdain, does not mean that Taoist minds were barren of other interests and ideas. It would have done the critics no harm if they had troubled to seek from the recluses the fruits of their highly original way of thinking; after all, if they had come upon more turnips than figs or peaches, they would not have been obliged to eat them!

Even now it is possible that accomplished Taoists are to be found in Taiwan and the environs of Hong Kong, or scattered among the Chinese communities in south-east Asia, from whom authentic knowledge of Taoist beliefs and practices could still be obtained, but the signs are not hopeful. Recently I chanced to hear that, at one monastery in Taiwan, there is now a hostel able to accommodate guests by the hundreds; that the hostel was built by businessmen – not out of simple piety but because of the place's reputation for the dreaming of prophetic dreams deemed to shed light on forthcoming business transactions! At Castle Peak in the New Territories opposite Hong Kong, a large Taoist temple has recently been erected. Known as the Abode of the Green Pine Fairies, it is altogether too palatial for those enamoured of the misty vagueness of the Valley Spirit or longing for the rugged simplicity of the Uncarved Block. Still, in these days Taoists can no longer take their pick among ten thousand hermitages and monasteries; it may be that the recluses residing in those grand surroundings include a handful of men truly conversant with the Tao. Yet, even if there are such people, they may be difficult to identify; for true Taoists are retiring men who shun the limelight and, were inquiries to be made, those of small attainment would be the most likely to come forward.

In case a search for genuine professors of Taoism is made, should it be found that even the most erudite recluses among them resemble Pien Tao-shih in being over-credulous, we may be permitted to smile discreetly behind our fans, but not to laugh and walk away scornfully, flapping our sleeves, for such men as Pien, though liable to start down devious paths, seldom departed so far from the Tao as to be beyond the periphery of its radiance, and there was always a chance that it would one day illumine their minds with the glorious lustre of sun and moon, making them gods.

Chapter 6

The Nameless: Taoist Mysticism

The One Mind, omniscient, vacuous, immaculate, eternal, the Unobscured Voidness, void of quality as the sky, self-originated Wisdom, shining clearly, imperishable, in Itself that Thatness ... To see things as a multiplicity, and so to cleave unto separateness, is to err – The Tibetan *Book of the Great Liberation*.

Therefore let desire be stilled while you contemplate the Mystery; when desires reign, you behold (only) its outward manifestations – Lao-tzû

Today there is a wide measure of agreement which on the physical side of science approaches almost unanimity, that the stream of knowledge is heading towards a non-mechanical reality; the Universe begins to look more like a great thought than a great machine. The old dualism between mind and matter disappears – Sir James Jeans

Taken by itself, the previous chapter would do scant justice to the Taoist sages, whose whole philosophy – whether in relation to statecraft, education or being – drew life from a mysterious root. The awe-inspiring implication of their teaching must somehow be conveyed, even at the cost of fumbling and stumbling. Near the heart of things, words fail and, as Lao-tzû put it, 'He who knows does not speak.' Words, so the teaching goes, can be transcended by directing the consciousness in upon itself; within the mind, shrouded by the mists that hover in deep valleys, lies a treasure discoverable only by direct intuition. Understandably Lao-tzû called it the Nameless – yet because this treasure, embedded in the consciousness of every sentient being, anteceded them all, he also called it the Mother of Heaven and Earth. It was from concern for others that the sage, ruefully aware of the limitations of words and concepts, went so far as to disregard his own dictum by writing a five-thousand-word treatise; the same compassion impelled his spiritual descendants the Ch'an (Zen) Masters and their admirers – those staunch upholders of the 'wordless doctrine' – to produce whole volumes of explanations and pithy aphorisms. Unbroken silence, like using sacred images for fuel on a winter's night, is altogether too extreme. All the same, the difficulty of finding words just to discuss ideas *about* the ineffable, to say nothing of trying to describe it, is truly formidable. Semantically, traps abound; conceptually, chasms yawn. Each assertion threatens to thicken the primordial mist instead of shedding light. To speak in terms of is and is not, of laudable and otherwise, is surely the antithesis of a canny approach to the non-dual Tao, but how else is one to speak at all?

To take just one example. In rendering the famous sentence from the *Tao Tê Ching* as 'The name which can be named is not the Eternal's name' rather than employing the more usual, but meaningless translation 'eternal name', I have inadvertently set up an entity, the Eternal. This naturally is a synonym for the Tao, but it attributes the quality of eternity to that which is beyond all qualities and pairs of opposites. 'God' is a still less appropriate synonym, conveying as it does the idea of a being rather than a state and, what is worse, of a creator standing apart from his creation. 'The Ultimate' or 'Ultimate Reality' is not much better, since it suggests something lying beyond the world of form rather than a One that is identical with and inseparable from the multiplicity of its creations. No wonder Lao-tzû preferred to call it the Nameless!

Chinese mystics (Taoist and Buddhist) are not alone in recognizing that perception of the Nameless is a wholly intuitive experience demanding such vivid and immediate awareness that the thinker and his thought, the beholder and the beheld, are one. Knowledge, discrimination, logic, analysis, reason and every variety of conceptual thought must be banished. None of them will serve. Therefore the need for perfect stillness, outside and in. Without, there must be no boundaries, the mind being free to penetrate all objects and perceive their interfusion; within, self-consciousness must be annihilated. The fruit of such intuition is a liberating transformation; the mind, freed from the tyranny of dualism and self-assertion, roves at will, transcending self and other, recognizing the ego as a ghost of what never was nor ever will be. Pure harmony results, a limpid perception of the seamless unity of the formless Tao and its myriad forms, be they people, animals or objects. Profound compassion stirs. Fear and anxiety vanish. Henceforth, ups and downs, good and bad, life and death, are one. Now is the secret treasure-house illuminated by a pearly gleam. The Tao itself is manifested as that which, penetrating, encompassing and interfusing each of the myriad objects, constitutes their real nature. That small fragment of mind which the adept has hitherto mistaken for his own is seen to be the universal mirror forever reflecting impartially the changing scene. Things come and go across its surface leaving no trace. When he recovers from his awe, he can scarcely help laughing; in retrospect his resemblance to the well-frog that mistook a tiny portion of the sky for the limitless heavens seems gloriously funny. If he does not laugh, it will be because the awe resulting from such an experience lingers long. Sensations of being encompassed in brilliance; of elation, bodily lightness – ecstasy even – these are the terms used by mystics of many faiths to describe the joy that crowns their sublime experience. Their unanimity on this (and on so very many other matters) points to their having travelled by various roads to an identical goal, besides increasing the likelihood of the experience's validity. The following summary of what I heard from an old gentleman trained wholly in the Taoist tradition who visited me not above two years ago is in most respects a typical exposition of mystical teaching.

'The Tao is to be found in inner stillness. It reveals itself as One – timeless, formless, all-pervading. In it all creatures and objects have their being. The same may be said of your gold-fish and the water in which they swim, but the likeness is only superficial. One could take a fish out of the water and put it back; but the separateness of creatures and objects either from one another or from the Tao is illusory. Apart from the totality which is the Tao, they have no being. The Tao and the myriad objects *are not two*! Unlike water which rises from the lake as vapour and flows back to it in streams, the Tao's creations do not rise from it, nor do they return to it, they and the Tao having never at any time been apart. They *are* the Tao. This faculty of being one and many simultaneously is a mystery that can be apprehended but not explained.

'When I speak of goodness and of beauty, I speak of the Tao. When I speak of bad and ugly, I speak of the Tao. Self is the Tao. Other is the Tao. Distinctions between opposites are false at the beginning, illusory in the middle, and erroneous at the end. If you suppose otherwise, you will be tormented by demons – demon longings, demon fears. You will struggle all your life against fiends of your own imagining, weighing gain against loss as though there could be anything in the entire universe that is not yours already. What wasted energy! What needless tears!

'It is not enough for you to suppose that you know these things. You must perceive them directly. Listening to sermons, memorizing classics will do you no good. You must look within your mind. Even then you will see nothing clearly, unless you lose awareness of a self that looks. There is no such person, I assure you – there is a looking, but no looker. Yet banishing the concept of being one who looks can be difficult. Therefore prepare yourself by limiting your desires, requiring nothing of the world beyond what is needed for sustaining bodily well-being. Meanwhile, practise the art of *kuan* (inner vision) daily. This will still the restless waves of thought and sharpen your awareness. Awareness must be acute, but objectless. No looker, no looked-at, just looking. Do you understand? I mean your mind must be indifferent to the objects it reflects, performing its function like a mirror. When there is no attachment, true seeing arises. With seeing comes serenity. Serenity puts an end to woe. In the absence of woe, joy will fill your body to overflowing. Certainty of the rightness of your doing and of the truth of your seeing will flush your cheeks and make your eyebrows dance.'

Though he spoke with the conviction that comes from direct intuition and what he said reminded me in many ways of a hundred Taoist and Buddhist expositions, taken as a whole it had a special Taoist flavour and an archaic one at that. That is to say, his interpretation of his direct intuition was strictly in the manner of the Taoist ancients, betraying nothing of the influence of later Masters. The mystical experience itself I would judge to be timeless and unvarying – not so its depth or degree, nor the application that is made of it. In the light of what was taught by later Taoist adepts as well as by Buddhists and mystics of other faiths, I am inclined to think that Lao and Chuang (like the friend whose words I have quoted), differed from these others in one of two ways. Either their experience was less intense, a series of intuitions that fell short of ultimate illumination, or else they did not draw (or thought it best not to reveal) certain awe-inspiring implications. To all appearances, those sages had no special goal beyond achieving the joyous serenity and absolute freedom that follow from becoming cheerfully indifferent to the most cruel blows which fate may hold in store. They did not insist that failure to achieve conscious union with the Tao prior to death might have tragic consequences.

In tracing the development of Taoist mysticism, one is bound to begin with Lao and Chuang. Since there are no authentic texts covering the two-and-a-half millennia separating them from the Yellow Emperor, one does not know the extent to which their predecessors anticipated their doctrine of mystical intuition. The art of wood-block printing had yet to be invented and no manuscripts penned by earlier mystics survive, unless one counts those fragments attributed to the Yellow Emperor which are concerned not with doctrine but with yogic method.

Typical of Lao-tzû's mystical aphorisms are the following:

'There is something that arose from chaos before the world was born. Silent and invisible, it exists of itself, unchanging. Penetrating everywhere, it never ceases. One may deem it the Mother of the World. Not knowing its name, I call it the Tao. If pushed to describe it, I should say it is big; yes, big and flowing; flowing and far-reaching, far-reaching and (yet) returning.

'The world had an antecedent that can be called its Mother. Knowing the Mother, you will come to know the child. Knowing the child, go back and hold fast to the Mother, then all your life you will be secure.

'Non-being is the name given to the source of the world's beginning. Being is the name given to the Mother of the Myriad Objects. Yet are these fundamentally one, differing only in name. Therefore let desire be stilled while you contemplate the Mystery; while desires reign, you behold (only) its outward manifestations.

'(Non-being and being) – these two are fundamentally the same, though different in name. Their sameness is what one calls a mystery. Mystery upon mystery – such is the gateway to all secrets.'

These selections, which touch upon some fundamental concepts of Taoist mysticism, can, if interpreted in the light of similar passages in the *Tao Tê Ching*, be interpreted as follows:

Since before the world was born, there has been the Tao. Silent and invisible, it is spontaneous, immutable, all-pervading, inexhaustible, the primal cause from which the whole universe derives its being. Lying beyond all categories of thought, it is vast, reaching to infinity and yet close at hand. By knowing the Tao one comes to know the multiplicity derived from it; whereas understanding of its individual manifestations cannot replace contemplation of the Tao itself as a means of achieving unshakeable security. (Security connotes the utter serenity that stems from viewing poverty and wealth, life and death, as equally welcome experiences; nothing can disturb one who welcomes everything without exception. The analogy of mother and child is of but limited application, for there are other passages in the *Tao Tê Ching* which make it quite clear that the Tao and its creations are not to be thought of as at any time apart. Probably it is used in the sense that mother and child are of one flesh and also that the formless preceded the world of form. Being and non-being are in fact identical.) This view coincides exactly with the Mahayana Buddhist doctrine that, while all beings are by nature void, there is no void standing *behind* the realm of form, void and non-void being two simultaneously valid aspects of the one reality. The identity of being and non-being is a mystery to be perceived only through intuition, which cannot be attained until inordinate desires and self-assertion have been eliminated; for as long as the 'self' is felt to be real, the formless aspect of the Tao can by no means be perceived. Resolution of the paradox that the Tao is simultaneously being and non-being, form and formlessness, is the gateway to the perception of all mysteries. Intellectual acceptance of their identity is not enough; it must be intuitively experienced and the intuition must be palpable. (There is a world of difference, for example, between the conviction that honey is sweet and actually knowing its taste from experience.)

Those familiar with the teachings of mystics of other faiths may notice that two elements are lacking in Lao-tzû's exposition. First, apart from the injunction to still desire, nothing is said about the method of seeking intuitions of the Nameless; as a matter of fact, the *Tao Tê Ching* does contain one or two apparent references to contemplative sitting, but none that is not also open to a different interpretation. Second, there is no hint of what most mystics look upon as a man's highest goal, that of death-transcending union with the nameless (the Godhead, Nirvana, etc.). It is possible to infer, then, that Lao-tzû was rather a quietist than a mystic in the full sense of the word. Was he perhaps one of those fortunate persons to whom intuitions of the Nameless came virtually unsought, thus obviating the need for special contemplative or other yogic practices? Again, was he content not to speculate about possible sequels to the present life, or did he regard the matter as one too sacred (or too difficult) to be touched upon in his exceptionally brief work?

With Chuang-tzû, the case is somewhat different. He fits in more closely with the general notion of a mystic. Whereas many passages in his work merely confirm or expand upon Lao-tzû's quietist tenets, there are some others which reveal familiarity with yogic exercises. Concerning the world's origin, he speaks of a Great Beginning, wherein was non-being from which arose a formless One that impregnated its myriad creations with its own *tê* or virtue; and he calls for a return to that virtue which derives directly from the Original Source. 'Being identical (with it), you will be empty; being empty, you will be great.' He declares that the Tao makes one of all things, be they little stalks or giant pillars, lepers or lovely women, things ribald or shady, grotesque or strange; hence wisdom lies in making no distinctions. Of special interest is his very practical advice for translating the wisdom gained through mystical intuition into a way of life. He asserts that one can be liberated from all cares and rendered impervious to shock, sense of loss or grief by a complete renunciation of dualistic thought. By accepting all that happens as the play of circumstance – dream-like play in that nothing can be truly apart from the immaculate perfection of the One which alone is real – it is possible to pass through life armoured against even the worst mischances. (I remember hearing this point explained by a Taoist who put it thus: 'When in a dream the dreamer becomes aware that the upraised sword exists only in his imagination, the glittering horror arouses laughter.')

Some writers make much of apparent differences between Lao and Chuang; however, the fact that the *Tao Tê Ching* merely hints with extreme terseness at matters which Chuang-tzû sets forth at length does not necessarily point to great differences of view-point, as a short work and a reasonably long one are not altogether comparable. Still, on the face of it, it does appear that, whereas Lao-tzû contented himself with extolling the majesty of the Tao, as a no-thing – utterly sublime, constant and eternal – Chuang-tzû gave more thought to the means of winning accord with it, though both agree that the prime necessity is the elimination of dualistic thought. Since opposites belong together, to cleave to one and abhor the other is plainly absurd. Fame and shame, wealth and want, life and death come and go turn by turn, so why make distinctions? How much better to accord freely with the Tao by accepting each transformation with undisturbed equanimity. Longing to be other than one is implies rejection of identity with the ever-changing, always constant Tao, whereas recognition of that identity banishes fear as well as disappointment; disaster does not exist for a man who cheerfully accepts the inevitability of unceasing change in his condition, sustained by his knowledge of that ultimate transcendence over change which is inherent in his being inseparable from the Tao.

Chuang-tzu, in enjoining glad acceptance of whatever may befall, was not advocating mere fortitude. For him, there was no question of stern submission to misfortune; what was needed was the wisdom to understand that every kind of up and down is as necessary to nature's pattern as are sunshine and storm, and that the pattern taken as a whole is perfect. He would have had no patience with a man who, standing amidst the smiling fields of summer, talked nostalgically of moon-lit snow, or who bemoaned the drabness of winter while amusingly grotesque silhouettes of naked branches were there to be enjoyed. Viewing all opposites as two parts of a whole, Chuang-tzû saw in death so little cause for tears that he was found singing and beating a drum during the obsequies of his wife, a lady of whom he had been genuinely fond!

Weakness and softness – as of water, infants, females – were qualities he extolled, perceiving that it is by yielding to circumstances that one conquers. He could see no sense in striving to grasp what lies out of reach or clutching at what is already on its way out. As to those woes which no philosophical or mystical insight can banish altogether, such as extreme want or mortal danger, his prescription for guarding against them was to be inconspicuous, lowly, unassertive, to give the impression of being incomplete, imperfect, of little value, so that rulers and robbers would pass one by.

Chuang-tzû's familiarity with yogic methods for cultivating direct intuition of the One is borne out by many passages of his work. It seems likely that he himself practised one or more of those involving closing the doors of the senses and raising the state of consciousness with the assistance of a form of yogic breathing for which the Taoist term is 'breathing like an infant', or 'breathing like a foetus in the womb'. This can be gathered from the following quotations, of which the opening sentence recalls the Ch'an (Zen) conundrum about the sound of one hand clapping.

'You have heard of flying with wings, but never of flying without wings. You have heard of the knowledge that knows, but never of the knowledge that does not know. Look into the closed room, the empty chamber where brightness is born! Fortune and blessing gather where there is stillness. But if you do not keep still – this is called sitting but racing around. Let your ears and eyes communicate with what is inside, and put mind and knowledge on the outside . . . Can you really make your body like a withered tree, your mind like dead ashes?

'When I speak of good hearing, I do not mean listening to others; I mean simply listening to yourself . . . If the gentleman can really keep his vital energies intact and not dissipate his seeing and his hearing, then he will command corpse-like stillness and dragon vision, the silence of deep pools and the voice of thunder. His spirit will move in the train of Heaven, gentle, easy in inaction, and the myriad objects will be dust on the wind . . . The essence of the Perfect Way is deep and darkly shrouded; the extreme of the Perfect Way is mysterious and hushed in silence. Let there be no seeing, no hearing; enfold the spirit in quietude and the body will right itself . . . Be cautious of what is within you; block off what is outside you, for much knowledge will do you harm. Then I will lead you up above the Great Brilliance, to the source of the Perfect *Yang*; I will guide you through the Dark and Mysterious Gate, to the source of the Perfect *Yin* . . . Smash your form and body, spit out hearing and eyesight, forget you are a thing away from other things, and you may join in great unity with the deep and boundless . . . Forget things, forget Heaven, and be called a forgotten of self. The man who has forgotten self may be said to have entered Heaven . . . Let his spirit ascend and mount upon the light; with his bodily form he dissolves and is gone.'

As to the more ascetic and acrobatic forms of yoga, they seem to have aroused Chuang-tzû's scorn. Speaking of Induction (to use Waley's rendering of the name of a contemporary school of yoga), he declares: 'To pant, to puff, to hale, to sip, to spit out the old breath and draw in the new, practising "bear-hangings" and "bird-stretchings", longevity their only concern – such is the life favoured by scholars who favour Induction.' Nevertheless, Chuang-tzû has traditionally been credited by the exponents of the internal alchemy with having been one of their number, for he remarks in one passage that 'the True Man breathes with his heels'. This has been taken by some to indicate his familiarity with a particular method of yogic breathing to which I referred in Chapter 4; however, others aver that the exercise was introduced much later by yogins who found it advantageous to employ a chance phrase culled from Chuang-tzû's work as a sort of 'scriptural authority'.

The fact that the yogic theory and practice known to the early sages had a great deal in common with Indian yoga led Waley to assume that, even as far back as the third century B.C., Indian influence had somehow made itself felt in China; but, to one familiar with the development of mysticism throughout the world, it seems unnecessary to stretch the imagination that far. It is observable that contemplatives belonging to many faiths have often arrived independently at rather similar methods of wresting the treasure from the secret store-house in the mind.

If, on the doubtful assumption that the views of each of the two sages are *fully* represented in their respective works, we take it that Chuang-tzû's cultivation of intuition by yogic methods was a step forward from Lao-tzû's quietism, we must still regard Chuang-tzû's teaching as an archaic form of mysticism because of his seeming lack of concern with achieving death-transcending union with the One. However, the matter cannot be judged with any certainty, as his utterances on death, some of which are quoted in my chapter on philosophy, vary so widely in their implications. There is a particularly macabre passage suggesting that he regarded the tranquillity of the grave as the most admirable form of serenity. In it he relates a fanciful conversation with a skull which pours scorn upon the notion of returning to life. Said the skull: 'Among the dead there are no rulers above, no subjects below and no chores of the four seasons.' Wrinkling its brow it added: 'Why should I throw away more happiness than kings enjoy?' Against this, the sage's putting into Lao Tan's (Lao-tzû's) mouth the words: 'Why don't you make him see that life and death are the same story?' can be taken in two senses – that there *is* a sequel to what is commonly termed death or that there being none just does not matter. Then there is the passage, 'How do I know that in hating death I am not like a man who, having left home in his youth, has forgotten the way back?' This could be taken to imply belief in a very desirable state of existence beyond the grave, but could equally be regarded as mere speculation analogous to the passage in which the sage, awakening from a dream of being a butterfly, speculates as to whether or not he is now a butterfly dreaming of being a man. On the other hand, the passage 'Some day there will be a great awakening when we shall know this is all a dream' very strongly suggests belief in a blissful state to come. Perhaps the key to the enigma is contained in the words 'That which kills life does not die; that which gives life does not live.' Interpreted in a mystical sense, this means that individual beings are mere shadows with no lives of their own, mere waves in the eternal ocean that lies beyond the dualism of life and death. This would accord with the Mahayana Buddhist philosophy that, in an ultimate sense, there are no beings to enter Nirvana, nor anything that has ever been apart from it. Yet, even if we accept the very likely hypothesis that Chuang-tzû and the Buddhist mystics were pointing to exactly the same truth, there remains a difference of approach. With Chuang-tzû there is no urgency to make sure of reaching the transcendental goal, no impulse to 'carry the fortress by storm'. It is as though he were content to let the future take care of itself, content with having won the freedom that arises from serene dispassion. He does not seem to share the concern of later Taoist mystics about the fading into nothingness of the *hun* and *p'o* souls of those who die without having experienced mystical intuition. Can it be that he assumes that everyone, whether conscious of the Tao or not, will be reabsorbed at death into its formlessness and thus share perpetually in its vast consciousness? It is more likely, I think, that he implies the non-existence of beings who seemingly live and die; in other words, all that really lives in each of us is the undying Tao, which each wrongly takes to be a separate entity belonging to or constituting himself. There is no way of knowing for sure. Unless we postulate that Lao and Chuang kept back certain teachings, believing it unwise or unnecessary to commit them to words, their philosophy, because of its focus on the proper living of this very life – the Here and Now – might reasonably be called mystical humanism. Though it falls short of certain later developments, it offers a very pleasant and at the same time admirable philosophy of life. The qualities to be looked for in its exponents include: quiet acceptance of the twists and turns of fate; a disinclination to interfere; a warm affection for beings both beautiful and ugly, arising from the perception of nature's seamless unity; a comfortable absence of self-consciousness and a spontaneity which, besides being delightful in itself, might beget rare skill in performing tasks involving co-ordination of hand and eye – Chuang-tzû was fond of relating stories about chefs, wood-cutters, carpenters, wheel-wrights and so on to illustrate this point. As simple frugality and distaste for ostentation would preclude any thirst for luxuries and expensive novelties, pleasure in simple things would be all the keener; moreover, feeling a zestful interest in everything that could possibly happen would certainly prohibit boredom. A man thus trained would be loved and valued by his friends, because never in the way; his inner happiness would prove infectious. Even in those relatively prosaic terms, his lot could be described as enviable, to say nothing of the likelihood of his being able to enter at will into the bliss discoverable in the 'secret chamber' of the mind.

The other literary sources from which we might hope to gain information about Taoist mysticism in its earlier days – the works ascribed to Kuan-tzû, Han Fei-tzû and Lieh-tzû for example – are so widely regarded as later compilations of material of varying and uncertain date that it is difficult to deduce any worthwhile conclusions from them or to put them into proper historical sequence. In the *Huai Nan-tzû*, written several centuries later, some attempt is made to analyse the works of the Tao in terms of the interaction of *yin* and *yang* – the positive and negative principles. A school of Taoism much concerned with the *yin* and *yang* grew up and so did another which associated its teachings intimately with the *I Ching (Book of Change)*, but neither of these schools is of direct concern to the development of Taoist mysticism. By the third and fourth centuries, the Tao was equated by some philosophers (Wang Pi among them) with what was called *pên-t'i*, the original substance of the universe; thus it ceased to be regarded as a no-thing or no-being and became *pên-wu*, pure being. The thoughts of another great Taoist philosopher, Kuo Hsiang, wandered off in the opposite direction; he held that the myriad objects transform themselves spontaneously, each acting in accordance with its own inherent principle. But to define the Tao and its workings is to leave the realm of intuitive experience and enter upon mere philosophic speculation. Perhaps those sages, while succeeding in attaining direct intuition of the Nameless, failed to recognize the futility of attempting to give concrete expression to the mystery. Scholars have ever been fond of precision, preferring literal 'truth' with all its limitations to the amorphousness that surrounds that which is beyond categorical exposition. How much more to be admired is yet another of Lao-tzû's terms for the ineffable – the Shapeless.

A particularly interesting development in the fourth century A.D. was Tao Shêng's doctrine of sudden illumination, which was later to exercise a lasting influence on the thinking of the Ch'an (Zen) Masters. For centuries, Chinese mystics continued to dispute whether direct intuition of the Tao is or is not instantaneous. Personally, I am inclined to think that the dispute can easily be resolved in true Taoist fashion by reference to water. Bringing cold water to the boil is a gradual process; yet, at a certain temperature, the change from non-boiling to boiling is sudden. In other words, for those not fortunately gifted with unsought intuition, preparation for attaining it is gradual and often arduous, but the intuition or illumination, when it comes, is of course instantaneous.

My use of the phrase 'intuition or illumination' reveals a quandary into which all students of Chinese and Japanese mysticism are bound to fall. For some reason the writings of various Masters fail to make a clear distinction between those light, passing intuitions of the Nameless now known in the West as *satori* and the final stage of illumination which Buddhists call Supreme Unexcelled Enlightenment. Though distinctive terms do exist for both of them, the manuals of meditation and books of anecdotes are often vague upon this point; it is by no means always clear whether a reference is to the supreme, eternally liberating mystical experience or to one or other of the preceding stages along the way. Some might say that there is no qualitative difference; but surely a young monk who has achieved his first *satori* is not identical (except in a potential or latent sense) with a Supremely Enlightened One, a Buddha!

The encroachment of Buddhist terminology into an essay on Taoist mysticism is inevitable. No one knows at what stage the two religions began to influence each other; but, though they maintained their separate identities all along, the interaction was tremendous. Each borrowed enormously from the other – even Tibetan Buddhism shows Taoist influence. It is now generally recognized that the Ch'an (Zen) School of Buddhism, though its *doctrine* remained entirely faithful to the Mahayana derived from India, owes an enormous debt to Taoism, which seems to have been the chief source of its methods, language, fondness for nature, special concern with the Here and Now and emphasis on *sudden* illumination, to say nothing of its art-forms, which are often indistinguishable from those of wholly Taoist inspiration. Such phrases as 'the Buddha-Mind is omnipresent', 'no thought (*wu-nien*)', 'a doctrine without words', 'forget self' are very close to Taoist aphorisms. Ch'an (Zen)'s informality, down-to-earthness, fondness for apparent absurdities, lavish use of paradox and of conundrums unsolvable by logic or conceptual thought seem like echoes of Chuang-tzû. However, this in the present context is by the way. Of much greater importance to our thesis is the likely influence of Buddhist thought on the later development of Taoist mysticism.

Buddhist mysticism can be bracketed with mysticism in its Christian, Moslem (Sufi) and other world-wide forms, in spite of being free of the least suggestion of theism; for, while sharing the Taoist conception of the Ultimate as a No-being, it is imbued with that sense of urgency which is found also in theistic mysticism – urgency to achieve not mere intuitions of the One but absolute and everlasting union. The One, which Chinese Buddhists often call the Tao, is equated with *Sunyata*, the Great Void in which all things have their existence and whose nature all things share. Full experiential knowledge of the world's void nature is called Enlightenment. The casting off of the last shreds of ego-consciousness so that, at death, there occurs a merging with the Void, is variously termed liberation, final illumination, and attainment of Nirvana. By this achievement both extinction and immortality are transcended, for it is recognized that from the first there has never been anything to extinguish, the ego-entity being a mere illusion; therefore nothing dies, but conversely there is no shadow of individuality left to be immortal. When 'the dew-drop slips into the shining sea', not a particle is lost, yet nothing remains that is distinguishable from the sea. It is also taught that, in reality, this ultimate experience is not an *attainment* but a full *realization* of a unity that in truth has never from the first been ruptured. The devotee's overwhelming thirst for this realization and the joy which it bestows are both described in terms which vividly recall the ecstatic language used by theistic mystics in describing their thirst for and attainment of union with the Godhead.

The gradual change that overtook Taoist mysticism, bringing it into line with mysticism generally, is susceptible to three explanations: first, that there was no change, that the seemingly lower-key quietism of Lao and Chuang was identical with mysticism in its fully developed form, but for the greater reticence with which it was propounded; second, that the change occurred as a direct result of Buddhist influence; third, that it occurred independently of Buddhism, being in fact inevitable, since intuitive experience of the One cultivated by Buddhists and Taoists alike was bound to lead to recognition of the possibility of a great death-transcending apotheosis. By Taoists this apotheosis, instead of being called Nirvana (Buddhist) or everlasting union with the Godhead (Christian), became known simply as Returning to the Source.

Thus, with the passing of time, the final goal of Taoist and Buddhist mystics became recognizably one, as it had been factually one from the beginning, but there remained a great difference in their thinking in regard to the alternative to achievement of the apotheosis in this very life. To Buddhists, that alternative was terrifying – aeon upon aeon of being tossed relentlessly by the waves of a dark ocean, undergoing the tribulations of existence after existence before once again attaining a state conducive to further progress. To Taoists, on the contrary, the alternative was merely cessation of existence – a prospect not likely to inspire actual terror except perhaps in the young. But how splendid, how dazzling was the goal contemplated for those who did succeed in achieving full illumination, that ineffable, ego-shattering experience by which the last shreds of ego-hood are burnt up, so that the individual merges forever with the Tao, albeit the physical body of an illumined one may continue to lead a wraith-like existence until death, whereafter no gradual fading into nothingness can take place, there being nothing left to fade.

The final step in the direction of unifying Buddhist and Taoist concepts was the embracing of the doctrine of rebirth by a certain number of Taoists. Unfortunately there is no means of knowing to what extent this development was general. My guess, based on the rather haphazard contacts with Taoists described in this book, is that only a relatively small minority ever became adherents of this essentially Hindu-Buddhist doctrine.

All of the foregoing applies only to the purely mystical aspect of Taoism. Devotees who entertained popular notions regarding the various heavens and hells, or who contemplated transmogrification into some sort of immortal state for its own sake, though numerically very important, have little to do with the developments just described. Incidentally, within the folds of both Taoism and Buddhism there were always large numbers of borderline cases, that is to say people who, though convinced of the possibility of Return to the Source (or Nirvana), felt so overwhelmed by the difficulties involved that they made no serious attempt to achieve that goal. Such people can be called mystics in the sense of holding mystical beliefs, non-mystics in terms of practice and experiential realization.

Finally we come to a very important insight, especially widespread among Buddhists: the identity of the immaculate Source with pure mind. This is a momentous concept; for, if mind alone is seen to constitute the whole stuff of the universe, then all mysteries are solved. To those who hold mind and matter to be separate, the limits to which the one can act upon and affect the other seem well defined; whereas, in the absence of this dichotomy, it can be readily appreciated that the power of mind to act on mind is unlimited. The Buddhist doctrine is that the spotless, illimitable Void perceived during mystical illumination is pure mind in its quiescent state, while the unending flow of appearances falsely conceived to be separate objects is pure mind engaged in the play of thought. To use a telling Taoist expression, *these are not two!*

Westerners, on first encountering the doctrine of mind only, are apt to ask for a definition. Does mind in this context connote the totality of so-called individual minds or a sort of over-mind, Mind spelt, so to speak, with a capital 'M'? Asians reared in the ancient traditions find the question puzzling. How can these be two?

This doctrine of mind as the only reality requires that a distinction be made between 'illusion' and 'delusion'. If the world did not exist at all, its seemingness would be a delusion, whereas the mystical doctrine is that what is perceived does in fact exist, but that faulty perception endows it with illusory qualities that distort its real nature. Entities are real, but not in the sense of being truly separate from one another, of having each its own-being. Container and contained are one; it and they are pure mind.

Both Taoists and Buddhists were agreed that mere intellectual understanding of the mystery of the Tao or Void is powerless to unbind the chains of woe. The true nature of oneself and all else must be consciously experienced; the truth must be made as tangible as the heat of the sun upon the skin. However, Buddhists emphasize much more strongly than did the ancient Taoist sages that banishing the mists of conceptual thought is a prodigious task involving skill and pertinacity. There has to be a turning of the adept's mind upon itself, a mental revolution, an intuitive experience of indescribable profundity. Both intellect and logic are enemies closely linked to the false perceptions at the root of human woe.

Progress with the yogic exercises aimed at achieving the ultimate experience of union may lead to the development of extrasensory perception or even of startling, almost magical powers; the adept is, however, warned not to attach much weight to them, to regard them as potentially harmful distractions likely to attract unwanted credit and renown. The true miracle lies in achieving an awareness that bestows greater powers than kings and emperors enjoy. Leaving the conquest of the world and of negligible fractions of illimitable space to others, the yogin bends his endeavours to the much greater feat of conquering himself. He thus becomes imbued with such wisdom and compassion that his very presence radiates a gay serenity that is palpable to others. The descriptions of illuminated beings and of those close to ultimate illumination, as recorded by mystics belonging to many faiths, are often lyrical. With increasing imperviousness to human error, human woe, there arises a sense of balance and harmony so perfect that withdrawal into a state of bliss can be achieved at will. The world loses its terrors; laughter comes so easily that accomplished adepts are frequently mistaken for simpletons. Death is no more to be feared than dropping off to sleep on a summer afternoon. As the mind, no longer fettered by duality, joyously recognizes its unity with pure, bright, illimitable Mind – the Tao, the Godhead – there comes a sense of being able to soar throughout the universe at will.

That the mystical experience is no fantasy is demonstrated by the extraordinary degree of unanimity found among mystics of every age and clime. If a reasonable allowance is made for three diversive factors – differences of religious and cultural background, the need of each mystic to employ terms familiar to those about him, and the immense difficulty of bending language to describe what lies beyond the furthest confines of conceptual thought – it is apparent that all the world's mystics have spoken with one voice of an experience common to them all. Since error spreads as easily as truth, this unanimity would lose much of its power to astonish, were it established that all mystics have been people exposed to a single tradition which, some two or three thousand years ago, miraculously spread throughout the world, leaping across the vast mountain-barriers and limitless tracts of wilderness or ocean which bounded the scattered centres of civilization in those days; but can anyone seriously suppose that certain groups within the ancient and medieval cultures of China, India, Egypt, the Middle East, classical Greece and Eastern and Western Christendom were *all* pervaded by an identical tradition – one, moreover, which in all but two cases formed no part of the orthodox religious teachings that flourished around them? Dismissing that supposition as too wild, we are left with but two alternatives – either we must believe that countless madmen and dreamers were visited by an identical fantasy, or else accept the mystics' enigmatic pronouncements as being rooted in direct intuitive experience of the 'Really So'!

Though I have had opportunities to enter more deeply into Buddhist than into Taoist mysticism, it was from a Taoist teacher,

Tsêng Lao-wêng, that I gained the highest insight that can ever be vouchsafed to a person of such ordinary attainments as my own. I recall his revelation with gratitude and awe. It stemmed from an experience so close to the heart of things that whether or not his exposition is held to reflect Buddhist influence matters not at all; for, beyond a certain level, all such distinctions fade. His belief in transfiguration leading to total absorption in the Tao was subscribed to by innumerable Taoists who were certainly not conscious of having inherited a mixed tradition, since it had been transmitted from one Taoist adept to another over a space of many centuries. I shall relate the story in detail, as being at once dramatic and fully representative of Taoist mysticism in its most developed stage. What I came upon so unexpectedly includes a fair sample of the teaching given to Taoist adepts in my day; its blend of humour and sincerity has such an authentically Taoist stamp that it would not be too far-fetched to find in it echoes of Chuang-tzû and the Ch'an (Zen) Masters, even though it dealt with a type of mystical experience that goes far beyond simple mystical humanism.

That the Master known as Tsêng Lao-wêng spoke from direct knowledge conferred by full illumination strikes me as unquestionable; for, though I do not possess the high intuitive powers required for detecting an adept who has reached the goal, Tsêng Lao-wêng's presence conferred a direct communication of bliss from heart to heart that was all the more remarkable in view of my own unadvanced state.

The year was 1947 and the place not a great monastery, nor even a hermitage in the ordinary sense, but a house in the northwestern precinct of Peking inhabited by less than half-a-dozen Taoists. Towards the end of World War II, they had been driven from their mountain retreat by guerrilla operations conducted by Chinese partizans against the Japanese invaders. Though, as refugees, the recluses adhered to the regimen to which they had been accustomed, they had exchanged their distinctive costume for the silk or cotton gowns worn by Peking laymen in those days, so as to avoid unwelcome attention. Since the end of the war, conditions in the countryside being too disturbed to permit a return to their hermitage, they had clung to their temporary refuge, not even bothering to acquire Taoist robes to replace those discarded when danger threatened. Probably their neighbours were unaware of their calling. My coming to know of their existence was due to a chance remark dropped by Yang Tao-shih, a young recluse whom I sometimes visited in the White Cloud Monastery. I had happened to remark rather tactlessly that, of the many wise hermits encountered during my wanderings, the few who had betrayed signs of being, as I fancied, closest to illumination had almost all been Buddhist.

'That may be so,' replied my friend, 'but I wonder if even one of them surpasses the Taoist recluse known as Tsêng Lao-wêng? Lao-wêng (Old Gentleman) is an unusual title for a recluse, but he dislikes being styled Immortal and, for reasons best known to himself, prefers now to pass for a layman. Few people even remember how he was styled in the days before he was driven from his mountain retreat.'

'His name is of no importance. I have noticed you are something of a cynic; so, if even you consider him an accomplished sage, he must be well worth meeting.'

'Ah, yes. But they say he is not fond of receiving visitors. That in itself is a sign of wisdom, don't you think? I love visitors, but then, unlike Tsêng Lao-wêng, I have no talents to hide. A true sage shrinks from the public gaze and, above all, from becoming a local curiosity, which to a man of his calibre can so easily happen.'

'All the same, do please try to arrange a meeting. I am all agog and I promise you it is not just idle curiosity.'

I could see that my good-natured friend regretted mentioning the elusive Master Tsêng, but I persevered until he could not courteously avoid a promise to try his best.

By the time that promise bore fruit, autumn had given place to winter and Peking had become a strangely silent city, so thick was its carpeting of snow. One day I dropped in at the White Cloud Monastery to find my Taoist friend huddled over a charcoal brazier, from which he obligingly detached himself just long enough to fetch a wine-kettle and a small earthenware jar from a shelf in the corner, braving the icy chill that seeped in through the windows of translucent paper.

'One needs friends on a day like this,' he exclaimed, beaming. 'I had no sooner wished for an excuse to broach this jar of peach brandy – a sure aid to longevity – than you appeared like one of those amiable demons who can be summoned by a flash of thought. By the way, Tsêng Lao-wêng has sent for you.'

'Tsêng Lao-wêng? Ah, but of course – now I remember. When did the message come?'

I saw from his face that it had been long enough ago for the question to be embarrassing; although, what with the pitiless wind and snow during the last few weeks and the distance from the monastery to my house, his not having notified me was excusable.

'A while ago,' he said rather too casually. 'Come to think of it, by now they may have left for Hangchow. You should have paid your respects to him much sooner.'

'Was that my fault?' I burst out, wafted by the fumes of the strong peach brandy beyond the bounds of Taoist courtesy.

'If you had been kind enough to visit me more often, then' – he handed me a slip of paper with the address.

It was no use regretting the number of times I had put off summoning a hooded rickshaw, inadequately quilted against the cold, for the long ride to his monastery. Now, of course, just in case Tsêng Lao-wêng were still in Peking, I should have to make an even longer expedition that very afternoon to a secluded section of the north-west corner of the city. There was nothing for it but to drink another warming cup of the mulled peach brandy and set out as soon as possible. I knew of no way of summoning one of the great city's half-dozen taxi-cabs at short notice, and horse-drawn vehicles were colder than rickshaws; so I had no choice.

An hour or two later, a draughty covered rickshaw set me down before the last house in a lane that petered out in the gigantic shadow cast by the city's northern ramparts. All that could be seen above the outer wall of this unobtrusive dwelling was some rooftops emerging from among the bare, snow-laden branches of the trees within its courtyards. The brasswork on the gate was green with verdigris and the scarlet-laquered door panels, far from showing up bravely against the sombre grey-brick wall, had faded to a dull, uneven pink. The early dusk of winter was at hand and it was obvious that callers seldom chose that hour, for there was no response to my repeated knocking until I had grown stiff with cold. Even then, one gate-panel opened only just enough for the gate-keeper to take stock of me.

'The Lao-wêng is not receiving,' he announced flatly. 'Their Reverences said nothing about a visitor.' Too cold and dispirited to face the prospect of a miserable journey home without first warming myself at a stove and drinking the hot tea unfailingly served to visitors, however inopportune their arrival, I persisted to the point of rudeness. At last the burly fellow stood back, opened the gate a little wider and gestured with his chin towards a doorway across the forecourt. The flagstone pathway had been cleared of snow earlier that day, but already it was half obliterated by small avalanches from the skeletal old fruit-trees rising on either hand.

Wishing that dour man had had the courtesy to lead the way and announce me, I watched him withdraw into the warmth of his quarters near the outer gate; then I hurried over to the doorway he had indicated and pounded on it with numbed fists. No one came. Too cold to stand on ceremony, I let myself into a small parlour that was very murky because so little light now filtered through the paper windows; but at least it was warm, thanks to an iron pipe zigzagging across the ceiling from a stove in an adjacent room. To the left was a door cloaked against the cold by a wadded curtain of blue cloth; that the room beyond was occupied could be deduced from a line of golden light just above the door-sill; still, what with the ponderous wooden door *and* the curtain, it would not be surprising if no one had heard my frantic pounding. Having no other way to make my presence known, I called out, as though expected, 'Wo lai-la! (I have come).'

Again there was no answer, and so I gathered courage to push aside the curtain and open the door beyond. In crossing the high sill, I stepped – into another century!

Lit by thick candles of crimson wax was a scene that might have been set in the T'ang dynasty over a thousand years ago. What little furniture there was, apart from the shelves piled with blue-cloth ivory-hasped book-boxes that lined the walls, had been so arranged as to leave a wide space in the centre. There, seated cross-legged on floor-cushions with their backs to the door, were three figures clad in long gowns the skirts of which had been tucked beneath them. Backs erect, heads just perceptibly inclined, they maintained such stillness that neither sound nor movement betrayed their breathing. Even from behind I could see that the one sitting closest to the further wall was an elderly person, for parts of a luxuriant white beard were visible on either side of his face. Clad in a layman's gown of coarse grey cloth, he had drawn up his hair in a bun and concealed it beneath a home-made cap of soft black material. His companions sat behind him and at a distance from each other, so that the three meditation-cushions formed the points of an equilateral triangle; this, I believe, had no esoteric significance, but was simply an arrangement that gave each meditator ample space. The younger men wore the high-necked gowns of wadded dark-blue silk that formed the winter garb of prosperous Peking merchants in those days; their close-cropped heads were bare like those of laymen; nevertheless one could sense that they were no amateurs at the art of meditation. There was no ikon to be seen, but smoke curled from a single stick of incense set in an antique tripod that stood to one side of the bearded figure.

As no one showed any awareness of my presence, I sat down cross-legged behind them, taking care to make no noise. The wooden floor was cold, but to have sat in a chair – and thus at a higher level than the recluses – would have been discourteous. Thirsty and tired, I hoped the meditation period would soon be over. To pass the time I studied a peculiarly fascinating wall-scroll, an ink-painting depicting a Taoist immortal making his way across an ice-bound river to a pavilion standing amidst a grove of snow-covered cedars. Executed with a masterly economy of brush-strokes, it suggested rather than portrayed this scene and yet presented it more vividly than a meticulously detailed oil-painting could have done. That the traveller was an immortal was apparent not from his costume but from his seeming to sweep forward with irresistible power, serenely unhampered by slippery, cracked ice or treacherous snow-drifts. I had seldom seen a painted figure so marvellously imbued with life. But gradually my interest in the picture waned, for I discovered with some surprise that inexplicable sensations of buoyancy and well-being had driven away both boredom and fatigue. Presently they became so intense that, had I had anything to eat or drink since those little cupfuls of peach brandy whose effect had worn off hours before, I should have suspected someone of doctoring it with some sort of euphoric drug. As it was, no one seemed aware of my presence, and even the longed-for cup of tea had not materialized. I cannot hope to describe the quality of those rapidly mounting sensations, but I remember smiling at the thought that a newly transmogrified immortal, very conscious of his weightless, jade-smooth body and freedom to soar effortlessly among the clouds, would be likely to feel something very much akin to them. Their source was not to be found within myself; after a while I recognized it as a strikingly intense form of the joy that comes from being in the presence of a person of great mystical achievement. If the holy sage's inner joy can communicate itself to others in such great measure, who can imagine the bliss that wells within the sage himself? Probably the authors of those Taoist texts which speak of immortals serenely winging their way over mountains and oceans were hinting in veiled language at the very sensations of which some emanations were now filtering into me. My thirst had vanished. Gone, too, was my shyness at the thought of having to explain my intrusion. In their place had come an exquisite happiness that was centred on nothing in particular, and a feeling (which should have been, but was not, alarming) that the entire cosmos, lovely, shining and beautifully ordered, was somehow contained within the narrow confines of my skull. Having said all this, I have gone but a little way towards conveying the richness of the experience, which, at the very moment when it seemed about to produce some sort of fabulous climax, ceased!

When the once-tall incense-stick had burnt down to its stub, the old man stirred and lightly tapped a bronze bell concealed from my view. Small responsive movements indicated that the other meditators had returned to their ordinary state of consciousness and were adjusting themselves to it, preparatory to rising. As for my own return, it had been brutally sudden; the source of my joy had been switched off like a light. By the time the vibrations of the little bell or gong had died away, I was my old self – anxious about my invasion of their privacy, rather tired and quite dreadfully thirsty.

Rising from their cushions, the recluses turned towards me, betraying not the least surprise at finding an intruder – a foreign devil at that – scrambling awkwardly to his feet in their meditation-room. The two younger men smiled a welcome and the bearded elder strode forward, throwing out his arm suddenly to prevent my prostrating myself as courtesy demanded.

'No ceremony, I beg you. Sit down and be at ease. Tea is

coming. You must think us remiss to keep you waiting so long for refreshment after your cold journey all the way from the White Cloud Monastery.'

I drew in my breath. Grinning puckishly as though amused at my regarding telepathy as a matter for astonishment, he motioned me to a chair and took one separated from mine by the width of a table just broad enough to accommodate the two bowls of pale-green tea now served by one of his disciples. The effect of this proximity was to restore something of the joyous serenity I had felt earlier, the difference in intensity being no doubt attributable to his having descended from the incalculably exalted level of consciousness attained during meditation.

'So kind of you to have hurried over.'

Hurried over? Indeed I had, but as my visit to the White Cloud Monastery had been made on an impulse, my friend there could not possibly have told the old gentleman to expect me that afternoon, and there was no obvious reason for the latter's knowing from where and at what speed I had come. Not for the first or last time in my life, I felt uncomfortable in the face of a prescience that makes one's thoughts seem visible.

'I should have hastened to pay my respects much sooner, but for ——'

Gracefully he waved his hand. 'No apologies. You came as soon as you could.'

Clutching at a simpler explanation, namely that he had been expecting some other visitor from the White Cloud Monastery, I blurted out: 'Venerable, are you quite sure you know who I am?'

'That, no!' he exclaimed, eyes crinkling with amusement. 'Such knowledge would be miraculous, wouldn't it? Does one ever know that much even about himself? If you can tell me truly that *you* know who you are, I must bow down to you as my Teacher.'

'*Please*, Venerable!' I answered blushing. 'I was speaking in a conventional sense. My insignificant name in its Chinese form is P'u Lo-tao and my humble cognomen Chu-fêng. Perhaps you were expecting——'

'I was expecting P'u Lo-tao and P'u Lo-tao is here. That's all that matters. I, as you may know, am the person generally called Tsêng Lao-wêng, so we need no further introduction. Another few days and you would have found us gone to Hangchow, as one of my pupils is suffering from the harshness of this northern winter. Please be as happy as I am that we have managed at least this one fortunate meeting.'

If a scholar's eye were to fall on my description of this incident, its owner might feel like complaining: 'Pooh-pooh, that mountebank recluse of yours guessed who you were from the fact of your being the one foreigner to seek him out. Naturally your friend at the monastery gave him your name when arranging for you to meet the old rascal. What you say about telepathy is just an instance of the cunning of those fellows.' Well, there was a great deal more to it than that. I have never lost the rather eerie conviction that Tsêng Lao-wêng had somehow known I would come that very afternoon; that as soon as I had entered the room he had sensed my presence at once and deliberately transmitted a share of the serene, object-free joy that was the fruit of his meditation. But when I pressed for confirmation that that was so, my halting question was characteristically answered by a peal of laughter. Had Tsêng Lao-wêng admitted to powers of foreknowledge and telepathy, *then* I should have had reason to doubt; had he denied them I would have been left guessing; for, among Taoists, the wielders of genuine powers, if they were saintly men, could no more be persuaded to confess to them than a Buddhist Arahat can be brought to admit to having crossed Nirvana's brink.

The tea, served in cups of unremarkable design that were replenished, when required, by the watchful disciple, was too delicious to be drunk without comment. Pleased by my enjoyment of its colour and fragrance, Tsêng Lao-wêng told me from what province and which mountain the thin green leaves had been carried and how the tea had been brewed in melted snow, the city's water-supply being unsuited to its delicate flavour. Presently he remarked:

'Your going to such trouble to visit me is flattering. How may I best be of service to you?'

'You mean, why have I come, Venerable? I have been longing to meet you ever since I heard our mutual friend describe you as an illumined sage.'

Tsêng Lao-wêng sighed and answered resignedly: 'Why do people talk so? Such words are tedious. You will find no sages here, just this old fellow and four or five other very ordinary men who are students of the Way. It must be disappointing for you.'

'Do not blame Yang Tao-shih, Venerable. He wished only to make me see for myself that Buddhists do not have a monopoly of wisdom.'

'And does seeing an old man distinguished by nothing more than an unusually bushy beard convince you that they do not?'

What could I say that would not sound like flattery, which he obviously disliked? 'Venerable, it is just that, as most of my teachers are Buddhist, I am ignorant about what Taoists mean by such terms as wisdom and illumination, and about their methods of approaching the Tao.'

He laughed. 'How strange. Can there be two kinds of wisdom, two kinds of illumination, Taoist and Buddhist? Surely the experience of truth must be the same for all? As to approaching the Tao, be sure that demons and executioners, let alone Buddhists, are as close to it as can be. The one impossible thing is to get a finger's breadth away from it. Do you suppose that some people – this old fellow, for example – are nearer to it than others? Is a bird closer to the air than a tortoise or a cat? The Tao is closer to you than the nose on your face; it is only because you can tweak your nose that you think otherwise. Asking about our approach to the Tao is like asking a deep-sea fish how it approaches the water. It is just a matter of recognizing what has been inside, outside and all around from the first. Do you understand?'

'Yes, I believe I do. Certainly my Buddhist teachers have taught me that there is no attaining liberation, but only attaining recognition of what one has always been from the first.'

'Excellent, excellent! Your teachers, then, are true sages. You are a worthy disciple, so why brave the bitter cold to visit an ordinary old fellow? You would have learnt as much at your own fireside.' (His harping so much on his being just an ordinary old fellow was not due to exaggerated modesty, being a play on the words of which his title, Lao-wêng, was composed.)

'Venerable, please don't laugh at me! I accept your teaching that true sages have but the one goal. Still, here in China, there are Buddhists and there are also Taoists. Manifestly they differ; since the goal is one, the distinction must lie in their methods of approach.'

'So you are hungry not for wisdom but for knowledge! What a pity! Wisdom is almost as satisfying as good millet-gruel, whereas knowledge has less body to it than tepid water poured over old tea-leaves; but if that is the fare you have come for, I can give you as much as your mistreated belly will hold. What sort of old tea-leaves do Buddhists use, I wonder! We Taoists use all sorts. Some swallow medicine-balls as big as pigeon's eggs or drink tonics by the jugful, live upon unappetizing diets, take baths at intervals governed by esoteric numbers, breathe in and out like asthmatic dragons, or jump about like Manchu bannermen hardening themselves for battle – all this discomfort just for the sake of a few extra decades of life! And why? To gain more time to find what has never been lost! And what of those pious recluses who rattle mallets against wooden-fish drums from dusk to dawn, groaning out liturgies like cholera-patients excreting watery dung? They are penitents longing to rid themselves of a burden they never had. These people do everything imaginable, including swallowing pills made from the vital fluids secreted by the opposite sex and lighting fires in their bellies to make the alchemic cauldrons boil – everything, everything except – sit still and look within. I shall have to talk of such follies for hours, if you really want a full list of Taoist methods. These method-users resemble mountain streams a thousand leagues from the sea. Ah, how they chatter and gurgle, bubble and boil, rush and eddy, plunging over precipices in spectacular fashion! How angrily they pound against the boulders and suck down their prey in treacherous whirl-pools! But, as the streams broaden, they grow quieter and more purposeful. They become rivers – ah, how calm, how silent! How majestically they sweep towards their goal, giving no impression of swiftness and, as they near the ocean, seeming not to move at all! While noisy mountain streams are reminiscent of people chattering about the Tao and showing-off spectacular methods, rivers remind one of experienced men, taciturn, doing little, but doing it decisively; outwardly still, yet sweeping forward faster than you know. Your teachers have offered you wisdom; then why waste time acquiring knowledge? Methods! Approaches! Need the junk-master steering towards the sea, with the sails of his vessel billowing in the wind, bother his head about alternative modes of propulsion – oars, paddles, punt-poles, tow-ropes, engines and all the rest? Any sort of vessel, unless it founders or pitches you overboard, is good enough to take you to the one and only sea. Now do you understand?'

Indeed I did, though not with a direct understanding firmly rooted in intuitive experience that matched his own; but I pretended to be at a loss, hoping his voice, never far from laughter, would go on and on and on; for, just as his mind when lost in the bliss of meditation had communicated a measure of its joy, so now it was emanating a warmth, a jollity that made me want to laugh, to sing, to dance, to shout aloud that everything is forever as it should be, provided we now and then remember to rub our eyes. I could have sat contentedly listening to him hour after hour, day after day. Overwhelmed with love and admiration only partly inspired by his words, I did not guess that he had yet a still more precious gift for me, one that would remain when the magic of his presence was withdrawn, the very secret that had been denied me by the Abbot of the Valley Spirit Hermitage, who had held the mystery too sacred to be lightly revealed.

Tsêng Lao-wêng's talk of rivers flowing into the ocean had put me in mind of Sir Edwin Arnold's lovely expression of the mystery of Nirvana, 'the dew-drop slips into the shining sea', which I had long accepted as a poetical description of that moment when the seeming-individual, at last free from the shackles of the ego, merges with the Tao – the Void. This I knew to be an intensely blissful experience, but it was Tsêng Lao-wêng who now revealed its shining splendour in terms that made my heart leap. Afterwards I wondered whether Sir Edwin Arnold himself had realized the *full* purport of his words. At a certain moment in our conversation when Tsêng Lao-wêng paused expectantly, I translated the beautiful line for him and was rewarded by a smile of pleasure and surprise. Eyes glowing, he replied :

'My countrymen are wrong to speak of the Western Ocean People as barbarians. Your poet's simile is penetrating – exalted! And yet it does not capture the whole; for, when a lesser body of water enters a greater, though the two are thenceforth inseparable, the smaller constitutes but a fragment of the whole. But consider the Tao, which transcends both finite and infinite. Since the Tao is All and nothing lies outside it, since its multiplicity and unity are identical, when a finite being sheds the illusion of separate existence, he is not lost in the Tao like a dewdrop merging with the sea; by casting off his imaginary limitations, he becomes immeasurable. No longer bound by the worldly categories, 'part' and 'whole', he discovers that he is coextensive with the Tao. Plunge the finite into the infinite and, though only one remains, the finite, far from being diminished, takes on the stature of infinity. Mere logicians would find fault with this, but if you perceive the hidden meaning you will laugh at their childish cavils. Such perception will bring you face to face with the true secret cherished by all accomplished sages – glorious, dazzling, vast, hardly conceivable! The mind of one who Returns to the Source thereby *becomes* the Source. Your own mind, for example, *is destined to become the universe itself*!'

His wise old eyes, now lit with joyous merriment, bored into mine. For a fleeting moment, I was able to share in the vastness of his inner vision. The bliss was so shattering that I was compelled to lower my gaze. For a person in my state of unpreparedness, prolongation of that flash of limitless insight would have been more than flesh and blood could bear.

Chapter 7

Dragons to the West? Prospects

In contemplating the demise of Taoism at the hands of a régime whose single-minded concern with creating a new society has given rise to a puritanical aversion to romance and mystery, I like to evoke a fantasy. I imagine a band of recluses rounded up by dedicated communist cadres, say in 1949, to undergo public trial by the people. Judged by the new standards, their offences have been grave. These mild, strangely coiffured men are alleged to have lived without toil and in relative luxury at the expense of victims cowed into supporting them by cunningly implanted superstitious fears. In particular they stand accused of purveying a criminally anti-social philosophy, of deluding the sick and dying with quack remedies, of propagating vile, degrading superstitions, and of serving as the lackeys of capitalist oppressors bent on exploiting the ignorance of the masses so as to perpetuate the evils of feudalistic tyranny – a formidable list of charges not easy to refute, in that the recluses' guilt or innocence depends entirely upon a subjective point of view.

The bewildered prisoners, herded under guard on to a specially constructed bamboo platform, can be seen above the heads of a throng of local peasants who surround them at a distance of perhaps twelve paces. In the intervening space, earnest young orators, voices harsh with righteous indignation, are working up the passions of the crowd. 'Parasites, bloated leeches, human bloodsuckers,' are but a few of the ugly images that pepper their invective. Meanwhile, a handful of farmers, former tenants of the monastery, having been persuaded for whatever reasons to back up these indictments, are shrieking accusations with such eloquence that, in the general fury and excitement, the most scabrous and far-fetched charges pass unchallenged. The crowd greets each further revelation with roars of execration for the two-faced monsters they had so misguidedly loved and trusted over the years. Fists are shaken, cudgels waved, lethal implements gripped menacingly.

'Incestuous dung-beetles!' screams the youngest of the cadres, her otherwise charming little face, now distorted by revulsion, framed by sleek bobbed hair and a jauntily perched cap. 'Call upon your devils before we slit your tongues. Let *them* save you from the people's wrath! You see, comrades? Even devils are ashamed to help these blood-drinkers! Death to the exploiters of the people!'

'Shaaaaah! (Ki-i-i-ill!)' roars back the crowd. As though taking her words as a signal, some enthusiastic youngsters break rank and surge towards the platform where the recluses, unconscious of wrong-doing, have been gazing about them, stricken by the swift transmogrification of erstwhile friends into avid foes. Strangely calm as the screaming youths surge towards the platform, fists and weapons raised to strike, these sad-faced hermits glance expectantly towards their Abbot, who nods and twirls his fingers in an esoteric gesture. The effect is shattering! Just as the foremost ranks make ready to leap upon the platform and rend their 'oppressors' limb from limb, the headlong rush is halted; swiftly pounding feet stop short, brace themselves against the pressure from behind and remain rooted to the ground; senses reel; and the ugly din gives place to sighs and muted cries of terror. Amidst breathless wonder, the cluster of men in antique garb is seen rising majestically into the air; decorous to the last, they try in vain to keep their robes from billowing wildly as they soar into a sea of clouds so deeply tinged with scarlet shot with gold as to proclaim the presence of an assembly of dragons. Concealed now from mortal gaze by this radiant cloud-screen, the recluses mount their steeds. Astride shimmering dragons or gorgeous unicorns whose bushy, sky-blue tails are extended in full flight, they wing their way towards the rim of the Western Ocean. The Abbot deftly steers his mount by pressing the golden scales with his knees, for he is ceremoniously clasping to his breast a gift intended for the worthy savants who will doubtless receive him on our shores – a crystal vial brimming with the elixir of immortality.

How should this fantasy proceed? Will my fellow barbarians value the Abbot's gift? Will they perceive in Taoism something of living worth or will it rouse no wider interest than do the beliefs of long-dead Incas and Egyptian pharaohs?

More than twenty years have passed since the day on which the recluses would have landed among us, and so some notion can be formed as to how their doctrines would have fared. Certainly Taoism seems unlikely to emulate Buddhism in setting down vigorous roots in western soil; nevertheless, English translations of Lao and Chuang are proliferating, for not only the Flower People and hippies but also all who seek to rid society of the oppressions and stilted conventions of the past naturally welcome a system of thought which, for all its antiquity, embodies their most cherished ideals.

Taoist abhorrence of violent and coercive measures, whether penal or parental; its distaste for puffed-up leaders, overbearing officials, tax-collectors, pompous pedants, smart alecks and greedy profiteers; its impatience with ostentation and stuffy convention; its joy in spontaneity; its insistence on the rightness of leaving people to follow their own bents so as to develop to the full the potentialities inherent in their natures; its closeness to simple, natural things; its tolerance and wry humour – each of these awakens a yea-response in hearts sickened by the bitter fruit of centuries of bungling. Moreover, besides confirming what people in the West, especially youngsters, are discovering for themselves, Taoism inculcates some special values – stillness, for example, *inner* stillness. For all its seeming inconoclasm, it strongly favours restraint and courtesy. The Taoist way is to do one's own thing spontaneously, but without a show of resentment towards those who differ. The other fellow, be he teacher, parent or whoever, has an equal right to be as he is and to do things *his* way, however misguided; he must not be subjected to discourtesy or rancour. If conflicts loom, Taoist wisdom bespeaks retreat. This attitude demands a certain maturity which Westerners, by temperament impatient, have still to acquire.

Certain passages from the Taoist sages may strike even relatively staid and contented people like fresh air streaming into an overstuffy room. One knows of Englishmen and Americans whose studies of Taoist philosophy have profoundly affected them as people. Indeed, whoever recognizes a need to rethink the whole range of concepts on which our traditional ideas of progress, development and education are based is likely to find inspiration in Chuang-tzû's laughing anarchism. His erudite turning of established beliefs inside out and upside down perhaps foreshadows a time when the teacher's role will be one of open-minded, unassertive prompting, rather than of pontification and command. Governments, unfortunately, are less amenable than educationalists to calls for sanity; it is hard to imagine a great Power voluntarily renouncing the use of coercion to impose its ideology and selfish interests on its friends and enemies alike; yet if statesmen can be persuaded to take a course in the works of Lao and Chuang, they may perhaps improve. As to those men lured by greed for wealth to court the risk of stomach ulcers, nervous breakdowns, crippling strokes and coronary thrombosis, the best that can be hoped of them is that they will not commit the supreme vulgarity of peddling Lao-tzû tee-shirts and Chuang-tzû dolls as a substitute for taking to heart the sages' teachings.

Taoism can provide a wide range of interesting matter for research, very different from those scholastic studies which aim to prove that this or that sage did not exist, or lived later than the century traditionally ascribed to him, or did not write the work that bears his name. It is hard to see the general usefulness of such endeavours; one wonders whether modern scholars, sinologists especially, write just to edify (or pique?) one another and to keep themselves in business. Whatever their motives, what they do is of course *their thing* and they are fully entitled to carry on with it, all the more so as they incidentally perform one very great service; when they bring their scholarship to bear on the task of carefully translating ancient texts, their work is of high value to posterity. Few people are better or worse off for knowing who did or did not compose the *Tao Tê Ching*, whereas countless readers have been edified by translations of its author's wisdom.

Among the aspects of Taoism into which research would be creative is the whole subject of rejuvenation. Since there is ample testimony to the unusual longevity achieved by advanced Taoist adepts and to their having maintained rude health and vigour to the last, one would love to know the secret. Was this achievement due merely to a healthy mode of living coupled with a freedom from anxiety, or did their practice of internal alchemy and dual cultivation play a decisive part? Was the dual cultivator's careful conservation of his *yang*-force – and this despite very frequent sexual intercourse – a main factor? I cannot accept the opinion of my friend Joseph Needham – greatly as I revere his works on the history of Chinese sciences – that Taoist white tiger and green dragon cultivation led merely to the deflection of the male semen into the bladder; for I have yet to learn that he or his fellow scientists – so meticulous in other matters – have reached that conclusion as a result of prolonged and properly controlled experiment. Considering how great a boon a simple way of achieving rejuvenation and vigorous longevity would be to those who lament the passing of their youth and mourn life's brevity, it is astonishing that no serious research has been devoted to the restorative method successfully employed by Taoists throughout the centuries. Even if a study of *yang*-force conservation were to produce a negative result, much would have been gained, for the field would have been narrowed and the way left open for identifying the true source of age-defying vigour.

Of less poignant interest, but not without exciting possibilities, would be research into the means whereby certain Taoists learned to pass over fire unscathed, to control the flow of blood to wounds, and to cause torn tissues to heal rapidly, leaving no scar. I prefer to say nothing of certain other skills such as levitation, or modifying the shape or position of external objects by power of mind, or achieving invulnerability to weapons; for, although such powers can occasionally be witnessed to this day (among Tibetan yogins, for example), adepts willing to demonstrate them to satisfy casual or scientific curiosity are so rare that few people credit their existence. Telepathy, on the other hand, is well known to exist and provides wide scope for research into its prevalence among Taoist and Buddhist hermits. Indeed, any research into the modification and enhancement of physical processes by means of mind-control would be richly rewarding.

As to contemplative exercises, meditation, special breathing, and similar means of achieving mystical perception of the Tao, though theoretically these should be Taoism's greatest contribution to the West, methods closely analogous to them may be studied at the various Buddhist institutions that have sprung up in our midst. It is doubtful whether the Taoist forms of these practices are so particularly effective as to add much to what Ch'an (Zen) and the Vajrayana have to offer; and, in any case, competent Taoist adepts would now be hard to find. In the absence of highly accomplished teachers, nothing worthwhile of this nature can be learnt. Making translations of Taoist manuals on yogic meditation would be no substitute, as the really essential instructions were customarily passed down from adept to disciple, the manuals being used only in conjunction with the oral teaching. Naturally, if an accomplished Taoist Master were somehow to be found, it would be extremely valuable to compare his methods with those used by the different schools of Buddhism, and it is probable that they would have the advantage of being particularly well suited to the psychological and spiritual endowments of certain people. Moreover, to mystics of whatever faith, the special disciplines employed by fellow-mystics belonging to different traditions are always of deep interest. For example, I have heard of no less than five separate endeavours by Catholic bodies or individuals to embody Buddhist meditational techniques into their own practice and, even among people who subscribe to no particular religion, there can now be found quite a number of zealous meditators.

Enough has been said to hint at the richness of the gifts to be expected, had that flock of recluses astride dragons and unicorns alighted on our shores. As they did not, one must conclude that they were beguiled by cloud-dwelling immortals encountered along the way and that they still linger in high abodes veiled from mortal gaze by rainbow-tinted mists. Who shall blame them? Two-and-a-half millennia of intolerance and defamation by Confucian bureaucrats and scholars, culminating in the total dispersal of their communities by the new régime, must have persuaded many a Taoist Immortal that wisdom lies in leaving this world of dust to its own devices. All the same, it is tragic that a way of life so worthy of affection and respect – even if some of its aspects now and then made one want to smile – should have vanished so swiftly and completely. For the grey mists of scientific technology, besides swallowing up all colour and romance, are fast depriving man of his most priceless endowment – a sense of mystery. Is it really more satisfying to accept that the moon is a dreary waste of rock and dust than to believe that its lovely orb is the glittering ice-palace of Tsang Ô, a goddess as lovely as she is unapproachable? Be very sure that Tsang Ô remains forever enthroned in her hall of ice. For the spacemen, her condescending to create dusty mirages to delude impertinent explorers was the greatest of good fortune. Had they beheld her face, the rest of their lives must have been spent in an agony of longing for a prize that the gods themselves have sought in vain since the world's beginning.